"THE WORLD'S EASIEST GUIDE"

— TO —

Finances

Randy Southern is a freelance writer with more than 50 books to his credit. A former product developer for David C. Cook, he lives with his wife and two children in Mount Prospect, Illinois.

James S. Bell Jr. is Executive Editor for Moody Press. He has compiled and abridged numerous classics. He is also the general editor of *The World's Easiest Guide* series as well as co-author of *The Complete Idiot's Guide to the Bible* and *The Complete Idiot's Guide to Prayer.*

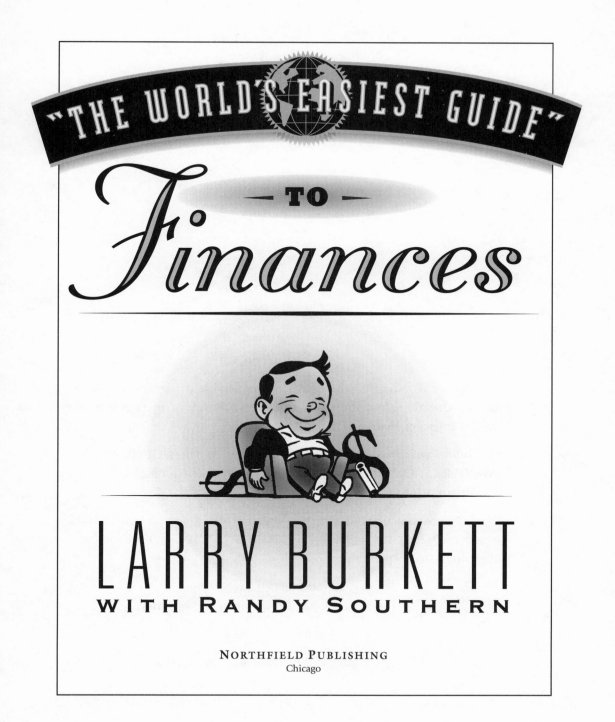

"THE WORLD'S EASIEST GUIDE"

⟶ TO ⟵

Finances

LARRY BURKETT

WITH RANDY SOUTHERN

NORTHFIELD PUBLISHING
Chicago

Editors: Jim Bell, Moody Press
Adeline Griffith, Crown Financial Ministries

ISBN: 1-881273-38-5

Printed in the United States of America

Table of Contents

TABLE OF CONTENTS

"THE WORLD'S EASIEST GUIDE"

Expenses

Forgive Us Our Debts… and the Interest Too, Please

SNAPSHOT

The knot in Ed's stomach tightened as he looked at the pile of papers on the table. *This can't be right,* he thought. *Maybe the mailman delivered our neighbors' bills by mistake. There's no way we owe this much.*

But the bills and statements in front of him, the ones that were all addressed to "Edward Pfaff," told a different story:

- ➤ $1,275 to Community Hospital for Becky's C-section and Michael's neonatal care

- ➤ $6,510 to VISA (payment past due)

- ➤ $3,280 to Discover Card

- ➤ $7,512 to Ford Credit ($419 monthly payment past due)

- ➤ $840 to Workout World ($40 monthly payment past due)

And that doesn't even include the mortgage and what we

> ## SNEAK PREVIEW
>
> **1.** You can get out of debt, but it will involve some tough choices and hard work.
>
> **2.** You need a financial counselor you can trust because some popular financial advice isn't very wise.
>
> **3.** The first step in getting out of debt is to stop borrowing.

owe Becky's dad, Ed reminded himself.

He glanced down at his paycheck stub and then at the figure on his calculator. *We can't even make minimum payments this month,* he realized. *And we just paid for new brakes on the Honda, so that means next month is going to be even worse!*

Ed shook his head and sighed. "Becky," he called out, "we need to talk. I think we may be in trouble."

* * * * * * * * * * * * * * * *

Telltale Signs of Debt

Do you have a bill or a loan payment that's past due?

Do you carry a balance on your credit card?

Do you ever get nervous about your financial situation and wonder how you'll ever be able to pay what you owe?

Do you ever try to disguise your voice when you answer the phone, just in case it's a collection agent calling?

Have your ever considered panhandling as a second career?

Do you have a bumper sticker on your car that reads, "I owe, I owe, so off to work I go"?

If you answered yes to any of these questions, chances are you're struggling with debt.

> ### PENNY FOR YOUR THOUGHTS
>
> Interest works night and day, in fair weather and in foul. It gnaws at a man's substance with invisible teeth.
>
> –HENRY WARD BEECHER

In ancient times, that might have meant a stretch in prison for you—or at least a future as a servant to your creditor. In those days, people didn't fool around when it came to money. One way or another, debtors paid what they owed.

Creditors today prefer a different method of imprisonment. What they'll do is offer you credit opportunity after credit opportunity until they've got your financial future locked up tight. It's not quite as dramatic as life behind bars, but it's just as effective. Anyone who's ever fallen into the easy credit trap can tell you that being surrounded by walls of debt *does* feel like a prison.

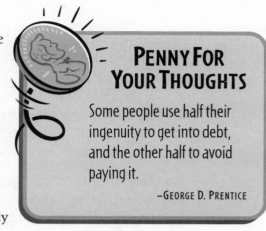

PENNY FOR YOUR THOUGHTS

Some people use half their ingenuity to get into debt, and the other half to avoid paying it.

—GEORGE D. PRENTICE

The good news is that there's a way out of your financial Alcatraz. The bad news is that getting out won't be easy. There are a few truths you need to accept right from the start.

1. You're not going to win the lottery.

2. A computer virus is not going to permanently wipe out all records of your debt.

3. Your creditors aren't going to let you off the hook because they think you've suffered enough.

4. Ignoring the problem will not make it go away.

If you're counting on a near miracle to rescue you from debt, we're going to ask you to hop on the first bus out of the Land of Make Believe and join us here in the real world—where it really is possible to escape debt, but only with a lot of hard work, tough choices, and personal sacrifice.

The Usual Suspects

Most debt is caused by three common financial mistakes, any of which can put you between a rock and a hard place faster than you can say, "What do you mean I've exceeded my credit limit!" Let's look at these three blunders to see why they're so dangerous—and so easy to make.

Mistake #1: Making the wrong long-term commitments

No, I'm not talking about marrying someone with expensive tastes (though that certainly could be a financial drain). I'm talking about buying big-ticket items that most people consider necessities, things like houses and cars. The long-term commitment to these purchases is in the payments. Today it's not unusual for car loans to be stretched out over seven years or more. And, believe it or not, it's now possible to get a *70-year* mortgage.

Seventy years—run that figure through your brain a couple of times. Let's say you bought your dream house when you were in your early 30s. With a 70-year mortgage, your kids, your grandkids, your great-grandkids, and your great-great-grandkids could all watch you write out your monthly payment. When you retired at age 65, you would still *owe* more on the house than you'd paid. You could even live to see Willard Scott IV wish you a happy 100th birthday on the *Today* show and still be survived by your payment book!

Fortunately, a 70-year mortgage is still the rare exception and not the rule. Even if you choose not to finance a house for seven decades, though, you'll find that most lenders will be happy to give you more than enough financial rope to hang yourself, if you're not careful.

The average mortgage today runs closer to 25 or 30 years, and even though that's considerably less than 70 years, it's still a hefty chunk of calendar. That's why buying a house is not a decision to take lightly. If you make a mistake in choosing a home, you'll feel the financial effects of it for years, even decades, to come.

That House Is Too Much

The most common mistake new homeowners—young married couples, in particular—make is buying too much house too soon. They look for a home based on what they want, not on what they can afford.

As long as we're spending all this money, they reason, *we should get something we really like*. And that's how the trouble starts.

PENNY FOR YOUR THOUGHTS

There are but two ways of paying debt: increase of industry in raising income, increase of thrift in laying out.

–Thomas Carlyle

From there, the preferences get more specific—and expensive.

➤ "A two-car garage would be a lot more practical and convenient than a one-car garage."

➤ "We're going to need a big backyard for when we have kids."

➤ "Wouldn't it be great to have a whirlpool tub in the master bathroom?"

➤ "Cathedral ceilings look so much better than regular ceilings."

➤ "The closer we are to the golf course, the better our resale value will be."

And like an idling taxi, the meter keeps running and running. Ten thousand dollars here. Five thousand there. When all of these extras (or, if you prefer real-estate jargon, *amenities*) are tallied, the final price usually bears little resemblance to the numbers the home-buying couple discussed when they first started talking about how much they could afford to spend.

PENNY FOR YOUR THOUGHTS

It is hard to pay for bread that has been eaten.

—DUTCH PROVERB

Talking yourself into paying for these extras is surprisingly easy to do, even without a realtor breathing down your neck. All you have to do is look at your future very, very optimistically. The reasoning goes something like this: "Right now, the monthly payments for this house are almost more than we can afford. But with raises and bonuses, our salaries are bound to get bigger and bigger each year, so in a few years we should be able to make the payments with no problem at all. And although we may struggle in the meantime, at least we'll be in the house we want."

Avoiding Mistakes That Grow with Time

It's not hard to spot the danger in this logic. First, if most of your income is going toward mortgage payments, how will you be able to afford things like a car, furniture, clothes, or even groceries? It's easy to underestimate these expenses when you're trying to shoehorn a big ole house payment into a little ole budget. Second, if you really have the ability to see that clearly into the future, why weren't you able to keep yourself out of debt? The fact is, regardless of how rosy your income potential seems right now, there's no guarantee that your future financial situation will be any better than your current one. Your salary may increase over time, but so will your cost of living.

If you're thinking of buying a house, there are two things you can do to reduce your chances of making a long-term mistake.

1. *Don't apply for a mortgage until you can afford to make a 20 percent down payment.* If your dream house is selling for $210,000, don't start packing until you have at least $42,000 to put down. If you can't afford that kind of down payment, you can't afford that kind of house. You may want to consider buying a smaller home or one in a less-expensive area.

2. *Make sure that your monthly housing costs take up no more than 38 percent of your Net Spendable Income (your income after tithes and taxes have been taken out).* I'm not just talking about mortgage payments here. Monthly housing costs include mortgage payments, plus all utility bills, home insurance payments, and maintenance costs (everything from new carpeting to cleaning supplies). Together these expenses should gobble up no more than 38 percent of your post-tithe take-home pay.

Cars and Credit Don't Mix

Car payments, on the other hand, should take no more than 0 percent of your Net Spending Income. You read that right: 0 percent. Zero. Zip. Nada. Goose egg. Null set.

If you'd like to acquaint yourself with the ins and outs of new car investments, here's an exercise you can try.

CRUNCHING NUMBERS

Monthly housing expenses (mortgage payments, utility bills, homeowner's insurance, maintenance costs) should equal no more than 38 percent of Net Spending Income (take-home pay minus tithe).

1. Withdraw $20,000 from your bank account.

2. Flush $4,000 of it down the toilet.

Purchasing a new car is like buying $20,000 worth of stock and finding out the next day that your investment is suddenly worth only $16,000. Most new cars lose about 20 percent of their value the day they're driven off the lot. And no matter how carefully you drive home, there's nothing you can do about it!

If you finance the car, the problem is even worse. Buying a new car on credit—that is, making monthly payments on it for years at a time—ranks right up there with buying lottery tickets or site-unseen real estate offers as one of the worst investments you can make. When you finance a car, you put yourself in the position of paying a premium—sometimes for as long as seven years—for an investment that gets less and less valuable every day.

Of course, that's not something you'll worry about the first few months you own your new car. Writing a check for, say, $419 each month will seem like a mere pittance for the pleasure of owning such a sleek, shiny driving machine.

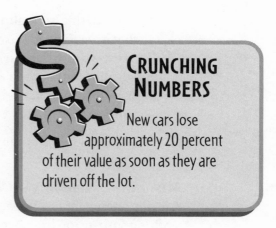

CRUNCHING NUMBERS

New cars lose approximately 20 percent of their value as soon as they are driven off the lot.

A year or so later, though, after the inevitable scratches and dings have taken their toll on the exterior and countless spilled sodas and muddy footprints have sullied the interior, $419 a month is going to start to seem a little pricey for such a *plain* car.

A few years after that, when the transmission is slipping, the timing belt is whining, and the brakes are squeaking, $419 a month is going to seem like an outrageous price to pay for "that hunk of junk in the driveway."

By that time, though, you probably will have decided to trade in that old car, even though you're not through paying for it, for a shiny new one. Like a lot of other people, you'll be putting yourself in the position of paying for two cars, one of which you don't even own anymore! Financial experts have a term for this type of arrangement: not smart.

Affordable Vehicles

Here are two helpful rules of thumb to keep in mind when purchasing an automobile.

1. *If you can't afford to pay cash for the car you want, find a car you can afford (or learn to love public transportation).* Escaping from debt is all about prioritizing your expenses. Your choice of transportation is a good example. There's nothing wrong with having a "dream" car. But are you

willing to sacrifice your financial health—your *family's* financial health—to own it? Committing yourself to monthly car payments, even for the automobile of your dreams, makes you a prime candidate for serious debt problems.

2. *Buy used.* If a car is affordable and in good condition, does it really matter that it was owned by someone else first? Are you willing to pay thousands of extra dollars just to be able to say that you're driving a *new* car? If so, who are you trying to impress? And for that matter, why would anyone *care* whether your car is a year old? Besides, as any car dealer with a semi-sincere smile can tell you, it's not a *used* car, it's just *pre-driven*.

(For more useful information on the dos and don'ts of making major purchases, check out chapter 4.)

Mistake #2: Trusting an incomplete budget

Trusting an incomplete budget each month is like walking across a raging river on a rotting suspension bridge. You may make it across once, maybe a couple of times, with no problems. But the more you keep trying it, the more likely you are to hit a weak spot, one that can't hold you up. Before you know it, you're on your way down—and soon you'll be in over your head.

PENNY FOR YOUR THOUGHTS

Be not made a beggar by banqueting upon borrowing.

–ECCLESIASTICUS 18:33

That's why it's important to be extremely thorough when you plan your budget. (For tips on how to anticipate and plan for future expenses, check out chapter 2.) If you don't plan for *all* potential expenses, you're just giving yourself a false sense of security.

For example, let's say you bring home just enough money each month to cover your tithe, your mortgage or rent payments, your car loan, your insurance payments, your utilities, your credit card bill ($150 maximum), and your grocery bill. If you have a few shekels left over for a good time on the weekend, you might be tempted to believe that you're doing okay money-wise. You might even fool yourself into thinking that you're financially stable.

But what happens if your dream car starts leaking real transmission fluid all over your driveway? What happens if your house's 15-year-old furnace gives up the ghost in the middle of your state's worst cold snap in 40 years? What happens if you break your ankle in a freak croquet accident? Worse yet, what happens if someone in your family gets tired of your budget restrictions and decides to put your credit cards through a major retail workout?

Automobile repairs, home maintenance, medical expenses, and spur-of-the-moment shopping sprees—these are just a few of the unexpected costs that have been known to assault unsuspecting budgets. The reason most people don't plan for these emergency expenses is simple: There's no room for them. Their monthly budget is already stretched tighter than a waistband at Thanksgiving, so there's no money left to set aside for future expenses.

When an emergency arises, you'll probably do what most other people do: pay for it with a credit card. And your already tight budget will be pushed beyond its limit. Instead of breaking even with a few dollars left over each month, you'll find yourself coming up a little short. Instead of a $150 credit card bill that you pay in full, you may have a $1,150 bill (depending on how expensive the emergency is) that you can't pay off. If you make your regular monthly payment of $150, that leaves a $1,000 balance in your account.

Of course, it won't stay $1,000 for long. Your credit card's interest rate will make sure of that. Every day that number is going to creep a little higher, and every day you're going to sink a little deeper in debt.

And that's just with one relatively inexpensive emergency. Imagine what would happen if a couple of unexpected expenses decide to double-team you. *Hasta la vista, budget.*

You can't avoid emergency expenses, but with some advance planning you can keep them from becoming budget killers.

Mistake #3: Buying when you shouldn't
Before all you bargain hunters out there get too excited, we should point out that I'm not talking about waiting for a "factory closeout offer" before you buy a new coffee table or waiting for a "13-hour sale" before you buy a new sweater. (Though

I do strongly recommend waiting for sales or special offers before you buy.)

No, what I'm talking about here are more far-reaching financial choices: buying decisions that are made out of ignorance (or at least a naive approach to finances) or indulgence.

For example, if you don't have a lot of experience in dealing with money matters, you may not recognize poor financial advice when you get it. As a result, you may fall for lies and half-truths like these.

> ➤ Maxing out your credit cards is okay, as long as you don't miss a monthly minimum payment.

> ➤ Buying a house is always better than renting.

If you can't spot the faulty logic in this advice, you might be tempted to splurge on things like clothes, furniture, or compact discs and then whip out the plastic to pay for it. Or, even worse, to purchase a house before you're able to afford it.

If you didn't know any better, you might assume that maxing out credit cards and buying a house as soon as possible are things everyone does—that this is the way twenty-first century finances work. (Unfortunately, you probably wouldn't be too far off the mark, but that's beside the point.)

Likewise, if you suffer from a chronic case of the "gotta-have-it" or if you have a hard time telling the difference between a want and a need, you'll find yourself susceptible to a different type of thinking—but one that's just as dangerous. I'm talking about mindsets like the following.

> ➤ Buy now and pay later, before you're too old to enjoy the things you want.

> ➤ You are what you own.

If you find happiness, fulfillment, or status in the things you own, you're bound to make more than your share of poor buying decisions.

Whatever the reason for your unwise buying habits, whether it's ignorance or indulgence, our credit-happy society is more than willing to exploit your weakness. If you can sign your name, chances are good that you can get a credit card. And if you can get a credit card, you have the ability to satisfy the impulse to buy whenever you want (until you reach your credit limit, of course).

With a flash of plastic or a signature on a dotted line, you can own things that your parents or grandparents had to save months, even years, for. With that kind of buying power at your fingertips, is it any wonder that you find yourself struggling with debt?

The problem with unwise purchases isn't always *what* you buy but *when* you buy it. A couch, a computer, or even a new bathtub could be considered an unwise purchase. If you haven't budgeted for it, your payment for that purchase will show up as debt. And the more unbudgeted things you buy, the bigger your debt will be.

PENNY FOR YOUR THOUGHTS

Creditors are a superstitious sect, great observers of set days and times.

—BENJAMIN FRANKLIN

The Great Escape

"That's great," you may be saying. "But I already know *why* I'm in debt. What I need to find out is *how to get out of it!*"

Good point. Knowing what causes debt is like knowing who passed you a cold virus. It may satisfy your morbid curiosity, but the information is not terribly useful in the here and now. What you really need is some helpful advice or "medicine" to make the problem go away.

Okay, if you're ready to tackle your debt problem, there are four things you'll need to do.

1. Stop borrowing.

Let's say someone left your bathtub faucet running and flooded your entire house. You're looking at about four feet of standing water everywhere. Now before you grab a bucket and start bailing, wouldn't it be a good idea to turn off the faucet? Otherwise, all your hard work would be just a waste of time, with more water pouring in as quickly as you can bail it out.

The same principle applies to your finances. Before you start working on strategies to clean up your flood of *debt,* you need to "turn off" your borrowing. If you don't shut down the source of the problem, all your efforts to become financially free will be just a waste of time, with more debt pouring in as quickly as you can pay it off.

Stopping your borrowing means not using credit of *any* kind. That includes . . .

➤ bank loans

➤ personal loans (not even from your wealthy grandmother or your college roommate who struck it rich with an Internet IPO)

➤ automobile financing

➤ payment plans.

But the best place to start—or make that *stop*—is with your credit card spending, since that's probably what started your debt problems in the first place.

Fortunately, most credit cards have a built-in feature that will help speed up the non-borrowing process. Here's what you'll need to do to activate this feature.

➤ Preheat your oven to 425 degrees.

➤ Grease a cookie pan.

➤ Place your credit cards on the pan.

➤ Bake for ten minutes.

Charbroiling your VISA card may seem like a crazy idea, but is it any crazier than paying interest on, say, a dinner you ate (and charged to your account) two years ago? If you pay for meals with your credit cards and then don't pay off the balance each month, that's exactly what you're doing! (*Oven roasting your credit card is a joke, of course—don't try it!*)

Easy credit is your enemy when you're trying to pay down a debt. By forcing yourself to pay for things with cash or a check, you'll be a lot less likely to buy stuff you can't afford.

Try putting your plastic shopping companions in a safe deposit box, in the bottom of a container of water in the freezer, or in some other place that's not immediately accessible. You may be surprised by how quickly the urge to buy passes if you have to go out of your way to retrieve your plastic. (Make laziness work for you!) The best thing you can do for your financial health is to teach yourself to live without credit.

It's important, though, that you take action *now*. Don't wait until after you make one more major purchase or until you pay off a certain loan. If you wait for the right time to stop borrowing, you'll never get around to doing it. There will always be "one more thing" you have to buy first.

2. Talk to an expert.

Find a trusted financial counselor to help you deal with your debt. Don't make the mistake of trying to fix the problem on your own. You're way too close to the situation to be able to look at things objectively. You need an extra set of eyes, preferably one belonging to an expert, to help you see the big picture. A trained financial advisor can help you understand the many options that are available to you and keep you from doing any more debt damage.

The first place to look for an advisor you can trust is your church. Don't believe the old saying that people who are heavenly minded are no earthly good. Many churches offer excellent financial counseling programs as part of their ministries. If yours does, make an appointment with one of the ministry leaders to find out what you need to do to join the program.

If your church doesn't offer a financial counseling ministry, talk to your pastor about your situation. He may know of someone—perhaps an accountant, a banker, or a business person in the

GLAD YOU ASKED

Should I consider declaring bankruptcy?

Depends on what your motives are. If you're being hounded by your creditors and need some time to work out a payment plan, then declaring bankruptcy might be the way to go. If, however, you're simply trying to protect your assets and wipe out your debts, declaring bankruptcy would be an irresponsible and cowardly route to take. If you make a commitment to repay money, you have an obligation–to your creditor, yourself, and the Lord–to honor it.

church or community—who offers free financial counseling for people in need.

You won't need to do a lot of preparation before you contact the counselor. In fact, all you'll really need to do is introduce yourself and explain your situation briefly ("I have about $20,000 of debt, and a collection agency is threatening to repossess my car"). The counselor will then schedule you for an appointment and tell you exactly what you need to do.

Working with Your Counselor

In the meantime, though, here are a few dos and don'ts to help you get the most from your counseling experience.

Do...

tell your counselor *everything* about your financial situation. Turn over all of your financial records, receipts, and contracts. Expenses that you consider insignificant—purchases such as a daily newspaper or a triple espresso on the way to work in the morning—may be helpful in giving your counselor an accurate view of your spending habits. The more information you give, the better equipped your counselor will be to help you.

Don't...

try to make your financial situation look better than it is by keeping information to yourself or hiding certain expenses or debts. No one's going to give you a gold star for good financial behavior or call your parents if you've been a naughty spender. So if you ordered a set of commemorative Dwight and Mamie Eisenhower salt and pepper shakers from the Home Shopping Network last night, 'fess up. It's okay to be embarrassed about your financial situation, but don't let your embarrassment keep you from getting the help you need.

Do...

be open to suggestions and new ways of looking at your finances and your daily living expenses. Your counselor may suggest strategies and solutions that you've never considered before—or that you don't really *want* to consider. For example, your advisor may suggest selling your second car and learning to live with just one in the family. Resist the urge to laugh in his face and give him 64 reasons why that's a lame idea. Instead, give the matter some serious thought. Consider whether it *is* possible for you to get by with one car for a while. By keeping an open mind when you talk with your advisor, you may discover some surprising debt-reduction strategies that actually work for you.

Don't . . .

be offended if your counselor says things that seem critical of your past financial dealings or decisions. The brutal truth is that you've made your share of financial mistakes. If you hadn't, you wouldn't be in the position you're in. That doesn't mean you're a bad person, and it doesn't mean you're a money moron. It means you're human—as fallible as the rest of us. Your advisor's job is to help you learn from your mistakes, so that you won't repeat them in the future. To do that, the advisor is going to have to point out what those mistakes are—whether you like it or not.

Do . . .

ask as many questions as it takes to help you understand the strategies your counselor suggests. After all, *you're* the one who has to put those strategies into action. If you don't understand why your advisor is asking you to do something, say so. Get an explanation that makes sense to you. When it comes to your finances, the only stupid questions are the ones you don't ask.

Don't . . .

expect your advisor to work miracles. He or she will not—repeat, *will not* . . .

> ➤ introduce you to a wealthy benefactor who will pay off all your bills for you

> ➤ find a legal loophole to get you out of paying what you owe

GLAD YOU ASKED

What is loan consolidation? Is it something I should consider?

Loan consolidation is when a person borrows a large amount of money at a relatively low interest rate to pay off other high-interest loans. Whether it's right for you depends on your situation. If you haven't taken care of the underlying problems that created your debt in the first place, you may find yourself worse off after consolidating your loans than you were before. If you keep up your spending habits, it won't be long before you have more high-interest loans to worry about–in addition to your large consolidation loan.

25

➤ set you up with a new identity south of the border to help you escape your creditors.

Getting out of debt takes a lot of hard work, dedication, and sacrifice. And there's nothing your financial advisor can do to change that.

3. Set up a budget.

One of the first things a financial advisor will do is ask you to make a list of all your monthly expenses. These will include mortgage or rent payments, utilities, grocery bills, car payments, credit card bills, and school loan payments.

Your counselor will then help you prioritize your loans and financial responsibilities, based on how far behind you are in your payments, how much you owe, and what the interest rates are. Together you will decide which debts should be paid immediately and which ones can wait for a while.

After you've made those decisions, the next step is to create a budget that sets aside enough of your monthly income to cover your expenses and start paying off your debt. In chapter 2 you'll find everything you need to know about setting up a budget, so there's no need to cover the specifics here.

The important thing to remember, though, is that a budget works only if you commit yourself to it. It's important that you treat it like a law and not like some general guideline. If your budget says to pay $150 a month on your VISA bill, pay $150. Don't write a check for $130 and pocket the extra $20 for spending money. Don't skip a payment and vow to pay double the next month. Despite your best intentions, you probably *won't* pay double the next month—and you'll find yourself even deeper in debt.

GLAD YOU ASKED

My creditors are really starting to get impatient. What should I do?

Personally contact the account manager of each of your loans. Fax each one a copy of your budget and your payment plan. Explain how much you can afford to pay each month and how much time you need to pay off the loan. If that doesn't work, get your financial counselor or a group like the Consumer Credit Counseling Service (CCCS) involved. Collection agents are more likely to listen to a third party, especially a financial professional, than to someone who owes money (and who would likely say anything to stall for more time).

4. Develop new spending habits.

If you're reading this paragraph, you probably need to change your spending habits. How can we make such a bold statement? Because you wouldn't be looking at this chapter if you weren't struggling with debt. And you wouldn't be struggling with debt if it weren't for your spending habits.

The key to changing those habits is controlling your impulse to buy. Here are a couple of tips to help you.

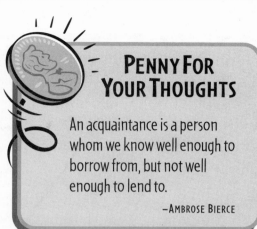

PENNY FOR YOUR THOUGHTS

An acquaintance is a person whom we know well enough to borrow from, but not well enough to lend to.

—Ambrose Bierce

➤ *Never spend money on anything that's not in your budget without first thinking about it for 48 hours (not continuously, of course—that would be a tad obsessive).* If you're an impulse buyer, a two-day wait may seem like an eternity. That's good. The more time you have to think about what you're doing, the less likely you will be to spend your money on something you don't need.

➤ *Always question yourself before you buy anything.* Here are some questions to get you started.

   a. Why do I want this? (Be honest here. Often people buy things because they're bored or unhappy or because they want to impress someone else, and *not* because they see something they really want.)

   b. Why do I *really* want this? (Just in case you were able to fool yourself the first time around.)

   c. How much use will I get out of it?

   d. Is this the best price I can get for it? Have I done enough checking around to make sure that I'm not overpaying? (Just make sure, as you drive from store to store comparing prices, that you don't spend more money for gasoline than the item is worth.)

   e. Considering my financial situation, is it a good idea for me to buy this?

If you can't give yourself convincing answers to these questions, you're probably better off not buying right now.

Return of the Living Debt

If you manage to get yourself out of debt, you deserve a lot of . . . well, credit. But don't start your victory dance just yet. The real trick is to *stay* out of debt. Think of that character in every horror movie who looks at the monster lying motionless on the ground and says, "Whew, I'm glad that's over." You know that's the cue for the beast to spring to life and start rampaging again.

The same thing is true with debt. It's dangerous even after it's been defeated. If you're not careful, it will spring to life when you least expect it and viciously attack your budget and your financial stability.

If you're serious about staying debt-free, there are three important things you need to do.

1. Identify your danger areas.

Think about the temptations, the spending habits, and the attitude toward money and possessions that got you in trouble in the first place. Write them down and put them in a place where you'll see them often. Share them with your family, your close friends, and your financial counselor. Ask the people you trust to warn you when they see your old habits or attitudes rearing their ugly heads again.

2. Enjoy your freedom.

Remember the constant pressure and tension you felt when your bills were overdue and you weren't sure how you were going to pay them? Compare that with the feeling of living debt-free (and actually being able to sleep at night). Once you've tasted financial freedom—really tasted it—you'll do everything you can to keep yourself from falling into debt again.

3. Master your plastic.

Keep in mind that as long as you carry credit cards, debt has a shot at a comeback in your life. Our advice is to get rid of them. But if you absolutely *must* use credit cards, make sure you set some strict guidelines about what you will and won't use them for. For example . . .

➤ Never use a credit card to buy something that's not in your monthly budget.

➤ Always pay the entire credit card bill each month.

➤ If you can't pay the entire bill one month, cut up the card and cancel your account. (Just make sure you pay off the balance first. Unfortunately, canceling your account does not cancel your debt.)

The Buck Stops Here

Think you're an expert on debt? Here's a quiz to see how much you know.

1. Which of the following is most likely to cause long-term debt problems?
   a. Buying books on how to avoid debt
   b. Leaving 20 percent tips
   c. Financing a car for four years
   d. Tithing

2. What's the first thing you should do when you find yourself in debt?
   a. Look for someone else to blame
   b. Book yourself on a daytime talk show to discuss your problem
   c. Invite your wealthy friends to dinner
   d. Stop borrowing

3. What can you expect from a financial counselor?
   a. A lot of taunting and teasing about your poor money-management skills
   b. Advice on how to set up a workable budget
   c. A bill that will plunge you even deeper into debt
   d. A sales pitch for his or her monthly newsletter

4. What's a good rule of thumb to remember when you're considering a purchase?
   a. Always wait 48 hours before buying something that's not on your budget.
   b. Beware a giggling salesperson.
   c. Real Rolex watches are not sold on street corners.
   d. The more you own, the happier you'll be.

5. Which of the following is true of debt?
   a. It's not something Christians have to worry about.
   b. The more you try to fix it, the worse the problem gets.
   c. It's unavoidable.
   d. If you're not careful, it's a problem you may have to overcome more than once.

Answers: (1) c, (2) d, (3) b, (4) a, (5) d

CHAPTER 2

Telling Your Money Where to Go

SNAPSHOT

"That's it," Carl announced in his best theatrical voice as he sealed the State Farm envelope. "The last bill of September has been paid."

"I'll alert the media," Karen murmured without looking up from her magazine.

"And I'm happy to announce that our financial outlook is good," Carl continued as he scanned his checkbook register, "as long as we don't spend another dollar until January."

"What? We're strapped for cash again?" Karen asked, dropping her magazine. "It seems like we go through this same thing every fall."

"It's September," Carl reminded her. "All of our major bills are due in September. The payments for your car insurance, my life insurance, and the house insurance all fall within a week of each other. When you add those to our regular monthly bills, it's a pretty big hit."

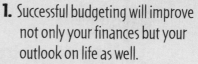

SNEAK PREVIEW

1. Successful budgeting will improve not only your finances but your outlook on life as well.
2. Many budgets are wrecked by hidden expenses that aren't accounted for.
3. If you want your budget to work, you need to set aside time on a regular basis to revise and update it.

"But if we know it's coming every year, we should be able to plan for it," Karen suggested. "That's what a budget is for."

"Which budget are you talking about?" Carl asked with a laugh. "The one we started on January 1 that lasted a week, the one we started in April that lasted three days, or the one we started in June that we didn't even get written?"

* * * * * * * * * * * * * *

For many people, a financial budget falls into the same category as a healthy diet. Sure, it's a good idea. Sure, there's a real need for it. Sure, the results can be dramatic. But . . .

There's also that sense of losing your freedom, of not being able to have what you want when you want it, of having your life controlled by a bunch of numbers on a piece of paper.

For one thing, there's the whole matter of sacrifice. Even nonfinancial types know that to make a budget work there's a good chance you'll have to cut back in areas you'd prefer not to cut back ("We have a four o'clock tee time—at the Putt-Putt course"). Then there's the hassle of trying to keep track of what you spend ("Can I get a receipt for that Happy Meal, please?"). Not to mention the headache of trying to make your numbers balance each month ("We would have been under budget this month—if it hadn't been for the mortgage and the car payment").

These complications explain why "tomorrow" is always the most popular day for starting budgets (and diets, for that matter).

So You Want to Start a Budget

The purpose of this chapter is not to talk you into starting a budget. (But you probably guessed that already from the decidedly discouraging tone of the opening paragraphs.) No, until you're ready to commit yourself to a budgeting lifestyle—and it is a lifestyle—all the encouragement in the world isn't going to do a thing for you, except maybe give you unrealistic expectations. And unrealistic expectations will sink your budget faster than a Caribbean cruise.

If you think the transition from spending freely to living on a budget will be smooth, or if you expect to see immediate results from your budget, you're going to be disappointed—and probably a little frustrated. And more than likely, you'll be tempted to pull the plug on the whole idea.

The truth is, an effective budget is going to require sacrifice, dedication, and work on your part. Sometimes it will require *a lot* of sacrifice, *a lot* of dedication, and *a lot* of work. That may not be what you want to hear, but it's what you *need* to hear if you're serious about budgeting. Call it tough love, financial style.

Of course, if that were the whole truth, only masochists and accountants would even bother with budgets. It's also important for you to know that once you get the hang of budgeting, once it becomes a natural part of your routine, you'll notice some significant changes—not only in your finances but in your outlook on life.

> **GLAD YOU ASKED**
>
> **Why do you say that budgeting is a "lifestyle"?**
>
> A budgeting mentality is not something that you can turn on and off at certain times of the month. If you're not committed to a full-time effort, you're not going to see much of a change in your financial picture. A single spending spree or even one moment of indulgence can wipe out months of hard work and planning.

Budget Benefits

If you plan and execute it right, a budget can...

> ➤ give you a sense of peace about your finances.

> ➤ help you determine what's really important in your life.

> ➤ give you a taste of financial success, regardless of your income level.

> ➤ improve your self-confidence.

> ➤ make you a smarter consumer.

> ➤ give you richer, more luxurious hair (okay, that might be stretching the point a bit).

You don't need an MBA to create a workable budget for yourself. You don't even need a college degree. In fact, you don't need anything except the desire to take

charge of your finances and the dedication to follow through on your decisions. That, and maybe a calculator. And a sheet of paper to write on. And a pen, of course—well, you get the idea.

If you're serious about grabbing the reins of your finances, read on. You'll find step-by-step instructions for creating a budget of your own.

First Things First

Before you start deciding where your income should go, you need to figure just how much you have to budget. This is called your Net Spendable Income, which sounds pretty impressive and complicated—until you realize that it's just a fancy name for the money you have left after tithes and taxes are deducted.

Determining your Net Spendable Income is not difficult at all. We'll walk you through the process, using Carl and Karen, the couple from the "Snapshot" scenario on page 31, as an example. You can find their budget in the Appendix. You'll also find a blank budget sheet there. We encourage you to plug in your own financial numbers in the appropriate categories to get an idea of how your budget might look.

Carl earns an annual salary of $48,000. (Karen just graduated from college and is currently looking for a job.) That $48,000 is Carl's gross income. (*Gross* in this case refers to pretax dollars; it's not a commentary on the way Carl makes his money.) Divide that amount by the 12 months of the year and you'll get a monthly gross income of $4,000.

$$\$48,000 \div 12 = \$4,000$$

From that amount we need to subtract a tithe. A tithe is the amount of your income that you give back to God via your church or other ministries. The word *tithe* means "a tenth," which kind of makes it obvious how much it will be. In this case, a tenth of Carl's $4,000 gross income is $400. (For more information on tithes, see chapter 16.)

$$\$4,000 \div 10 = \$400$$

Now let's figure taxes. Unless you're self-employed, your taxes (like Carl's) are probably taken out before you receive your paycheck. How much is deducted depends on your income level and other factors that are irrelevant right now. In Carl's case, 20 percent of his gross income is deducted through federal withholdings, Social Security, and state and local taxes. Twenty percent of $4,000 is $800.

$$\$4,000 \times .20 = \$800$$

When you subtract that amount from $4,000, you'll find that Carl is left with $3,200 per month after taxes.

$$\$4,000 - \$800 = \$3,200$$

We've already determined that Carl's monthly tithe is $400, so we need to subtract that amount from the after-tax total, which leaves him with $2,800.

$$\$3,200 - \$400 = \$2,800$$

So Carl's monthly Net Spendable Income—the amount he has left from his original $4,000 after tithes and taxes—is $2,800. That figure is his starting point for creating a budget. If you plugged in your own numbers along the way, you too should have a starting point for your budget— your very own Net Spendable Income total!

CRUNCHING NUMBERS

To calculate your Net Spendable Income, divide your annual gross income (your salary) by 12 to get your monthly gross income. Divide that total by 10 to get your monthly tithe. Subtract your tithe from your monthly gross income. Then subtract from that total the amount of taxes you have taken out of your paychecks each month. The amount you're left with is your Net Spendable Income.

Cutting Up the Pie

Now that you know how much money you have to budget, your next step is to identify where it needs to go. How you design your budget is up to you. If you want to use a cutting-edge computer program, click away. If you prefer to write a list of your expenses on a monthly basis, scribble to your heart's content. If you choose to copy the sample budget sheet in the Appendix and fill it out each month, that's fine too.

What's really important is that you account for *all* of your monthly expenses, both real ones and potential ones, in your budget. The sample budget that we'll be guiding you through is divided into 12 categories. Depending on how thorough you care to be, you may choose to divide yours into more or fewer categories.

Let's take a look at the dozen different paths your money may take after its departure from your bank account. Using Carl and Karen's finances as a model again, we'll go through the budget categories one at a time, explaining what each category includes and giving you tips on how to determine a specific amount to set aside for it.

1. Housing

This major category includes all expenses associated with your home. Your mortgage or rent, property taxes, homeowner's or renter's insurance, utilities, and maintenance costs all fall under this heading. Let's take a closer look at each of these expenses.

Your mortgage or rent payment is probably the easiest expense to figure because it's a set amount every month. Carl and Karen have a monthly mortgage payment of $900. As is the case for many homeowners, their property taxes are included in their mortgage payments.

Like your mortgage or rent payment, your homeowner's insurance bill is also probably pretty predictable. However, instead of paying this bill monthly, as you do with your mortgage or rent, chances are you pay it annually (once a year) or semiannually (twice a year). If you pay the bill annually, you'll need to divide the total by 12 to get your monthly amount. (If you pay it semiannually, you'll need to divide it by 6.) Carl and Karen pay $348 a year in homeowner's insurance, so their monthly cost is $29.

$$\$348 \div 12 = \$29$$

Utilities are a little trickier to average, because the amounts aren't always consistent. Depending on the time of year and the area in which you live, your electricity and gas bills may fluctuate by as much as $100 or more from month to month. What you'll need to do is figure out a monthly average, based on how much you've paid during the past 12 months. If you're an organized packrat, this won't be much of a chore. Just go to your "Utility" file and pull out your gas, electric, water, and phone bills for the past 12 months.

If, on the other hand, your filing system consists of shoving things in drawers or—gasp!—throwing them away, you may have your work cut out for you. If you can't find bills for the past 12 months, take a look at your check register. Trace your payments back 12 months and make a note of each check you wrote for utilities and how much it was for. If your past check registers are shoved in a drawer somewhere, try calling the utility companies and asking for a record of your past bills.

Once you have your figures for the past 12 months, add them and divide the total by 12 to get your monthly average. For example, here are the totals for Carl and Karen's past 12 electric bills.

September	$ 77.54
October	$ 56.77
November	$ 48.46
December	$ 55.53
January	$ 63.44
February	$ 54.92
March	$ 55.65
April	$ 54.73
May	$ 48.67
June	$ 52.77
July	$100.96
August	$ 98.56
TOTAL	**$768.00**

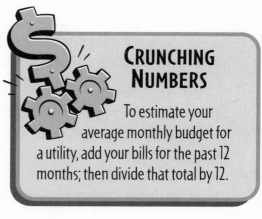

CRUNCHING NUMBERS

To estimate your average monthly budget for a utility, add your bills for the past 12 months; then divide that total by 12.

Divide the total by 12, and you get $64, Carl and Karen's average monthly electric bill.

You'll notice that for nine of the past 12 months, Carl and Karen's electric bill was less than their monthly average. That's important because they need the money that's left over in the budget to cover the other three months—the air conditioning months—when their bills exceed their budget.

Don't Forget the Other Expenses

Repeat this addition-and-division procedure for your gas bills, water bills, and phone bills. Utility bills that are fairly consistent, such as cable and sanitation (garbage collection), don't require such work. All you need to do with them is write down the amount of your monthly payment.

If you're wondering why Carl and Karen's budget figures always seem to work out to nice, round numbers, it's because Carl and Karen are fictional, and fictional characters don't have to worry about decimal points and fractions. You, on the other hand, as an actual person, *will* have to worry about decimal points. Depending on how precise you want your budget to be, you may round off your totals to the nearest dollar or the nearest cent.

PENNY FOR YOUR THOUGHTS

Annual income twenty pounds, annual expenditure nineteen nineteen six, result happiness. Annual income twenty pounds, annual expenditure twenty pounds ought and six, result misery.

—Charles Dickens

Maintenance expenses include any repair work or remodeling your home may need. That's not to say your house will require a certain amount of repair every month. Instead, this category serves more as a savings fund for when remodeling or repairs are necessary. If you're not sure how much to set aside each month for maintenance, start with at least 5 percent of your monthly mortgage payment. If you're planning a major, Bob Villa-type project on your house, you should probably double or triple that amount.

With Carl and Karen's $900 mortgage payment, their minimum monthly maintenance budget would be $45, which is 5 percent of $900.

$$\$900 \times .05 = \$45$$

If you think of any additional housing expenses that we haven't covered, write them down in the category marked "Other."

2. Food

For many people, buying groceries is a continuous process. There's usually one big trip to the store each week for meals and supplies for the next seven days. However, that trip is often supplemented by three or four side trips to pick up milk, eggs, chips, ice cream, or anything else that was forgotten the first time around.

These multiple shopping excursions are important to keep in mind when you budget, because there's a tendency to consider only that one big trip to the store each week when you estimate how much you spend on groceries. If you don't include *all* of your weekly grocery purchases, your estimate will be too low—and you will not be a happy camper in "Budgetland."

Keeping track of all your food runs may be a hassle, but in time you and your budget will be glad you did it. Perhaps the best method for maintaining an accurate total of grocery expenses is to post a sheet of paper on your refrigerator door and write down the amount of each purchase as soon as you walk in the kitchen.

After you've compiled two months' worth of grocery expenses—enough to reflect your true spending habits—add them and divide that number by two to get your monthly average. For example, Carl and Karen ran up a total of $430 of grocery expenses over a two-month period. Dividing that number by two gave them a $215 monthly food budget.

$$\$430 \div 2 = \$215$$

GLAD YOU ASKED

What should I do with the leftover money in my budget—like, say, when my gas bill is less than what I budgeted?

If you're thinking about buying something with it, forget it. It's not really "leftover" money, anyway; it's budgeted funds that haven't been spent yet. Leave it in your checking account so that you can use it to pay for future bills that exceed your budget. On your budget sheet (or in a separate ledger), keep a running total of your surplus funds—and your debits—for each category. At the end of your budget year, you should have close to a zero balance in each category. If you don't, you'll need to make some adjustments in your next budget.

Another word of warning here: Don't purposefully underestimate your grocery totals to make your budget look better. For you golfers out there, that's like cutting a few strokes off your actual golf score to improve your handicap. All you're really doing is creating unrealistic expectations for yourself. If it doesn't reflect the truth, you're the one who will pay the price for it in the end.

Lowballing your grocery expenses is a good way to blow your budget before you really get a chance to put it into action.

3. Auto(s)

Your vehicle expenses include your car payment(s), your automobile insurance premiums, your fuel bills, your charges for oil changes and other regular maintenance, and depreciation allowances.

Your car payment is a set amount—Carl and Karen pay $410 a month, for example—so all you have to do is write the amount in the proper place on your budget sheet.

Your insurance premium is also probably pretty stable, unless you've had an accident or collected a few speeding tickets lately. Carl and Karen pay a $276 premium semiannually (twice a year). That works out to $552 a year. Divide that total by 12, and you get a monthly auto insurance budget of $46.

$$\$552 \div 12 = \$46$$

Setting aside $46 every month greatly reduces the financial hit Carl and Karen will take when their big $276 insurance premium comes due twice a year.

Your monthly fuel bills can be estimated in the same way you estimated your grocery budget—by keeping track of each purchase for a total of two months, adding them up, and then dividing the total by two. For example, Carl and Karen's gas purchases over a two-month period added up to $190. Dividing that figure by two gives them a monthly budget of $95.

$$\$190 \div 2 = \$95$$

You can anticipate your car's maintenance costs by consulting your owner's manual for a suggested service timetable. Once you know what needs to be done over the course of a year, you can investigate the price of each service to get an estimate of how much you can expect to spend annually on maintenance. For example, Carl and Karen have their car's oil changed every three months at $22 a pop. That works out to four oil changes a year for a total of $88. On top of that, they pay $125 for an annual tune-up and $15 for a tire rotation. Counting just these *expected* expenses, Carl and Karen are looking at $228 annually for car maintenance.

$$\$88 + \$125 + \$15 = \$228$$

Dividing that total by 12, they get a monthly maintenance budget of $19.

$$\$228 \div 12 = \$19$$

Obviously, the older your vehicle is, the more money it will take to keep it running well. You may need to budget twice as much as Carl and Karen do. As they say in the car business, your mileage may vary.

Very few cars age gracefully—and the ones that do are usually owned by people who don't have to worry about depreciating value anyhow. That's why you need a depreciation fund in your budget.

Your depreciation fund is the money you set aside each month to repair your car if something were to go wrong with it or to replace it with a new (used) one. (There's more about the dos and don'ts of car buying in chapter 4.) Ideally, the amount you set aside should be enough to keep the car in good driving condition or to replace it every four to five years. Carl and Karen try to set aside $30 a month for their car's depreciation fund.

4. Insurance

Unless you're self-employed, it's likely that most of your personal or family insurance costs are handled through your employer and deducted from your paycheck. But even if you don't actually write checks for your insurance, it's still a good idea to include your deducted payments in this category to give you a complete picture of your financial landscape.

PENNY FOR YOUR THOUGHTS

Insurance: paying for catastrophe on the installment plan.

—ANONYMOUS

You can probably get the exact figures you need here from your paycheck stub. A quick glance at Carl's paycheck stub shows that he gets paid twice a month, and that he has $90 taken out of each paycheck for medical insurance, $21 taken out for dental insurance, and $6 taken out for life insurance.

Add those figures together and you'll find that Carl has $117 of insurance costs taken out of each paycheck.

$$\$90 + \$21 + \$6 = \$117$$

But since Carl receives two paychecks a month, he'll need to multiply that number by two to get his monthly insurance budget, which is $234.

$$\$117 \times 2 = \$234$$

If your insurance costs are automatically deducted from your paycheck—if you're not writing checks for them each month—they may not seem "real" to you. But these figures are a necessary part of your budgeting considerations. The more you know about where your money is going, the better equipped you'll be to make wise decisions in allocating it.

This category also includes any supplemental insurance you may have purchased—health, life, disability—that is not associated with your home or automobile. Again, if you pay your premiums annually or semiannually, you'll need to divide those totals by 12 or 6, respectively, to get your monthly insurance budget.

5. Debts

The quicker you eliminate this category from your budget—by paying it off, not just by erasing it—the rosier your financial future will look. We'll deal more with debt-reduction strategies in chapter 7. For the time being, though, you need to make sure that *all* of your debts are accounted for in your budget. That includes credit cards, bank loans, student loans, and personal loans (from, say, a friend or family member).

The good news is that since most of your loans probably have predetermined payment amounts you won't need to do much arithmetic here. Just add your various monthly payments and plug them into the proper categories. For example, Carl and Karen's minimum payment on their VISA bill is $38 and the minimum payment on their Discover card bill is $52. (There's more about credit card debt and the dangers of making minimum payments each month in chapter 1.) On top of that, their student loan payments are $80 a month. Add those numbers together and you'll see that Carl and Karen have a $170 (minimum) monthly budget for repaying their debts.

$$\$38 + \$52 + \$80 = \$170$$

You can see the incentive for eliminating this category. Once it's gone, Carl and Karen will have an extra $170 in their budget each month—a nice chunk of change they can use for savings or investments.

6. Entertainment

This is one of the broadest categories in anyone's budget. We could list three pages of entertainment activities that fit under this umbrella and still not mention some of your favorite pastimes. Let's just say that everything from vacations to club dues, from movie tickets to compact discs, from inline skates to computer games, from restaurant meals (yes, that includes fast food) to babysitting costs are included here. Put it this way: If you do it for fun or relaxation, and it costs money, it belongs here.

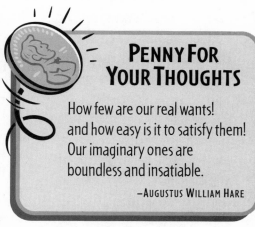

PENNY FOR YOUR THOUGHTS

How few are our real wants! and how easy is it to satisfy them! Our imaginary ones are boundless and insatiable.

—Augustus William Hare

You know the drill by now. To get an accurate idea of how much you spend on entertainment, you'll need to write down every entertainment-related expense you have for two months. Sure, it's going to be a pain to keep track of every dollar you spend for movie rentals and CDs, but it's important that you do it.

What makes it especially tough to get a handle on these expenses is that many of them are paid for with whatever spare cash you have on hand. You see something you want, and you throw down some bills to get it without thinking twice about it. Until now. Now, you not only have to think twice about it, you have to write the expense down.

After you've cataloged two months' worth of entertainment purchases, add the results and divide by two to get your monthly average. For example, at the end of two months, Carl and Karen added the amounts on their entertainment expense sheet and found that they had spent a total of $272. They divided that figure by two and came up with a monthly entertainment average of $136.

To avoid a budget overlap with the debt category, make it a point not to use your credit cards for entertainment-related purchases. A no-cash, no-purchase policy might also help you cut down on your entertainment spending (and make cash available for other budget categories). Credit cards have a way of silently encouraging you to overspend when you don't mean to. They make buying too painless and too easy. If you're having to peel off Lincolns, Hamiltons, and Jacksons to pay for your fun, you have a more tangible sense of just how much you're spending.

GLAD YOU ASKED

Why is accuracy so important in setting budget amounts? Why can't I just estimate how much I spend on entertainment and other categories?

Chances are, your estimate will be significantly off. Unless you're tracking every penny you spend, you'll find that it's easy to forget or overlook certain expenses. And each expense you forget throws your budget off a little more.

7. Clothing

For many people, clothes shopping is a seasonal activity. That means keeping track of your expenses for two months, as you did with groceries and utilities, may not give you an accurate figure for your clothing budget.

That leaves you with two choices. The easy way out is to estimate your annual clothing expenses, based on your best recollections of past shopping sprees. Do you buy a new ensemble every month? Every two months? Twice a year? How much do you generally pay for an ensemble? What about your spouse and your kids? How much does it cost to keep them looking sharp?

Keep in mind that it's better to overestimate your spending habits than it is to underestimate them. If you shortchange yourself when it comes to buying clothes, this category may turn out to be a budget buster.

Your other option is to comb through your receipts and pore over your check registers for the past year to see if you can piece together a more accurate picture of your attire-related spending. Obviously, that's a pretty tall order, especially when you have to include work clothes, casual clothes, workout clothes, school clothes, shoes, and even underwear. But the more accurate figure you get, the better able you'll be to determine a monthly average that works for you.

Carl and Karen searched through their receipts and came up with a total of $1,080 of clothing purchases in the past year. Dividing that number by 12, they calculated a monthly clothing budget of $90.

$$\$1,080 \div 12 = \$90$$

As was the case with entertainment purchases, it's best to pay for clothing with cash, not credit cards. Not only does it help you keep the debt and clothing categories separate, it also lessens your chances of overspending or spending money you don't have.

8. Savings

This is the Rodney Dangerfield of the budget world. It gets no respect. When finances get a little tight, it's the first category that gets sacrificed to make things right. And although trading future financial stability for immediate relief may seem like a good decision in the short term, eventually that choice will come back to haunt you.

You *need* to set aside money for savings each month. Not only does it give you a reserve to draw on in emergency situations, it's a key element in smart financial planning and eventual financial freedom. What's more, having a stash of cash at your disposal can give you peace of mind about your finances.

9. Medical

This category covers insurance deductibles—the part of your medical bills that you are required to pay—and other expenses not covered under insurance. These expenses might include contact lenses, orthodontic work, and medicine (both prescription and over-the-counter). If you have a pet, you also should include medical costs (veterinary/medicine) for your animal(s) in this category.

If you and your family enjoy good health, you might be able to get away with as little as $20 a month in this category. If, on the other hand, you or anyone else in your home suffers from a chronic illness or affliction, that amount will increase significantly.

Because medical expenses are generally unpredictable, your best bet for getting an accurate monthly average is to add your out-of-pocket medical bills for the entire past year and divide that total by 12. For example, based on the medical bills in their files, Carl and Karen spent $252 last year—above and beyond their insurance coverage. That works out to a $21 monthly average.

$$\$252 \div 12 = \$21$$

Depending on the health and medical condition of you and your family, your monthly average may look a lot different from that.

10. Miscellaneous

Think of this as the junk drawer of your budget—the place where you put all the things that won't fit anywhere else. Miscellaneous expenditures include daily coffees or sodas, newspapers, dry cleaning, haircuts, manicures, allowances, Christmas gifts, and magazine subscriptions.

Though these expenses may seem minor and insignificant, this is usually the place where budget battles are won and lost. There is real danger in underestimating your miscellaneous expenses when you create a budget. If you don't have enough money set aside for everyday necessities and little luxuries, your only choice is to dip into other budget categories for it. And once you start dipping, you jeopardize your whole budget.

To get an accurate reading of your miscellaneous spending . . . well, you know the procedure by now. Say it with me: For two months, you'll need to keep track of every dollar you spend that's not accounted for in other budget categories. Once you have two months' worth of miscellaneous expenses on paper, add them and divide them by two to get your monthly average. Carl and Karen came up with a total of $190 worth of miscellaneous expenses. Dividing that figure by two gave them a $95 monthly average.

$$\$190 \div 2 = \$95$$

On top of that, you'll need to consider all of the presents you purchase over the

GLAD YOU ASKED

How much should I set aside for savings each month?

The obvious answer is as much as possible. But even a little is better than nothing. Squirrel away a few dollars here and a few dollars there, and before you know it, you'll have a burgeoning nest egg–or at least enough to keep you from panicking when things go bad.

course of a year. For example, how many people do you buy birthday presents for? How about Christmas presents? Anniversary gifts? How much do you usually spend on each person for each occasion? Carl and Karen estimated their annual gift spending to be about $600. Dividing that amount by 12 gave them a monthly average of $50.

$$\$600 \div 12 = \$50$$

By adding this number to their previous total, Carl and Karen calculated a total monthly miscellaneous budget of $145.

$$\$95 + \$50 = \$145$$

Obviously those "insignificant" monthly expenses can add up pretty quickly!

11. Investments

Think of this final category as a bonus—a reward for careful budgeting and spending. Any money you have left over at the end of each month (aside from your stash for utilities and other running categories) can be funneled into this category, where it can be put to work collecting dividends for you.

At first, the investment category may be just a space filler in your budget. Chances are, you won't *have* any leftover funds to invest. That's okay. In time, as you learn to live within your budget and as you gradually lower your debt, you will be pleasantly surprised to find some extra cash lying around at the end of the month, just waiting to be put to good use.

In chapter 5, many of the different investment options available to you will be explored. For now, just remember that the sooner you start investing, the sooner you'll establish a budget that will *allow* you to invest, and the bigger your eventual payoff will be.

12. School/Child Care

If you don't have kids, you can skip to the next category right now. If you do have kids, though, you'll need to take into account their impact on your budget. Are you covering their college tuition? Are you sending them to a private elementary, middle, or high school? Are you paying for child care while you're at work? If you answered yes to any of these questions, add those expenses to your budget. If you pay any of these bills annually or semiannually, divide by 12 or 6 to get your monthly average.

Living with a Budget

You've identified your Net Spendable Income. You've calculated your average monthly expenses for every category known to the modern consumer. You've neatly categorized all of your figures on a specially designed financial sheet.

You're a lean, mean budgeting machine.

PENNY FOR YOUR THOUGHTS

Budget: a method of worrying before you spend money, as well as afterward.

–Dorothy Malone

Now all you have to do is learn to live with the financial restrictions you've set for yourself. And that shouldn't be a problem—at least not for the first couple of hours after you finish your budget. Beyond that, things might get a little dicey as the urge to splurge comes over you. . . and you start thinking about the "way things used to be"—back when you had complete freedom to spend your money any way you wanted, before you chained yourself to a set of totally unreasonable financial guidelines that no one in his or her right mind would ever have agreed to.

Okay, maybe your opinion of budgeting won't change quite that radically. It's safe to say, though, that you will experience your fair share of frustration and temptation as you try to make your budget work. Here are a few tips to help you begin a budgeting lifestyle.

Make budgeting a part of your weekly routine.

Set aside a certain time each week to organize your bills, write checks, and update your budget. It won't take a major chunk of time; five or ten minutes may be all you'll need. What's important is that you make budgeting a necessary part of your week—no different from, say, doing laundry. Not only will this keep your budget fresh in your mind, it also will give you a chance to spot early signs of trouble. For example, if you notice that your grocery bill is unusually high after two weeks, you may be able to make some adjustments to stay within your budget, instead of being unpleasantly surprised at the end of the month.

Don't tolerate excuses.

Chances are, you're going to think of some pretty plausible-sounding reasons why you should chuck your budget. Here are a few of the most popular ones.

➤ "When I write it all down, it's depressing."

➤ "I work hard for my money, so I should be able to spend it however I want."

➤ "I've already blown my budget this month, so I might as well keep going."

➤ "I'm too young to worry about a budget."

➤ "I'm too set in my ways to change my spending habits."

➤ "I'm just not a budget kind of person."

➤ "I'm not poor—I don't need a budget."

It's important that you recognize these "reasons" for what they really are: the excuses of quitters.

Keep things in perspective.

Living within a budget does require discipline and sacrifice, which can be tough for some people. However, it should *not* be a miserable experience—for you or your family. Rather than focusing on all of the things you have to give up for your budget, concentrate on the benefits you will gain from it—stability, peace, future security, not to mention the surplus for "fun" items (such as a vacation) that you're building each month.

> **PENNY FOR YOUR THOUGHTS**
>
> Anyone who lives within his means suffers from a lack of imagination.
>
> – LIONEL STANDER

If you have kids, give them a sense of ownership in the budgeting process. Post your weekly budget totals in a place where your entire family can see them. Encourage everyone in the household to come up with his or her own money-saving ideas.

Be flexible—but not too flexible.

After a few months, you may need to make some adjustments to your budget. If your family is going to bed hungry every night, you probably should consider increasing your Food budget. If you have leftover cash at the end of each week (stop laughing— it's theoretically possible), you may want to decrease your miscellaneous funds.

Do *not* make these changes to accommodate a sudden whim, though. Wanting a new leather coat is not a good reason to increase your clothing allowance. Pay attention to what's working and what's not working in your budget, and make your changes based on that information.

Try, try again.

Living on a budget is like quitting a bad habit. Sometimes it takes several tries before you succeed. You may not be able to live within your budget the first month you try it. Or the second. Or the third. That's okay. There's no shame in failing, as long as you are giving it your best effort and learning from your mistakes. Figure out where your vulnerable areas are—based on your unsuccessful past budgeting attempts—and make allowances for them in your next budget. With a little experience and a lot of dedication, you will succeed.

The Next Step

Are you satisfied with the way your budget numbers came out? Are there things you would prefer to change—categories that you would like to slim down and others that you would like to beef up? You can. In the next chapter, we will be looking at specific ways to sculpt your budget so that it provides maximum benefits for you and for your family.

 ## The Buck Stops Here

Think you're an expert on creating a budget? Here's a quiz to see how much you know.

1. What can a budget do for you?
   a. Give you a sense of peace about your financial situation
   b. Protect you from creditors
   c. Keep you from ever going into debt
   d. Improve your social skills

2. Which of the following is not one of the twelve budget categories?
   a. Entertainment
   b. Debts
   c. Miscellaneous
   d. Gambling

3. What is the best way to calculate your average monthly electric bill?
   a. Assume that your daily electric usage totals $1.89 and then multiply that number by 28, 29, 30, or 31, depending on the number of days in the month.
   b. Add your bills for the past 12 months and then divide that total by 12.
   c. Add $2.03 to the previous month's bill.
   d. Determine how much a month's worth of electricity is worth to you and pay that amount.

4. What is the danger of underestimating your clothing budget?
   a. *Looking* like you underestimated your clothing budget
   b. Losing your "Preferred Shopper" status at your favorite stores
   c. Having to wear a $15 pair of Keds with a $200 Tommy Hilfiger ensemble because you couldn't afford matching shoes
   d. Blowing your budget out of frustration with an ill-advised shopping spree

5. Which of the following is true of living on a budget?
   a. You can't really call it *living*; it's more like *surviving*.
   b. The younger you are, the easier it is.
   c. Flexibility is important.
   d. It comes naturally to most people.

Answers: (1) a, (2) d, (3) b, (4) d, (5) c

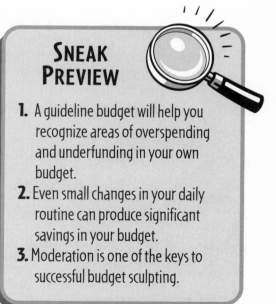

CHAPTER 3

Budget Sculpting

"**S**o how does our new budget look?" Karen asked as she peered over Carl's shoulder.

"Well," Carl began with an air of authority, "if you subtract our total monthly expenses from our Net Spendable Income. . ."

"Save the financial jargon for when we have an accountant," Karen requested. "Just give me the basics—in English."

"We're $4.00 short of meeting our budget each month," Carl explained.

"*Four* dollars—that's all?" Karen asked excitedly. "We could find that much under our couch cushions or in your pants' pockets each month!"

"Yeah," Carl reminded her, "but that number will change if we ever have kids. Or if we ever want to invest in anything. Or if we ever want to have any

SNEAK PREVIEW

1. A guideline budget will help you recognize areas of overspending and underfunding in your own budget.
2. Even small changes in your daily routine can produce significant savings in your budget.
3. Moderation is one of the keys to successful budget sculpting.

kind of savings whatsoever."

Karen's mouth dropped open. "You mean, that negative $4 balance doesn't include money for savings or investments?"

"No," Carl said. "So unless you have a secret fortune stashed away somewhere, we'll need to cut our budget."

"We could start with that health club membership you've used twice in the past year," Karen suggested helpfully.

"I've used it *three* times, thank you very much," Carl corrected her. "Besides, I was thinking we could start by cutting back on the Christmas gifts we buy for your mom, since she returns everything anyway."

Karen gave Carl a stern look. "This budget-cutting stuff isn't going to be fun, is it?" she asked.

"No," Carl replied. "Something tells me we're not in Kansas anymore, Toto."

* * * * * * * * * * * * * * * *

Hope for Your Finances

If you followed the step-by-step instructions in Chapter 2, you now have a fairly complete picture of your financial situation, like it or not. Don't forget, though, that the numbers on your budget sheet are changeable. The results can be improved dramatically, even if your Net Spendable Income is currently cowering in fear at the size of your monthly expense total.

PENNY FOR YOUR THOUGHTS

They way to stop financial joy-riding is to arrest the chauffeur, not the automobile.

—WOODROW WILSON

So don't tear up your budget sheet and resign yourself to being "financially challenged" for the rest of your life. There is hope for you and your finances. All you need to do is learn how to sculpt your budget to fit your future financial goals.

In this chapter, you'll find practical tips for slimming down the bloated areas of your budget and pumping up the weak ones. Specifically, you'll learn how to. . .

➤ judge the condition of your current budget.

➤ identify areas that need improvement.

➤ redistribute funds within your budget.

➤ cut your monthly expenses.

Making the Grade

How good or bad does your current budget look?

Tough question, isn't it? Your answer probably depends on whether the grading is being done on a curve or on a straight scale. If it's a curve, you probably can find people whose financial situation makes yours look positively peachy: the girl at the office who jokes about living from paycheck to paycheck, the single mother at church who is struggling to make ends meet, the neighbor who lost his shirt day-trading on his computer. Compared to their financial ledgers, your budget probably looks like a masterpiece of fiscal responsibility.

But what if the grading is done on a straight scale—A, B, C, D, or F? Would your budget be closer to the dean's list or academic probation?

Warning Signs

There are some obvious warning signs of a faulty budget, of course. A negative balance at the bottom of your financial sheet, for example, should be a clue that all is not well. But how do you know *how bad* your situation is?

And what if there *isn't* a negative balance at the bottom of your financial sheet? What if you have numbers plugged into every budget category—including savings and investments—and still have a little left over at the end of each month? Does that mean you're ready to graduate from "Budgeting University" and move on to more advanced studies?

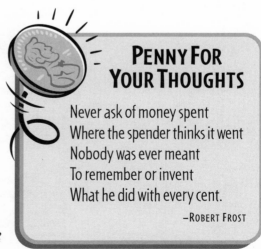

PENNY FOR YOUR THOUGHTS

Never ask of money spent
Where the spender thinks it went
Nobody was ever meant
To remember or invent
What he did with every cent.

—ROBERT FROST

Or is there something else you need to learn?

Put simply, how do you know whether your budget is something that needs to be followed or something that needs to be changed?

Wouldn't it be great if there were a simple chart that broke down your budget and gave you an idea as to how much of your Net Spendable Income should go to each category? Better yet, what if you could find a chart like the one below?

Playing the Percentages

The following chart is a guideline budget—repeat, a *guideline* budget. It is not the universal standard that all budgets are measured against. It has not been endorsed by your Local 431 Accountants' Union. It is not the secret to Bill Gates' success.

It is simply a model designed to demonstrate how your Net Spendable Income might best be divided among the 12 budget categories. The suggested percentages

GUIDELINE BUDGET

1. Housing	25 to 38 percent
2. Food	10 to 15 percent
3. Auto(s)	12 to 15 percent
4. Insurance	5 percent
5. Debts	5 percent
6. Entertainment	5 to 7 percent
7. Clothing	5 to 6 percent
8. Savings	5 percent
9. Medical	4 to 5 percent
10. Miscellaneous	5 to 8 percent
11. Investments	8 to 13 percent
12. School/Child Care	5 to 10 percent

for each category will help you recognize areas of overspending and underfunding in your budget and give you a target range of numbers to shoot for.

If you're a math whiz, you've already figured out that the next step is to convert your budget numbers into percentages so that you can compare them with the target ranges in the guideline budget.

To calculate the percentage of a specific budget category, all you have to do is divide the amount budgeted for that category by your Net Spendable Income. For example, Carl and Karen have $1,187 budgeted for housing costs each month. When you divide that amount by their Net Spendable Income of $2,800, you get .4239285.

CRUNCHING NUMBERS

To calculate the percentage of your Net Spendable Income that is being allocated to a specific budget category, divide the monthly budgeted amount for that category by your Net Spendable Income.

$$\$1,187 \div \$2,800 = .4239285$$

Slide that little decimal point over two places, round off to the nearest whole number, and you've got 42 percent.

Using the same simple procedure, Carl and Karen calculated percentages for all 12 of their budget categories. (You'll find their budget in the Appendix.) Here are the percentages they came up with. (Because they are fictional characters, Carl and Karen don't mind sharing details of their personal finances with you.)

CARL AND KAREN'S GUIDELINE BUDGET

1. Housing	42 percent
2. Groceries	8 percent
3. Vehicle(s)	22 percent
4. Insurance	8 percent
5. Debts	6 percent
6. Entertainment	5 percent

7. Clothing	3 percent
8. Savings	0 percent
9. Medical	1 percent
10. Miscellaneous	5 percent
11. Investments	0 percent
12. School/Child Care	0 percent
Total	**100 percent** *(with no savings)*

When you compare Carl and Karen's figures to the suggested percentages of the guideline budget, a few things become obvious.

1. The percentages for Housing (+4 percent), Vehicles (+7 percent), and Insurance (+3 percent) are all too high, according to the Guideline Budget.

2. The percentages for Food (–2 percent), Clothing (–2 percent), and Medical (–3 percent) are too low, according to the Guideline Budget.

3. The fact that Carl and Karen don't have any School/Child Care expenses gives them 5 percent of their Net Spendable Income to apply to other categories.

4. The fact that they aren't putting any money toward Savings or Investments leaves them vulnerable to future financial emergencies.

In order to balance their budget better, Carl and Karen will need to cut back in some areas and increase others. Chances are, the same thing is true for your budget.

GLAD YOU ASKED

So what if my housing takes up more than 38 percent of my budget, or if my car takes up more than 15 percent? As long as it all adds up to 100, what's the big deal?

If you have most of your income tied up in a house or a car, what will you do when an emergency situation arises and you need money? With no available funds to draw from, you'll probably have to go the credit route. And in the process, you'll create a whole new set of budgeting problems for yourself.

The good news is that no matter how little resemblance there is between your percentages and those of the Guideline Budget, there is hope for your financial future. With a little work, patience, and sacrifice—okay, a *lot* of work, patience, and sacrifice—you can sculpt your budget like an artist sculpts clay. By cutting a little here and adding a little there, you can gradually transform your budget into a financial strategy you can be proud of.

A Change Will Do You Good

Let's take a look at some of the different budget categories to see if we can find some obvious areas to cut.

Housing

If you have a bloated budget, it's a good bet that you'll find some telltale bulges in your Housing category. Many homeowners, in a quest for the house of their dreams, overextend themselves financially. They reason that the ultimate payoff—a house they can be proud of—is worth the risks. The most serious of those risks, of course, is an unworkable budget.

PENNY FOR YOUR THOUGHTS

Cast but a glance at riches, and they are gone, for they will surely sprout wings and fly off to the sky like an eagle.

—Proverbs 23:5, NIV

If your Housing expenses are standing between you and a healthy budget, there are a variety of options to consider. Perhaps the most radical one is downsizing: moving to a smaller, more affordable home. What would your budget look like if you cut your monthly mortgage payments by $300 or more?

Of course, in the time it took you to read that last paragraph, you probably had 20 good reasons flash through your mind as to why moving to a smaller house or one in a more affordable neighborhood is completely out of the question. And that may very well be the case, but if your housing expenses are demolishing your budget every month, you should at least give the idea some thought. (For more information on buying a house without sacrificing your budget, see chapter 4.)

Your mortgage is not the only place you can cut expenses in your Housing

CRUNCHING NUMBERS

Increasing your insurance deductible will decrease your premium.

category. Check your homeowner's insurance policy. You might find a little flab there as well. To trim the fat from your policy, contact representatives from at least three different companies and ask them to give you their best quotes for your insurance coverage. You may be surprised at the enormous difference in prices from one company to another.

After you decide which company's coverage is best for you, your family, and your budget sheet, you can cut your expenses further by raising the deductible (the amount you would pay if something were to happen to your home) on your policy. So instead of paying $250 of the damages if, say, the tree in your front yard were to drop in for a visit during a lightning storm, with an increased deductible you might pay $500.

Raising your deductible allows you to cut your premiums (the amount you pay for your policy every six months or every year)—sometimes by a significant amount. And cutting your premiums means cutting your monthly Insurance category, which is the whole purpose of this exercise.

Utilities Savings

The final category you'll want to look at is your utilities, where you can find plenty of cost-cutting opportunities if you know where to look.

Want to save on your telephone bill?

➤ Shop around for the best rates—even if it means listening to those annoying salespeople who call just as you're sitting down to dinner. Don't let them get away with telling you that you can save 50 percent on long distance bills and 30 percent on local calls. Pin them down on specifics. Find out how much you can expect to pay for each call you make. Ask questions to make sure there are no hidden costs in the prices you're quoted. Use the quote from one company to see if you can get a better offer from another. Figure out which offer makes the best financial sense for you and your family, and go with that.

➤ Place your long distance calls during reduced rate hours as much as possible. What you lose in spontaneity, you'll make up for in extra budget funds. Work out an arrangement with your out-of-state friends and family to alternate calls each week (or month) so that one of you doesn't get stuck with a super-sized telephone bill.

➤ E-mail, e-mail, e-mail.

Electricity Savings

Want to trim your electricity costs?

➤ Keep your thermostat set at a moderate temperature (68 to 70 degrees in winter, 74 to 78 degrees in the summer). Use blankets and layers of clothing to keep warm and more fans to stay cool. Resist the urge to fire up the heating unit the first time you get a few goose bumps. Hold off on blasting the air conditioning the first time you begin to perspire. Don't go overboard with this, though. No amount of savings is worth making life miserable for yourself or your family. Hint: If you find penguins nesting in your master bathroom or Bedouins setting up camp in your den, you'll know you've gone too far temperature-wise.

➤ Close all vents in the unused rooms of your house so that you're not heating and cooling areas that don't need it. If you live in a two-story home, close most of the vents upstairs in the winter. The rising heat from the first floor should be enough to keep things warm.

➤ Buy 130-volt light bulbs, which last five times longer than regular bulbs. Use low watt bulbs in places that don't require direct lighting. If anyone asks about it, smile and explain that you prefer a romantic atmosphere in your home.

GLAD YOU ASKED

Am I putting myself at risk with a high deductible?

Not necessarily. The difference in deductible costs that you would pay if you ever had to file a claim would more than likely be offset by the amount you save from paying lower premiums year after year. (For more information on your best insurance options, see chapter 8.)

PENNY FOR YOUR THOUGHTS

A penny saved is a penny to squander.

—AMBROSE BIERCE

Water Savings

Interested in cutting your water bills?

➤ Don't leave the faucet running while you brush your teeth or wash your hands. Wasting water like that makes about as much sense as pumping gas into a trash can after you've filled your tank. Either way, you're paying for the runoff.

➤ Don't do half loads of laundry. Always fill the machine to capacity. If that means waiting a couple of days to wash your clothes and being forced to wear second-string ensembles from the back of your closet, so be it.

➤ *Take no more than one shower or bath a week. Cleanliness and personal hygiene are wildly overrated.

➤ *Replace the grass in your lawn with Astroturf. Remember, what doesn't grow doesn't need watering.

*Okay, so there is such a thing as going *too* far in your quest for lower utility bills.

But that doesn't change the fact that you can make a serious dent in your Housing category just by implementing a few minor changes to your everyday routine.

Food

Does this scenario sound familiar? You're in a grocery line and you're in a hurry. It's been a long day and all you want to do is pay for your items and go home. The only thing standing between you and the automatic exit door is. . . an extreme shopper. You know this person: carries a coupon organizer the size of a concordance; files rebate offers alphabetically and cross-references them according to percentage of savings, expiration date, and manufacturer's geographic location; examines grocery receipts like an IRS auditor looking for questionable deductions; and considers *The Price Is Right* to be educational programming.

The next time you find yourself in line behind an extreme shopper, instead of muttering under your breath while you pretend to read tabloid headlines, see if you can pick up a few tips. Like it or not, if you want to reduce your Food budget, you're going to have to get serious about the shopping process.

First, you'll need to become acquainted with grocery pricing strategies. Sales and special offers tend to occur cyclically. In the soft drink aisle, Pepsi products may be on sale one week and Coca-Cola products may be on sale the next. In the pasta aisle, buy-one-get-one-free offers on spaghetti sauce may occur every six weeks or so. Many grocery retailers begin their weekly storewide sales on Thursday and continue them through the weekend.

With a little experience (and maybe a little note taking) you can start to anticipate these sales cycles. Then you'll be able to stock up on products when they're on sale, so you won't have to buy them when they aren't, saving money in the long run.

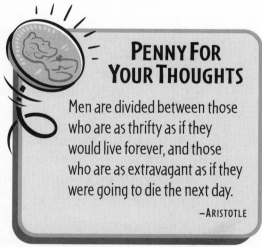

PENNY FOR YOUR THOUGHTS

Men are divided between those who are as thrifty as if they would live forever, and those who are as extravagant as if they were going to die the next day.

—ARISTOTLE

Comparative Shopping

If you shop at more than one store in your area, you'll need to learn to recognize bargains when you see them. Keep track of the prices of several key grocery items at different stores to see which retailer offers the best price for each item. For example, let's say you find a box of Bran Flakes cereal for $3.99 at Joe's Grocery. Is that a good price? How does it compare with the price at Sue's Supermarket a few blocks away? These are questions you'll need to be able to answer if you're serious about cutting your Food category.

One of the best strategies for reducing your Food expenses is planning your meals in advance. If you will take the time to plan a full menu for the week, right down to the last vegetable, salad, and Jell-O side dish, you can head to the supermarket with an exact list of items and ingredients to buy. Without a menu, you may be tempted to wing it on your grocery excursions: you wander up and down the aisles, picking up anything that looks good to you.

In the spirit of giving you more for your money, I've decided to throw in 10—

count 'em 10—bonus tips for reducing your grocery bill, all at no extra cost to you, the consumer!

1. *Never trust an electronic scanner.* Double-check the receipt to make sure that the advertised price is the price you're charged. You may be surprised by the amount of overcharging you catch.

2. *Don't go to the store when you're hungry.* In a battle of wills, a grumbling stomach will beat a cost-conscious brain every time. Walk into a store with an empty one (stomach, not brain) and you'll be walking out with more than you intended to buy.

3. *Bring a calculator to the store to keep track of your grocery total.* With a running tally, you'll know exactly how much more budgeted money you have to spend. So if you know that a pint of Häagen-Dazs will put you over your intended budget for the week, you'll probably be less likely to buy it. (We say *probably* because when quality ice cream is involved, human behavior can be quite unpredictable.)

4. *Cut back on the paper products you use.* Instead of paper plates and cups, use your everyday dishes. (What, a little dish washing is going to kill you?) Instead of paper napkins, use cloth ones. If people notice, they may assume you have class and sophistication.

5. *Avoid prepared foods, such as frozen dinners, pot pies, cakes, and cookies.* Instead of paying extra for someone else's labor, prepare these foods yourself.

6. *Buy generic or store-brand products instead of name brands.* If you were to take a blind taste test, you probably wouldn't be able to tell the difference between "off brand" products and name brands. So the question that begs to be answered is, How much is a fancy label worth to you?

7. *Clip and save coupons–but only the ones that will actually help you save money.* Coupons for products that you weren't planning to buy anyhow are not your friends. Neither are "sale-priced" items that still cost more than their generic counterparts. Don't be taken in by unhelpful coupons, or they may cost you money in the long run.

8. *When possible, buy your food in bulk quantities from discount stores.* The initial cost obviously will be high; however, when you factor in how long the food will last, you'll find that your savings are significant. In addition to cutting your grocery costs, you'll also get a strenuous cardiovascular workout as you attempt to wrestle 20-pound boxes of cereal and 50-pound bags of rice from the shopping cart to your car.

9. *Stay out of convenience stores.* In most cases, convenience is a luxury you pay through the nose for. Most mini-retailers charge twice or even three times as much as their supermarket counterparts for certain grocery items. They can do that because people in a hurry are willing to pay those prices. With a little advance planning and a willingness to be inconvenienced occasionally, you can avoid convenience store price gouging.

10. *Leave your children at home when you shop* so that you're not constantly bombarded with requests for candy, cookies, sweetened cereals, and every other sugar-coated item in a bright package.

Auto(s)

Is it possible that the sight of polished fiberglass can trigger a chemical reaction in the brain that causes it to temporarily shut down its centers of logic and reason? How else do you explain the decision of an otherwise intelligent and rational person to fork over tens of thousands of dollars for a brand new car that loses almost a quarter of its value the second he or she takes ownership?

If you want to keep the vehicle category from being the villain in your budget plans, do not buy a new car. Let's see that again in capital letters: DO NOT BUY A NEW CAR. If you're reading this chapter to learn how to cut your budget, the last thing you want to do is hop into a car fresh off the

GLAD YOU ASKED

When I eat at a restaurant or pick up some fast food for my family on my way home from work, should I include those charges in my grocery budget?

No. If you include eating out in your grocery budget, you may be tempted to think of restaurant meals (even fast-food meals) as viable alternatives to home cooking. They're not—at least, not from a financial perspective. (I'll leave nutritional issues for another book.) Instead, they should be considered "special events," similar to movies or concerts, and charged to the Entertainment category of your budget.

assembly line for a ride in the express lane to debt. (In chapter 4, you'll find out more about why new cars are among the worst investments you can make.)

That's not to say that used cars—especially *reliable* used cars—come cheap. They don't (usually). But often that word "used" (or "pre-driven," if you prefer) can mean the difference between a four-figure price tag and a five-figure one. With a little planning, patience, and wisdom, you can find the car that's right for you without running your budget off the road.

Making the Purchase

Here are a few tips to get you started.

➤ The cheapest car to drive is usually the one you're already driving.

➤ Pay cash for your car, if possible. Otherwise, get a loan from a credit union, bank, or wealthy family member, rather than from the car dealership. One of the problems with applying for a loan from a dealer is that any gains you make in negotiating the price of the car can be lost through a simple accounting trick in your finance agreement—and you may not even know it happened.

➤ When you negotiate the price of the car, don't include your old car as a trade-in. You'll usually make more money selling it on your own.

➤ Avoid double car payments. If you're still making payments on the car you have now, don't try to finance the car you want to buy. If that means repairing your old car and waiting another year to buy a new (used) one, so be it. If your budget is in need of cutting already, you do not need a second car payment.

➤ If possible, talk to the previous owner of the car before you buy it. Most people will tell you the truth about the condition of the car, if you ask. It would be a shame to get stuck with a money-guzzling lemon just because it didn't occur to you to ask the person who sold it to you how it runs.

➤ If you have to deal with a car salesperson, don't allow yourself to get caught up in his or her pitch. Know the type of car you want and the price you're prepared to pay *before* you go the dealership. Be willing to walk away if you don't get it. Remember, there's always another place to find a good car.

If you're not planning to get rid of the car you have now, you can also find ways to cut your vehicle budget by keeping it in good running condition and making smart financial decisions.

Maintaining Your Own Vehicle

Here are a few tips for you to consider.

➤ Set up a written maintenance chart for your vehicle so that you have a detailed record of its service history. Follow the suggested maintenance schedule in your car's owner's manual. The more preventive maintenance you give your vehicle, the more miles it will give you.

➤ Check your vehicle's gasoline rating and use the cheapest fuel recommended. Why pay for filet mignon if your car is happy with ground beef? (Metaphorically speaking, of course. In reality, it's best to keep all beef products away from your car's gas tank.) Note: Avoid cars that require high-test.

➤ As we suggested for your homeowner's insurance, contact representatives from at least three different companies and ask them to give you their best quotes for your auto insurance coverage. Your policy should include liability coverage (to pay for damages if you are at fault in an accident) and perhaps collision or comprehensive coverage (to pay for repairs to your car if you are at fault in an accident). Your deductible (the amount you would pay if something were to happen to your car) should be at least $100. Remember, the higher your deductible is, the less your premiums and your monthly auto insurance budget will be.

GLAD YOU ASKED

Are there times when it's best not to even file a claim and just pay for the damages myself? Absolutely. There are repercussions to filing an insurance claim. Your premium payments may increase. Your claim may be rejected. Your agent might even stop sending you calendars at Christmas. You need to decide whether the situation is serious enough to warrant getting your insurance provider involved. (For more information on your best insurance options, see chapter 8.)

Insurance

Chapter 8 offers more insurance tips than you can shake an actuary at, so there's no need to go into a lot of detail here about life insurance, medical coverage, and supplemental policies. We will point out, however, that you may be able to make some significant cuts in your budget simply by rethinking your insurance needs. (In case you're wondering, an *actuary* is a statistician who calculates insurance risks and premiums.)

What it boils down to is this: If you view insurance as an investment—or as anything but a way to provide for your family's financial needs—you may be overestimating your monthly insurance budget.

By choosing less expensive, but still viable, insurance options, you can free funds to use in other areas of your budget. For example, buying term life insurance instead of whole life can reduce your premiums (and your monthly budget) significantly. Likewise, you can reduce your medical insurance costs by eliminating hospitalization coverage in your policy. (However, if you suffer from a chronic illness, hospitalization coverage may be a worthwhile investment for you.)

Your best bet is to find an insurance agent you can trust, one who is more concerned about providing for your family's needs than for his or her own.

Debts

In the battle to establish your budget and make it strong, debt is your enemy. Your best military strategy is to send as many troops—led by George Washington, Abraham Lincoln, Alexander Hamilton, Andrew Jackson, Ulysses S. Grant, and Ben Franklin—as you can spare to defeat your foe. The quicker your debt is paid off, the safer your budget becomes.

And once your debt is paid off, you'll never have to worry about it again, and everyone will live happily ever after. The end.

Not quite, Cinderella.

You see, with 11 other budget categories demanding attention, very few people can spare the funds they need to pay off—or "defeat"—their debts in a short period of time. What's more, even if you manage to pay off your *current* debts, you are not guaranteed protection from future debts.

Unless you attack the root of the problem—your spending habits and attitude—your debt problems will be back . . . with a vengeance. And after winning the battle, you may end up losing the war.

Chapter 1 provides a comprehensive look at debt—what causes it, how to avoid it, and how to get out of it once you're in it—so anything we dwell on here would just be overkill.

Okay, here's the overkill. If you're serious about reducing your debt budget, the best thing you can do is take your credit cards out of commission. Cut them up, burn them, lock them in a safe-deposit box, or bury them in your backyard—just make them inaccessible. Force yourself to use cash or checks to pay for your purchases. If you can't afford to pay that way, don't make the purchase until you can.

This won't be easy, especially if you're a quick-draw artist with your credit cards. But when you learn to do without plastic, you'll see the results in your budget. Your savings and investments will rise up and smite your debt.

Entertainment

This seems like the most obvious place to cut your budget, doesn't it? Compared to mortgage payments and food for your family, entertainment expenses seem like a trivial way to spend money.

Isn't it a little hard to justify throwing away cash for a movie, concert, or even dinner at a restaurant with your spouse when there are so many other "serious" things to do with your income?

Not necessarily.

PENNY FOR YOUR THOUGHTS

The mass production of distraction is now as much a part of the American way of life as the mass production of automobiles.

–C. WRIGHT MILLS

It's likely that you can find several ways to reduce your entertainment budget. But it's important that you don't get carried away with your cutting. Remember, your goal is to create a *healthy* budget, and eliminating most of your entertainment funds isn't considered healthy. All work and no play makes Jack a prime candidate to become disillusioned with his budget.

Having said that, let's look at a few tips for *trimming* your entertainment budget.

➤ Plan your vacations during off seasons whenever possible. Instead of paying top dollar for accommodations during heavy traffic times (Florida during spring break, for instance), wait until the tourist trade has slowed to a crawl to take advantage of off-season incentive offers.

➤ Alternate paid entertainment, such as movies and concerts, with free activities, such as board or card games.

➤ Limit yourself and/or your kids to one sports league.

➤ Develop a home workout program that will allow you to let your health club membership expire.

Clothing

When you looked at the guideline budget and saw 5 percent next to the Clothing category, you probably had one of two reactions: Either you thought that seemed like an awful lot to spend on clothes each month or you assumed the number was a misprint because there was a "0" missing.

If the thought of cutting your clothing budget makes you break out in a cold sweat or start humming "The Impossible Dream," relax. Reducing the amount you spend on your wardrobe doesn't have to be a riches-to-rags story. You can do it as gradually or as radically as you're comfortable with.

PENNY FOR YOUR THOUGHTS

Art produces ugly things which frequently become beautiful with time. Fashion, on the other hand, produces beautiful things which always become ugly with time.

—JEAN COCTEAU

If you prefer the gradual approach, your first step might be to buy only items that are on sale. That way, you can still dress in the style you prefer, for the most part, while pocketing a few bucks in savings here and there.

Once you get the hang of scaling back your clothing expenditures, you might take the next step and try shopping in less expensive stores than you're used to. Instead of searching for name brands and hot designers, look for clothes that look good on you—and in your budget. As your shopping patterns change, eventually so will your attitude toward clothes. You'll find that a healthy budget is even more satisfying than a to-die-for wardrobe.

If you have kids, especially toddlers and infants, the problem of clothes shopping is compounded. You know how it is. You can't walk through a mall without seeing adorable outfits that would look just perfect on your children.

But you know what else your kids would look good in? College. Especially if you have enough money saved to send them there. The way to build that kind of nest egg is to start a pattern of savings now. And the way you do that is by resisting the urge to buy clothes that your kids will grow out of before you have a chance to cut the price tags off.

Here are a few more tips for reducing your clothing budget.

➤ Make a written list of your family's apparel needs and buy clothes out of season whenever possible. With kids' clothes, you may have to estimate the size your fast-growing children will be when the items you buy are in season again.

➤ Buy outfits that can be mixed and used in multiple combinations. It will make your wardrobe seem a lot bigger than it really is.

➤ Hang out at factory outlet stores whenever possible. Name brand items at off-brand prices is a tough combination to beat.

➤ Shy away from dry-clean-only fabrics. Save yourself money in cleaning costs.

➤ Locate some good consignment (nearly new) stores and shop around. You may be surprised at the great bargains you'll find.

Medical

Preventive maintenance is the key to reducing your medical budget. You can avoid costly dentist bills by eating right and brushing your teeth regularly—and by teaching your children to do the same.

Taking proper care of your body through diet, rest, and exercise will help reduce your susceptibility to illness, injury, or general body malfunctions. Regular checkups often can nip potential problems in the bud and prevent them from becoming serious physical and financial catastrophes.

If you're looking for a more specific reduction tip, try generic drugs. (Don't try them *now*—just when your doctor prescribes medicine for you.) When you need a prescription filled, ask your pharmacist to recommend generic alternatives. They are much less expensive, but just as effective, as name brand drugs.

Don't Go Overboard

Moderation is a key to successful budget sculpting. Remember, there's a fine line between being frugal with your money and being a tightwad. What ultimately separates the two is attitude and motivation. Frugal people save money because they think it can be used better in other areas of their budget. Tightwads save money because they're reluctant to let it go.

Be careful that as you work to become frugal you don't lose sight of your goal and wind up in the Tightwad Zone. It's okay to be concerned about cutting budgets and saving money; it's not okay to be obsessed with it.

If you find yourself spending way too much time thinking about your budget and ways to shave a few extra dollars from it, or if you find that financial matters have taken priority in your life over your personal relationships, take a break from budget-cutting for a while.

Remember, sculpting a healthy budget is one of the most productive and healthy things you can do for your family—as long as you don't sacrifice anything truly important in the process.

 ## The Buck Stops Here

Think you're an expert on budget revisions? Here's a quiz to see how much you know.

1. What is budget sculpting?
   a. The process of creating three-dimensional art using butter knives and Play-Doh

    b. A fancy term for wadding up your financial sheet in frustration when you can't make your numbers work

    c. The illegal practice of changing numbers in a company's financial records to cover up evidence of embezzlement

    d. The process of cutting expenses in certain budget categories and adding funds to other categories

2. What can a Guideline Budget help you do?
    a. Justify spending 40 percent of your income on a new BMW roadster.
    b. Recognize areas of overspending in your budget.
    c. Make your friends think that you've taken advanced accounting courses.
    d. Keep you from having to make a budget of your own.

3. Which of the following is a recommended method for cutting your housing budget?
    a. Moving to a more affordable home
    b. Painting the exterior of your home black and orange to decrease the property value
    c. Declaring yourself a "conscientious objector to mortgage payments"
    d. Renting rooms to complete strangers

4. What is the greatest threat to your budget?
    a. Wealth
    b. Debt
    c. Terrorists
    d. "How-to" financial books

5. What's the best way to tell if you've crossed the line between being frugal and being a tightwad?
    a. Friends start referring to you as Ebenezer.
    b. You find yourself counting out corn flakes for your kids' breakfast.
    c. Store cashiers start to cry when they see you in their checkout line.
    d. You find yourself thinking more about your finances than about your personal relationships.

Answers: (1) d, (2) b, (3) a, (4) b, (5) d

CHAPTER 4

The Big Stuff

SNAPSHOT

"**W**hat did you think of that personal finance book you were reading the last time I saw you?" Ken asked as he and Brady made their way up the ninth fairway.

"Oh, don't get me started on that," Brady replied. "They had a formula in there about when you should buy a house, based on how much you have to put down and how much of your budget the payments take up."

"Yeah?" Ken asked. "And what did you find out?"

"Based on what I'm making and saving now," Brady said, "I should be able to afford a decent two-bedroom house in about seven years."

"Seven *years*?" Ken questioned. "You sure that wasn't a typo? Maybe they meant seven months."

"No, the guys who wrote it were real conservatives," Brady explained. "They thought debt was, like, the scariest thing in the world."

"Then my finances would make their hair stand on end," Ken said. "If I waited until I could afford

> ### SNEAK PREVIEW
>
> **1.** No matter how necessary they may seem, major purchases (such as a house and a car) can do permanent damage to a budget if they are not planned well.
>
> **2.** The most common, and most serious, mistake new homeowners make is buying too much house for their budget.
>
> **3.** For most families, buying a used car makes more financial sense than buying or leasing a new one.

something before I bought it, I wouldn't even be playing golf right now."

"And you're okay with that?" Brady asked.

"Well, I'll probably never be nominated for 'Personal Financier of the Year,'" Ken replied. "But I figure I can either be miserable waiting to buy something or be miserable trying to pay for it. I choose door number two."

"So your whole financial strategy is to choose the lesser of two miseries," Brady concluded.

"Hey, it works for me and my creditors," Ken replied with a grin.

* * * * * * * * * * * * * * * *

Normal Needs

The typical American family might have . . .

> ➤ a father
> ➤ a mother
> ➤ two kids
> ➤ a dog
> ➤ a cat
> ➤ a goldfish
> ➤ a house
> ➤ at least two cars
> ➤ a suburban address with a big mortgage

We have no statistical evidence to support this list. In fact, with the diversity that exists in our country, the idea of a "typical" American family has little or no practical value.

Our purpose in creating this list was to get you thinking about what *you* consider typical. Which items on the list did you question? If you grew up in a single-parent home, you might have objected to the notion that a family can't be called typical without a father or mother. And you probably know of typical (or at least semi-typical) families with more or fewer than two kids and no pets. And with rural and urban populations booming, the suburbs certainly can't be considered the home base of normalcy.

The two items that might have escaped your scrutiny were the house and the car. After all, every family owns a house and a car, don't they? Isn't that the way things work? You get a job and have a family, a place of your own, and an automobile.

What no one ever mentions, though, is how to pay for these things. If you're not careful, major purchases, such as a house and a car, can do serious damage to a young budget.

Let's take a look at how you can make major purchases without sacrificing your financial health.

A Home of Your Own

"Every time you write a rent check it's like throwing money away."

More than anything else, it's this financial principle that causes most people in their early-to-late twenties to begin their house search. And why not? After all, who wants to pay money to some landlord when you could be investing it in a home of your own?

There's certainly nothing wrong with that reasoning. Building equity in a house through mortgage payments does make more sense than giving money to a landlord. . . as long as you can afford the house.

There's always a catch, isn't there? In this case, it's your budget. If you can't squeeze a mortgage payment into your financial plans without overloading yourself with debt or taking funds away from other important areas, it's not time for you to own a house yet.

Paying rent to a landlord may be a bitter pill to swallow each month, but it beats the misery of trying to make mortgage payments you can't afford and wondering when the bottom is going to drop out of your finances.

PENNY FOR YOUR THOUGHTS

A man builds a fine house; and now he has a master, a task for life; he is to furnish, watch, show it, and keep it in repair the rest of his days.

–RALPH WALDO EMERSON

Commitment Shy?

The average mortgage spans up to 30 years. Now, before you move on to the next paragraph, take a moment to consider the previous sentence again. The payment period for an average house covers *three decades*. Babies born on the day of your first payment will have kids of their own and be approaching middle age on the day of your last payment.

That's a long time to be making mortgage payments. If you're hesitant to commit to such a long-term expense, you have good reason to be. Buying the wrong home, or even buying the right home at the wrong time, can set off a chain of harmful financial effects that you'll feel for years, even decades, to come.

If that's not enough to scare you—if you've determined that purchasing a house is in your best financial interest—you'll need to consider four questions.

1. *Is your job secure enough to take on a mortgage*? If you're not sure about your future employment prospects, hold off on the mortgage until things become a little more settled.

2. *How long do you plan to stay in the area?* If you think you'll be around for a while—five to seven years, at least—you should consider the possibility of buying a home.

3. *What is the economy like in the area in which you want to buy?* You don't want to get stuck with a house you can't sell because of poor location. When it comes time to buy, look for an area that is growing substantially or is expected to grow substantially in the next few years.

4. *What is the cost of living in that area?* If it's higher than what you're used to, your budget probably will have to be reworked to account for the increased costs.

A House Is a House, Of Course, Of Course

When you start your search for a place to call your own, one of the first questions you'll need to consider is what kind of home will best suit your family's needs right now.

We've narrowed the list of options to five: new house, used house, "fixer upper," condominium, or pre-built (mobile) home. Let's take a look at the pros and cons of each one.

PENNY FOR YOUR THOUGHTS

Our houses are such unwieldy property that we are often imprisoned rather than housed in them.

–HENRY DAVID THOREAU

New house

One of the obvious benefits of buying a new house is that you're not forced to live with the decorating decisions and lifestyle choices of previous owners. You don't have to walk around on orange and brown carpet until you can afford to redo it. You don't have to watch TV in a room that smells like a stale ashtray, courtesy of the family of smokers who lived in the house before you. You don't have to think of creative ways to hide the crayon drawings on the bedroom wall.

With a new home, you have the freedom to decorate according to your taste. You can prevent odors from running amok. You get to decide where the stains will go.

Building your own house (not with your own hands, but through contractors and construction workers) gives you the added advantage of being able to design your living space exactly as you want it.

How surprised would you be to learn that the major disadvantage of buying or building a new house is the cost? This is especially true with those who go the building route.

With few exceptions, people who choose to build a new house end up spending more money than they intended. Every little change to the construction plan, every little glitch in scheduling, means more money out of pocket for the homeowner. On top of that, overseeing the project requires a great deal of time and mental effort.

Used house

The two biggest advantages of buying a pre-owned or "used" house are that you don't have to worry about additional construction charges being added to your bill and that you get more for your money in the form of extras—appliances, curtains, curtain rods, towel racks, treated lawn—that the previous owner leaves behind. They may not seem like much . . . until you have to pay for them yourself. Then you realize just how much difference the "little things" make in the cost of owning a home.

The disadvantage of buying a used house is the wear and tear that the place has already undergone. You can make an educated guess about the condition of the house based on what you see, but you can't know for sure what it has endured at the hands of its previous owners and against the forces of nature.

That's why, before you decide to buy a house you really like, you should do a thorough check of the heating and air conditioning unit, the roof, the hot water heater, the kitchen appliances, and the bathroom fixtures to make sure that they are in good condition.

If you were born without the do-it-yourself/home-repair gene, you may choose to hire a professional to do the inspection for you. Then you can decide whether to purchase the house as is or back out of the deal.

Fixer upper

The advantage of buying a home in need of serious repair work is that you can get it for a relatively low price. If you have the skill, the time, and the patience to do the work yourself, you may be able to make a nice profit on the house when you eventually sell it.

The disadvantages are the insecurity and inconvenience that come from living in a run-down house, wondering when the next major repair need will rear its ugly head. And don't forget that a fixer upper requires additional budget funds for repairs.

If you choose to buy a fixer upper, be sure to check the house thoroughly, including the foundation, plumbing, and wiring, so that you'll have a good idea of how massive your repair project is going to be.

Condominium

The primary advantage of a condominium is that you don't have to worry about yard work or other outdoor chores. Most of those tasks are taken care of by professional crews hired by the condominium association. Other people enjoy the sense of belonging they feel in a condominium community.

The primary drawbacks are the fees required in addition to your mortgage, including common area maintenance fees, club fees, and other expenses that come from living in a private community.

Pre-built (mobile) home

Some people would never consider buying a manufactured home because of their preconceived notions about this type of living—not to mention the mobile home's reputation as a tornado magnet. But that doesn't change the fact that people from all walks of life have purchased manufactured homes and are quite happy with them. Pre-built houses give people better housing than they could afford otherwise, and it satisfies the needs of their families.

Unfortunately, buyers of manufactured houses face the same problem that new car owners must deal with: depreciation. A new pre-built home will lose about 25 percent of its total value when it leaves the sales lot.

If you decide to buy a mobile home, look for a previously owned model so that you can avoid the problem of depreciation.

CRUNCHING NUMBERS

A pre-built home loses about 25 percent of its value as soon as it is driven off the sales lot.

The Big Oops

The most common mistake new homeowners—young married couples, in particular—make is buying too much house too soon. They look for what they want and not for what they need, so they end up with everything they desire but nothing they can afford.

They might start out with good intentions—everyone does—but along the way they begin to confuse their wants with their needs. Instead of looking for the two-bedroom house they need now, they start thinking about how it also would be nice to have a guest room and maybe even a room that could double as a home office. So they start eyeing four-bedroom houses.

Instead of looking for one-car garages (since only one of their cars is worth putting in a garage), they start looking ahead to when they might have two nice cars. So they start checking out homes with two-car garages.

Instead of focusing their search in the areas they know they can afford, they start branching out to more expensive neighborhoods and playing the "what if" game ("What if we borrowed the absolute maximum that our bank is willing to lend us? We could buy one of those really nice houses!").

The High Cost of Housing

Meanwhile, their budget is hemorrhaging green stuff all over the place. An extra ten grand here and five grand there can make a big difference in the final price of a house, as well as in the monthly mortgage payments. Unfortunately, many people don't realize that they've bought too much house until a month or so after they move in, when it's too late.

If you're thinking of buying a house, there are two things you can do to reduce your chances of making such a mistake.

1. *Don't apply for a mortgage until you can afford to make a 20 percent down payment.* If you really want a house that goes for, say, $180,000, you'll need at least $36,000 in savings to use as a down payment. If you can't afford that kind of down payment, take it as a sign that the house is too expensive for you right now. Your best bet is to start looking at smaller homes or homes in less expensive areas.

2. *Make sure that your monthly Housing costs take up no more than 38 percent of your Net Spending Income (your income after Tithe and Taxes have been taken out).* You'll notice that I didn't say your *mortgage payments* should take up no more than 38 percent of your Net Spending Income. No, your monthly Housing costs include much more than mortgage payments; they include utility bills, home insurance payments, and maintenance costs. *Together*

these expenses should account for no more than 38 percent of your post-tithe take-home pay (incomes of $50,000 or less).

Few things in life are more exciting than buying your first home. But it's important that you not let your excitement overwhelm your judgment and your hard work to stay financially stable. Otherwise, your dream home may become your ultimate nightmare.

CRUNCHING NUMBERS

Monthly Housing expenses (mortgage payments, utility bills, homeowner's insurance, maintenance costs) for a family of four should take up no more than 38 percent of Net Spending Income (take-home pay minus tithe).

Car Talk

The second major purchase might actually be considered minor compared to the cost of a house. Even so, it can make a huge difference in your budget totals. The purchase we're talking about is an automobile (this category could include a motorcycle, truck— whatever).

If you make the wrong vehicle purchase, or even the right purchase at the wrong time, you risk long-term damage to your budget and your financial health. It's that simple.

If you're not apprehensive at the thought of buying a vehicle, you may not be thinking enough about it. Let's take a look at what's involved in the buying process to see if we can increase your apprehension a little. Let's suppose that your vehicle will be a car.

First Things First

The first question to address is whether a car is really necessary for you at this point in your life. Think about why you want a car. Are there alternative methods for getting where you need to be? What about walking or riding your bike? Not only would you get more exercise, you would also . . . yada, yada, yada.

Who are we kidding? Of course you need a car. You wouldn't be reading this section if you hadn't already made up your mind about that. Maybe your parents are getting rid of their second car, leaving you without wheels. Maybe your friends are tired of hauling your vehicle-less body all over the place. Maybe your old car finally lost its long battle with "junkies."

PENNY FOR YOUR THOUGHTS

After all, what is a pedestrian? He is a man who has two cars— one being driven by his wife, the other by one of his children.

—ROBERT BRADBURY

Whatever your circumstances, one truth remains constant. If you don't have a car, there's nothing we can say to convince you that you don't need one. So we won't even try.

Instead, we'll help you weigh your need for a vehicle against your financial situation so that you'll know what's right for you and your budget— *before* you find yourself across the desk from a smiling salesperson holding out a contract for you to sign.

Automobile Investment and Other Oxymorons

As we mentioned earlier, compared to the expense of a house, the purchase of a vehicle may seem like a relatively minor investment. The truth is, though, it's neither minor nor an investment.

Unless your official job title is "sultan" or unless the employees of Microsoft all call you boss, you probably can't buy a car without feeling the effects somewhere in your budget. So the purchase could hardly be called *minor*.

As for the notion that a vehicle is an *investment*, how many investments do you know of that decrease in value every day you own them (aside from Internet stocks)?

A car is a purchase. You don't buy it with an eye toward making money on it in the future. You buy it to use, to run down, to devalue. Then, when you're done with it, you get rid of it and buy another one.

Knowing the difference between an investment and a purchase may seem like an insignificant aspect of buying a car, but it's not. Your attitude and mindset play a major role in your purchase of a vehicle. If you can convince yourself that you're *investing* instead of spending, you'll be more likely to pay more than you should.

Let's Talk Money

Speaking of spending, how much do you expect to pay for a car? Ten thousand? Fifteen thousand? As much as it takes to get the car you want? Actually, the answer should depend on your savings account.

The best strategy for buying a vehicle is to save the money ahead of time so that you can pay the entire bill as soon as you get your car. That way you avoid having to pay thousands of extra dollars in interest charges. In fact, you will be *earning* interest every day your money stays in the bank.

Pay Cash If Possible

For most people, though, the thought of paying cash for an automobile falls into the same category as our national leaders achieving world peace or the Chicago Cubs winning the World Series—heartwarming ideas but unlikely to occur in this lifetime.

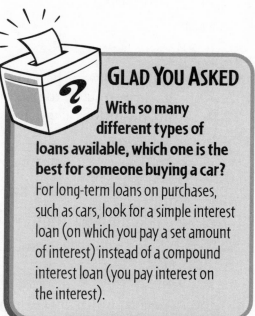

GLAD YOU ASKED

With so many different types of loans available, which one is the best for someone buying a car? For long-term loans on purchases, such as cars, look for a simple interest loan (on which you pay a set amount of interest) instead of a compound interest loan (you pay interest on the interest).

If you're like most people, you'll need to arrange financing to buy a car. That means you'll need to borrow it from a bank or credit union. Your first job, then, is to find the lowest possible interest rate for your loan. You do that by shopping around. Find out what rate your bank is offering and compare that with what other banks and credit unions are offering. A credit union will generally give you a better rate than a bank, but you have to be a member first.

Chances are, your car dealer will be more than happy to finance your loan. Don't let that happen. It may seem convenient—fill out a few forms right there in the dealership and it's done—but it's the most expensive way to finance a car loan. You almost always get a better deal if you get a loan elsewhere and just pay the dealer cash for the car.

Even if you can't pay the full amount for your car, you should be prepared to put down a sizable chunk for a down payment. Remember, the more you pay up front, the less you'll have to borrow; the less you'll have to borrow, the less interest you'll pay.

Crunching Numbers

Most lending institutions require a down payment of at least 10 percent for car loans.

Most banks, credit unions, and other lending institutions require a 10 percent down payment. So if you want to borrow money to buy a $15,000 automobile, you'll be expected to pay $1,500 up front. Your lender wants to make sure that you have a personal stake in the loan so that you'll be less likely to bail out of your payments later.

The Three Little Options

You have three choices when it comes to getting a car. (Actually, you have four, but for the purposes of this chapter, we'll rule out grand theft auto.) You can buy a new one, lease a new one, or buy a used one. Let's take a look at the pros and cons of each option.

Buying new

You know what's great about owning a new car?

1. The full warranty protects you from paying for costly repairs.

2. You don't have to worry about what a previous owner has done to it.

3. Banks will offer you a slightly lower interest rate to finance it.

4. Nothing beats the smell of the interior.

You know what's not so great about owning a new car?

1. It loses 25 percent of its value the moment you take ownership of it.

2. A quarter of your investment is gone before you start the ignition.

3. You lose one out of every four dollars you put into the car as soon as you drive it off the lot.

4. By the time you get it home, it is worth 25 percent less than what you paid for it.

To add insult to injury, air fresheners now come in new car scents. So any old beater can have that fresh-from-the-factory smell that you paid five figures for.

And did we mention that new cars immediately lose 25 percent of their value? That means when you pay $20,000 for a new car, you get something that's worth about $15,000. Think of it as leaving a $5,000 tip for your car dealer.

Don't Buy New

From the moment you sign your name on the contract, you'll have a debt greater than what your car is worth. And the depreciation doesn't stop there. By the end of its first year, your new car will have lost 30 to 40 percent of its original value. If, for some reason, you had to sell it, you'd still owe the bank more money than you could get for it. So you would be making payments for a car you no longer owned.

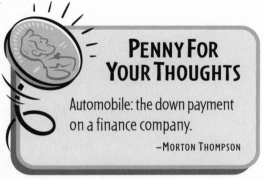

PENNY FOR YOUR THOUGHTS

Automobile: the down payment on a finance company.

—MORTON THOMPSON

Maybe you're okay with the idea of buying a car that loses its value or owing more on it than it's worth. If that's the case, here are four tips you'll need to keep in mind as you shop around for the best price.

1. Investigate all of the different options and packages available for the car.

2. Find the one that best suits your needs and your budget.

3. Choose the color you prefer.

4. Wait a year or so until you can buy the car used.

The final word on buying a new car is . . . don't.

Leasing

This concept surely began as a joke or an idle conversation between two car salespeople.

Salesman A: Wouldn't it be funny if we could get a guy to make monthly payments for a car but then not give him the car when the payments are done?

Salesman B: You mean, we would still own the car after the poor sucker has put his money into it for years?

Salesman A: Exactly. We could then turn around and sell the car as used and make even more money from it.

Salesman B: There's no way anyone would fall for a scheme like that.

Salesman A: He might if we convinced him it's more convenient not to own a car. We could sell him on the idea of getting a new car every couple of years or so.

Salesman B: Oh, so you're saying that people would keep paying for car after car but never actually own any of the cars when the payments are all made?

Salesman A: Yeah, we could call it leasing.

Salesman B: Leasing, huh? Look, you'd better stay out of the service department for a while. I think you've been sniffing too much exhaust. When people pay for something, they want to get something in return. Your leasing idea ranks right up there with your idea for selling extra rust protection on cars.

Hidden Dangers of Leasing

Here's a rule of thumb to keep in mind when you're looking for a vehicle: If a salesperson tries to talk you into something, it probably is not in your best interest to agree to it. And the more he or she tries to talk you into it, the less likely it is to benefit you.

With that in mind, you should know that one of the first questions a car salesperson is going to ask you is whether you're considering a lease. Unless having too much money is a problem you face every day, your answer should be "No." And the firmer your answer is, the less likely your salesperson will be to bring up the topic again.

Leasing works only for people who (a) always want to drive the newest model car, (b) only want to drive vehicles covered by the manufacturer's warranty, and

(c) can afford to pay top dollar for the privilege.

If that's not enough to talk you out of leasing a car, consider these additional costs.

➤ If you drive more than a certain number of miles—usually 10,000 a year—in your leased vehicle, you will pay an extra charge at the end of the lease. (Car dealers don't want you to put extra miles on *their* cars.)

➤ If you decide to pay off a lease early, perhaps because you find another car you really want, you will be charged a penalty so high that it probably would have been better for you to buy the car in the first place.

P.S. Don't buy a new car either.

Buying used

Automobile salespeople prefer to call them *experienced vehicles* instead of *used cars* (much in the same way that they themselves would prefer to be called *accuracy-challenged*, instead of *deceitful*).

However you choose to phrase it, the fact is that if a car has been owned or used before, it's a, well, *used car*. But that doesn't necessarily mean that it's already seen its best days or that it's a meltdown waiting to happen.

If you buy a "new" used car, one with 10,000 to 15,000 miles on it, you probably don't have to worry about getting a lemon. The way most automobiles are made today, you're going to get high mileage out of them—as much as 150,000 to 200,000 miles. So 15,000 up front isn't going to make much of a difference. (If you're wondering who gets rid of a car after 15,000 miles, reread the previous section on leasing.)

Even if you're buying a *used* used car—one that's, say,

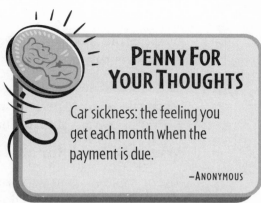

PENNY FOR YOUR THOUGHTS

Car sickness: the feeling you get each month when the payment is due.

—ANONYMOUS

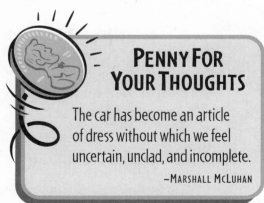

PENNY FOR YOUR THOUGHTS

The car has become an article of dress without which we feel uncertain, unclad, and incomplete.

—MARSHALL McLUHAN

five years old and has 60,000 miles on it—you can still get a good deal if the previous owner took care of it and gave it regular checkups.

The reason a used car sells for so much less than a new one is that you're not paying the 25 to 40 percent first-year depreciation that's included in a new car price. (Did we mention that buying a new car is not a good idea?)

Where to Look for a Car

The best place to start your search for a used car is with those closest to you. Let your family, friends, and fellow church members know what you're looking for. Find out if they know of someone who has an automobile for sale. The more of a connection you have with a seller—even if it's a "friend of a friend" relationship—the less likely it is that he or she will try to deceive you about the condition of the car.

The next places to look are dealerships that stock "pre-driven" vehicles. This is where you'll most likely find "new" used vehicles, late-model cars that were traded in for new ones, leased, or repossessed.

Your third, and least desirable, option is the classified section of your local newspaper. The problem with this method is obvious. You don't know the person doing the selling, so you have no way of knowing whether you should trust him or her. What's more, the seller doesn't know you, so he or she has no reason to give you a good deal—or even to be honest with you.

PENNY FOR YOUR THOUGHTS

Everything in life is somewhere else, and you get there in a car.

—E.B. WHITE

Pulling the Trigger

Let's say you've done your research and found the car you want. Now comes the ugly part: negotiating a price and closing the deal.

If you decide to buy a used car from a dealership, keep in mind that the powers-that-be generally try to make twice as much profit on a used car as they do on a new car. That means there's plenty of mark-up for you to knock down in your negotiations with the salesperson.

Your first offer should be substantially lower than the dealer's asking price—but not too low. Regardless of how shrewd a negotiator you are, offering $37 for a two-year-old Honda Accord isn't likely to inspire a flurry of counteroffers.

Do your research on the year and model of the car you're considering so that you know what it's worth. Say, for example, the car you want is worth $8,000. If the dealer is asking $10,000, make your first bid $6,000. More than likely, your bid will be rejected, so walk away. If you're not in a hurry to buy, you'll have a tremendous advantage over the dealer, who is definitely eager to sell.

The salesperson will probably phone you the next day to make a counteroffer of, say, $9,000. You know that's more than the car is worth, so you should decline. Explain that your final offer is $8,000. If the salesperson wants your business, that's the price he or she will have to meet.

Chances are, your salesperson will agree to the price—but only after a lot of dramatic pretenses about arguing with his manager and pulling all kinds of strings to make it happen.

As they say in commercials, no reasonable offer will be refused.

Questions for the Individual Owner

If you decide to buy from an individual, do yourself a favor and phone first. Ask the following questions to see if the car is worth investigating further.

> ➤ Is there rust? If so, where?

> ➤ How many miles are on the odometer?

> ➤ What's the gas mileage?

> ➤ How many previous owners had the car?

GLAD YOU ASKED

What is the best way to deal with a car salesperson?

As paranoid as it may sound, your best bet is to assume that your salesperson is working against you. Most car salespeople work on commission, which means the more money you pay for a car, the more money they will make. That doesn't leave them with a lot of incentive to find you the lowest price possible (though they will probably tell you that's exactly what they're trying to do). That means you need to do your research before you encounter a salesperson. Check the Internet, talk to people who know cars, and do whatever else you can to arm yourself with the information you need to get the car you want at the price you want to pay.

➤ What repairs have you had to make? How recently were they done? How expensive were they? What still needs to be done?

➤ How are the tires? the brakes? the window glass?

➤ Has it been in any accidents that you know of?

If, from your conversation, you judge that the owner has taken care of the vehicle and isn't trying to unload junk, make an appointment to see the car. If you don't know much about cars, drag along a friend or family member who does.

Regardless of where and how you make your purchase, remind yourself that if you are willing to wait, research, and haggle, you can find a car that you and your budget both like.

One More Thing

No matter how necessary a major purchase may seem, keep in mind that wrecking your budget to get it is not the solution. Remember, making mortgage payments is not the same as owning a house. Making car payments is not the same as owning a vehicle. The pleasure of having a house or car can be very quickly overwhelmed by the pressure of trying to keep it.

If your budget is financially sound, stay faithful to it. Make your major purchases when it's right for your budget, not when it feels right to you. When the balance sheet is totaled, you'll be glad you did.

The Buck Stops Here

Think you're an expert on making major purchases? Here's a quiz to see how much you know.

1. What is the mistake many people make when they purchase something major such as a house or car?
   a. Not trusting their realtor or salesperson
   b. Spending more than their budget allows

    c. Giving their credit card to a complete stranger

    d. Buying a red house and a white car, instead of vice versa

2. What's the problem with paying money to a landlord?
    a. Whenever you try to count it out for him, he or she shouts out random numbers to make you lose track and start over.
    b. Considering the condition your apartment's in, the landlord should be paying you to live there.
    c. You know he or she's just going to gamble the money away.
    d. It's money that could be used each month to build equity in a house of your own.

3. When do most new homeowners realize that they've bought too much house?
    a. When someone comes to install a chandelier in the nursery
    b. When they're given their own private zip code
    c. About a month or so after they move in, when it's too late to correct the problem
    d. When they are forced to implement a long-distance feature on their in-house baby monitors

4. What kind of car should you be looking for?
    a. Sporty
    b. Affordable
    c. Foreign
    d. Red

5. What is the problem with buying a new car?
    a. In a matter of seconds it will lose 25 percent of its value.
    b. Your friends will suddenly be ashamed for you to see their old cars.
    c. People will assume you're wealthy and start asking for loans and donations.
    d. Because most new cars have to be shipped from overseas, the destination charges alone will cost you $7,500.

Answers: (1) b, (2) d, (3) c, (4) b, (5) a

Financial Planning

CHAPTER 5

Finding Employment for Your Money

SNAPSHOT

"Good morning, Lee," Maria said as she climbed into the car with her coworker. "Did you see Roni-Corp was up two-and-a-half yesterday?"

"I don't want to talk about it," Lee grumbled.

"I thought you were going to buy some last week when you were online," Maria said.

"I changed my mind and bought Warders instead," he said quietly.

"Warders?" Maria said with a grimace. "Didn't you know they were being investigated for securities fraud?"

"No, I must have missed that courtesy call from the CEO while I was away from my desk," Lee said through clenched teeth. "If I'd known about the investigation, I wouldn't have sunk $500 of my hard-earned money into it."

"*Sunk* being the operative word," Maria quipped.

"Oh yeah," Lee said with a humorless chuckle. "It sunk like a stone."

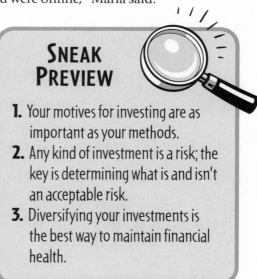

SNEAK PREVIEW

1. Your motives for investing are as important as your methods.
2. Any kind of investment is a risk; the key is determining what is and isn't an acceptable risk.
3. Diversifying your investments is the best way to maintain financial health.

"I've got to hand it to you," Maria said, shaking her head. "You have the most consistent track record of any day trader I've ever met."

"You've got that right," Lee acknowledged. "Eight investments, eight big losers. I just don't get it. You read every day about some pink-cheeked teenager who's made a fortune day-trading. Meanwhile, I consider it an achievement if my companies are still in business a week after I invest in them."

"Are you going to retire now with a perfect record?" Maria asked.

"Actually, I'm thinking of writing a self-help book," Lee replied. "It'll say, 'Here's my strategy for investing; do the opposite, and you'll make a fortune.' I'll call it The *Sadim Touch*."

"Sadim?" Maria asked.

"It's Midas spelled backwards," Lee explained. "Everything Midas touched turned to gold, whereas everything I touch dissolves into dust."

* * * * * * * * * * * * * * *

How much do you really want to know about investing?

Are you curious about . . .

➤ how a stock fund with an operating expense ratio of 1.4 percent per year compares to the national average?

➤ why bond mutual funds produce higher yields than money funds?

➤ who first decided that pork bellies would make a valid commodity in the free market system?

Or would you just like to know where you can get a fairly decent return on your money?

Many people probably fall into the latter category. The inner workings of Wall Street hold no appeal for them. The words *venture capital* don't pique their interest. The NASDAQ is not a priority in their lives.

But that doesn't mean they wouldn't mind getting in on the ground floor of the next big Internet venture.

This chapter treads the line between information and advice. The bad news is that you won't find the stock tip that allows you to retire to the French Riviera within the next six months. The good news is that you won't have to endure any lengthy discourses on the 1986 Tax Reform Act.

PENNY FOR YOUR THOUGHTS

'Tis money that begets money.

–THOMAS FULLER

Our goal is to introduce you to the basic principles of investing and to equip you with the information you need to make wise investment decisions.

Why in the World Do You Want to Invest?

Before we get into the *hows* of investing, let's talk briefly about the *whys*. Why do you want to risk your hard-earned money on the chance that you might make even more? You may think this is an irrelevant question, but it's not. Your motivation for investing will play a major role in your decision-making process.

Most people's reasons for investing can be divided into five categories: greed, laziness, ego, competition, and provision. Let's take a look at each of these motivations to see how it can affect your investment strategies.

Greed
Greed doesn't necessarily involve Scrooge-like penny-pinching or a Trump-sized desire for acquisitions. Greed is simply wanting more than you need.

In the realm of investments, the question you must ask yourself is this: How much is enough? This isn't a question that's usually answered with a dollar figure. The answer usually comes in the form of a description like . . .

➤ "I just want a little more than I have right now."

➤ "I want enough to be financially secure when I retire."

➤ "I want to have enough so that my kids will never have to work a day in their lives."

➤ "I want to have enough to hire Bill Gates to repair my computer."

People who lose big on the stock market or in other investment opportunities usually do so because of greed. And it's not always just a matter of going overboard in the amount they invest.

Being dissatisfied with what you have or what you're earning also makes you vulnerable to shady salespeople. Most get-rich-quick schemes rely heavily on greed to blind would-be investors to the truth.

PENNY FOR YOUR THOUGHTS

A businessman is one who buys at ten and is happy to get out at twelve. The other kind of man buys at ten, sees it rise to eighteen, and does nothing. He is waiting for it to rise to twenty. When it drops to two he waits for it to get back to ten.

—V.V. NAIPAUL

Usually, greed is what motivates high-income professionals to risk money in questionable tax shelters. Most of them could pay their taxes and still have plenty to live on comfortably, but the desire to hang on to a little more causes them to take foolish risks.

And if greed is your motivation for investing, that same desire may cause you to make foolish choices as well—choices that might end up costing you dearly in the long run.

Laziness

At first glance, this reason may have you scratching your head. Greed is understandable; it makes sense. But laziness? What does that have to do with investing? Just this: People often try to use investments as a quick-fix solution to a problem they've ignored for years.

People who don't plan well, financially speaking, during their younger days, will eventually be confronted with the error of their ways. Maybe it's the specter of their kids' college bills that does it—or the prospect of their own retirement.

Whatever the cause, they are suddenly faced with the fact that they've wasted prime savings time during which they could have established a nest egg. In an effort to make up for their earlier failing, they jump into the investment pool with both feet.

In short, they panic and try to generate in five years what they should have saved over the past 20 years.

If you're wondering why that realization might cause such an intense reaction, consider the following numbers.

Let's say you figure out that you'll need $200,000 by the age of 65 in order to retire comfortably. And let's say you have $5,000 a year to invest.

➤ If you start investing your annual $5,000 when you're 30, you would need to earn about 0.77 percent interest per year on your money to reach your goal. (For the sake of comparison, consider this: Your bank's lowliest savings account—the one it offers to 10-year olds cashing in their piggy banks—probably pays triple that amount.)

➤ If you wait until you're 45 to start saving, you'll need to earn 6.7 percent interest per year to reach your $200,000 goal by the time you're 65.

➤ If you wait until you're 55 to start saving, you'll need to earn 28.7 percent per year to reach your goal. You'll also probably have to become a loan shark or mobster, since no one else collects that kind of interest over such a long period of time.

You can see why people who wait too long to address their future financial needs might get panicky and be tempted to take excessive risks in their investment choices. There's a tendency to settle into a "lottery" mentality, as they look for that one magic investment that will make them rich.

But if you're not willing to sacrifice and do the hard work of setting aside a little money every month, year in and year out, for your future, you can't legitimately expect your investment portfolio to do the work for you.

Ego
This might just as accurately be called insecurity or jealousy. The way it usually starts is that you see someone who has more than you do and decide that it's not fair. Once the self-pity subsides, you get the urge to do something about your financial situation.

If your job doesn't provide you with the kind of funds you need to live the lifestyle of your choice, your only other legitimate option is the investment market. However, if it's ego that's driving you, you'll soon find yourself humbled—and probably discouraged—by the market. To compensate and to soothe your wounded pride, you might overextend yourself the next time you invest. And that's where the trouble begins. The last thing you want to do is go into debt for an investment—no matter how hot it looks.

Competition

To some people, making money is simply a game. They have no particular attachment to the cash; it's winning that's important to them. If they're not competing against other investors, they're competing against the market or even against themselves.

This is perhaps the most dangerous motive of all. For people looking for the thrill of competition, investing can become a habit every bit as devastating as alcoholism or drug addiction. Competitive investors are often willing to sacrifice everything—including their family, friends, and faith—just to be part of the game. They become totally absorbed by—if not obsessed with—the act of investing.

Provision

Compared to motives like greed, ego, and competition, investing to provide for your family's needs seems downright noble. If you can earn enough in your investments to supplement your retirement fund, your children's education expenses, and perhaps even the down payment for their first homes, more power to you.

Know Your Motivation

If you allow yourself to be motivated by greed, laziness, ego, or competition—if you lose sight of what's really important, you become vulnerable to making foolish decisions about your money.

GLAD YOU ASKED

How do I know whether a financial advisor is good or not?

The rule of thumb is, if a financial advisor makes more money for you than he or she costs you, he or she is pretty good. Your best protection against getting burned, though, is to check the advisor's track record. Ask for at least five references from clients who have worked with the advisor for at least three years. If an advisor refuses to give you his or her references, move on to the next candidate.

If, however, you're motivated by a desire to provide for your family, you may adopt the motto that guides most doctors: "First, do no harm." Knowing that your family's future is at stake—that it literally lies in your hands—may cause you to be less tempted by get-rich-quick schemes and more dedicated to finding investments that are reasonably safe. (For more information on how to invest during different stages of your life, check out chapter 7.)

Risky Business

There is no such thing as a risk-free investment. Any time you give your money away with the hope of receiving more back in the future, you run the risk of losing your investment.

The general rule is, the greater the potential return on your investment, the greater the potential risk. In other words, no guts, no glory. You have to spend money to make money. But remember, money does talk. It usually says, "Goodbye!"

Risk is not necessarily bad. You could argue that the free market system is built on risk. It's risky to start your own company. It's risky to put your company's fate in the hands of shareholders. However, the potential rewards can make the risks seem worthwhile.

It's when risk goes beyond common sense that you get into trouble. Some investment risks are disasters waiting to happen. Keep in mind that the wrong risk at the wrong time can wreak havoc on your financial well-being—both now and in the future.

The key to smart investing is not necessarily to avoid risk but to evaluate it carefully before you venture in. Don't allow yourself to be blindsided by a possibility you hadn't considered. Weigh the pros and cons of a risk—with your spouse, if at all possible—then decide whether you're willing and able to absorb the possible loss.

If you're not able to, don't be foolish. Let the opportunity go. There will be plenty more where it came from.

PENNY FOR YOUR THOUGHTS

'Tis sweet to know that stocks will stand
When we with daisies lie,
That commerce will continue,
And trades as briskly fly.

—EMILY DICKINSON

103

Risk Reduction

There are three things you can do to reduce your risk in investing.

1. *Don't get involved with things you don't understand.* Most dishonest salespeople depend on their customers' lack of knowledge. They know that it's hard to convince savvy people to do things they shouldn't do with their money. If you don't have the experience to understand the financial reasoning behind an investment opportunity or the wisdom to be able to sort through the details of it, your best bet is to back away from the opportunity and keep moving. Stick with investments that make sense to you. (Or expand your knowledge base so that you can have an informed opinion about a wide variety of financial topics—whichever you prefer.)

2. *Don't risk money you can't afford to lose.* What happens when a "can't miss" investment opportunity comes along during a "can't afford" financial period of your life? You may be tempted to borrow the money—perhaps against your home or from savings accounts earmarked for your kids' college education. It's important that you resist that temptation. When you risk borrowed money in any investment, you're being foolish. When you risk money borrowed from other budget categories, you're being stupid.

3. *Don't make a quick decision.* One of the key elements in most get-rich-quick schemes is the need for a quick decision. You may be asked to make up your mind about an investment opportunity based on sketchy details and possibly unreliable facts. Some opportunities may even offer special consideration for getting in early. Don't fall for these schemes. With few exceptions, a good investment opportunity today will still be a good opportunity a few days from now. Take time to do some research—to weigh the pros and cons of the opportunity—before you commit your money.

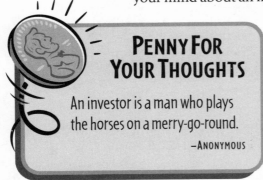

PENNY FOR YOUR THOUGHTS

An investor is a man who plays the horses on a merry-go-round.

—ANONYMOUS

Diversification: Six Syllables of Wisdom

In our ever-changing economy, no one can say for sure what will be a good investment over the next 10 years and what will be a bad investment. It's reasonable to assume that necessities such as food, housing, transportation, and health care will retain their value. But even these commodities have had their down cycles.

Who would have believed 50 years ago that farmers today would not be able to sell their products for what it costs to grow them?

Who would have imagined that in a nation of 100 million drivers, who own 70 million cars, an investment in one of the three big car companies would go sour?

What's a poor investor to do?

Actually, your best strategy is the advice you've heard since childhood: Don't put all your eggs in one basket.

Since there is no such thing as a sure thing, it makes no sense to have all your investment funds wrapped up in one stock—or even one type of stock. One major down cycle in that stock's performance could be enough to have you singing the blues.

That's why diversification, spreading your investments across a variety of areas— is essential to long-term investment stability. I'm not just talking about splitting your money between stocks and bonds, though. I'm talking about investing in some assets that are "paper"—such as stocks and bonds—and some that are real—such as real estate.

I would suggest you invest in assets that are not totally dependent on one country's economy. A portfolio with European stocks and bonds, Japanese companies, and Eastern bloc mortgage loans in it could sustain a drop in any one of the areas.

This may seem too complicated for someone with $1,000 to invest for future college needs, and it is. But for others, with, say, $10,000 to invest toward retirement in 30 years, diversification is a necessity.

The Seven Worst Investments for Beginners

For rookies, the worst investments are those whose risks outweigh their potential gains. And although there are many different ways to measure risk, perhaps the simplest is to look at the percentage of people who buy into an investment and get their money back and then to look at the percentage of people who receive a return above their investment.

Based on these criteria, here are seven of the worst investments you can make if you're not an expert investor.

Bad investment #1: Commodities speculation

Commodities trading is the buying and selling of materials for future delivery. If that seems pretty straightforward and easy to understand, hang on—things are going to get a whole lot murkier.

An offshoot of commodities trading is the *option contract*, which gives you the right to purchase a futures contract at a future date.

PENNY FOR YOUR THOUGHTS

I'm more concerned with the return **of** my money than I am the return **on** my money.

—Will Rogers

Huh?

What that means is that, as an investor, you pay a fee for the right to buy a contract at a future date. If the price of the commodity (which could be soybeans, oil, or anything else that is bought and sold) goes up while your contract is in effect—while you "hold the option"—you may choose to exercise the option and purchase the contract. More commonly, though, you would resell the option itself for a profit.

If the price of the commodity decreases while your contract is in effect, you can drop the option and forfeit your option money—leaving you with nothing to show for your speculating adventure.

The advantage of options, as opposed to buying an actual futures contract, is that the risk is confined to the amount you paid for the option. In a futures contract, the risk is potentially much greater (but so is the payoff).

The bottom line is this: Unless you can go to bed at night with the understanding that everything you've worked for your entire life can be lost while you sleep, stay out of commodities trading.

Bad investment #2: Partnerships

When it comes to investing, the most common type of financial partnerships are *limited partnerships*. Here's how they work. According to the contract, one person is named as the "general" or managing partner; everyone else involved in the investment, which typically involves real estate transactions, are named as "limited" or nonmanaging partners.

The purpose of a limited partnership is to confine the liability of the nonmanaging partners to their financial investments only. If the deal goes south, the limited partners lose only what they put in. They aren't held accountable for any other financial burdens, such as lawsuits, contract defaults, and future losses.

At least that's the way limited partnerships are *supposed* to work.

Unfortunately, the IRS has different ideas. Your friendly government revenue service came up with a concept it calls *recapture* to make sure that limited partners can't walk away scot-free when the IRS is owed money.

When a property is sold or foreclosed, some or all of the property's previous tax deferments become due and payable. Often this involves mucho dinero. And limited partners who believe they can't be touched by recapture soon find out how wrong they are.

The explanation of how recapture applies to limited partners requires about three times more information than you probably care to receive. So I'll just say that, as a limited partner in a venture, it's possible that you could someday be stuck with a five-figure (or even six-figure) tax bill as a result of your involvement in the partnership.

Bad investment #3: Tax shelters

The purpose of a tax shelter is to defer (delay paying) income taxes so that you can use that money to invest. And even though that may seem like a good financial strategy, you probably won't have to look hard for people who can tell you what a mistake it is.

Many investors have lost everything they own—literally, *everything*—in tax shelters. In fact, the only people who regularly make money from tax shelters are salespeople, attorneys, and accountants. (If that's not a strong indictment against them, I don't know what is.)

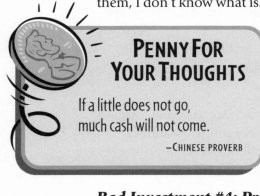

PENNY FOR YOUR THOUGHTS

If a little does not go, much cash will not come.

—CHINESE PROVERB

The fact is, unless you are willing to spend years in court and boatloads of money on accountants and attorneys, you will not beat the IRS at their own game. Think about it. Not only can they use your own money to fight you, they can change the rules in the middle of the game!

A good rule of thumb is to pay what you owe the IRS and find safer ways to make your money.

Bad Investment #4: Precious metals

Unlike stocks and bonds, which have a well-organized and highly competitive market, precious metals have no such market. In the precious metals market, a small group of investors and traders have the leverage to dictate prices and prevent you from making the kind of profit you could make with other commodities. Here's why.

In precious metals, you can buy contracts for future delivery in the commodities market, just as you can with virtually any other commodity. However, purchasing the actual metals themselves is a privilege limited to relatively few traders around the country.

These traders or dealers mark up the price of the metals, from 5 percent to as much as 12 percent, when they sell them. Then when they repurchase the metals they make an additional premium by way of a discount from the quoted retail price. Essentially, investors buy at retail and resell at wholesale. It's a system that works against the common investor, and it's one that you should probably shy away from.

Bad investment #5: Gemstones

Diamonds are forever. Unfortunately, the same can't be said of their investment value. The main drawback with dabbling in the gemstone market is that most novices tend to buy high and sell low. (And you don't have to be a Wall Street whiz to identify the weakness of that equation.)

The problem is that the average investor can't tell the quality or value of gems. He or she must rely on expert evaluation.

There are grading organizations that will swear to a gem's quality, clarity, and estimated value. But unless you can resell to the same dealer that sold you the stone, you have no guarantee that the next trader will accept that evaluation.

Even if the original dealer does agree to purchase the gem(s), there is no guarantee that you will get the current market value. In fact, the very idea of a "market value" for gems is a fuzzy concept at best. The prices are not quoted daily in the way that company stocks are.

With the odds stacked against you, your only real chance of making money on a gemstone is to sell it to someone who has even less knowledge than you do—and that solution certainly is not recommended.

Bad investment #6: Collectibles

Collectible coins, stamps, cards, and other unique items can be quality investments for knowledgeable buyers who take the time and effort to become good at what they do. This section isn't directed toward them. Neither is it directed to hobbyists who don't really care about the value of their collections.

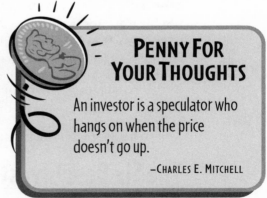

PENNY FOR YOUR THOUGHTS

An investor is a speculator who hangs on when the price doesn't go up.

—Charles E. Mitchell

This section is for novice investors who think they make a profit in the collectibles market. If you fall into that category, fall out of it.

Novice collectors who attempt to resell coins (or stamps or Pokemon cards or Beanie Babies) at the listed market price quickly discover that the price they paid for the items was retail and the price they are offered for them is wholesale.

Dealers buy low and sell high, so investors are forced to resell to dealers at a substantial discount. Again, not exactly primo investing strategies—for you, at least.

Bad investment #7: Stocks

Stocks—a bad investment? Yes, if you're a novice.

As with gemstones and collectibles, if you know what you're doing, you can make some decent cash in the stock market. But if you're an average investor, determining which stocks will do well and which ones won't may be beyond your capabilities. With the proliferation of Internet and communications companies, market analysis has become a highly technical field that very few investors are equipped to handle.

This is not meant to discourage you from maintaining stock, such as that offered by the company you work for, in your portfolio. I just want to discourage you from investing in stocks based on your "gut" feelings. Wouldn't it be terrible to find out that you lost your kids' college education on a feeling that turned out to be indigestion?

If you were to invest regularly in "blue chip" stocks and hold on to them for a couple decades or so, you probably would do all right in the market. But that's not the way most novice investors operate. They're too busy looking for the big score. They hear about a golden opportunity and rush to get a piece of it. Of course, by the time they hear about the stock, the price probably has peaked.

As the market turns down, the buyer suddenly panics and wants to sell to avoid taking a big loss. As a result, the net transaction is a loss.

And so it goes in the stock market.

The Six Best Investments for Beginners

Enough of the doom and gloom. Let's talk about *good* ways to invest your money. Although no investment should be considered foolproof, here are six of the safest and most sensible investments available to you.

Good investment #1: A home

Without question, the best overall investment for most Americans is a home.

Residential housing values have kept pace with inflation and appreciated approximately 4 percent a year on average. And even though that rate doesn't make it a standout in terms of growth investment, it does make it the best performer for the average investor.

What's more, a home serves a purpose beyond investment. It's something you can use while it appreciates (increases in value). Few other investments can make that same claim. (Try getting some use out of pork bellies while you wait for them to appreciate.)

Your best investment strategy is to make the ownership of your home your first priority. After that, you can use the money you were putting toward your monthly mortgage payments to start your savings for retirement or your children's education.

If it's extra incentive you're looking for, try this. If you pay off your home mortgage before your kids leave for college, by the time they graduate you can have enough money saved to pay for their entire education.

The easiest way to retire your mortgage early is to pay an extra amount—say, $100—on the principal each month. In the scope of your six-figure mortgage, a hundred bucks a month may not seem like much of an investment. In time, though, you will begin to see what a difference Benjamin Franklin (the man on the $100 bill) can make.

> **GLAD YOU ASKED**
>
> **Are there any publications you would recommend for a beginning investor?**
>
> *Consumer Reports* magazine has established credibility in the financial world by not accepting advertisements from any source, thus minimizing the possibility of favoritism or bias in their reviews. Once a year the magazine analyzes insurance, mutual funds, and a host of other financial products. Do yourself a favor–buy the issue and study its contents carefully before you make up your mind about where to invest your funds.

Here's an example of two different approaches to investing that illustrates the wisdom of investing in your home first.

Let's say the Marshall family and the Robinson family both have identical mortgages: a 30-year payment period, a 10 percent interest rate, and a loan of

$100,000. What's more, both families have determined that they want to invest $100 per month.

The Marshalls decide to add the extra $100 to each monthly mortgage payment until their loan is paid off. After their mortgage is retired, they decide to invest the amount of their mortgage payment (plus the extra $100) each month in a retirement account that pays 6 percent interest.

Here's what the Marshalls' financial picture looks like:

> ➤ $100,000 mortgage at 10 percent interest for 30 years = $315,720

> ➤ $100 per month additional payment saves $90,033 in interest.

> ➤ The Marshalls' home is paid off in 19 years.

> ➤ Their mortgage payment of $877 a month, plus the extra $100 a month, invested in a retirement account at 6 percent interest for 11 years = $182,947 (approximately).

The Robinsons decide to invest their $100 per month in a retirement account that pays 6 percent interest. Meanwhile, they continue to make their regular monthly mortgage payments for the life of the loan—30 years.

Here's what the Robinsons' financial picture looks like:

> ➤ $100,000 mortgage at 10 percent interest for 30 years = $315,720.

> ➤ The Robinsons' home is paid off in 30 years.

> ➤ $100 per month invested in a retirement account at 6 percent interest for 30 years = $100,953.

By paying off their mortgage before starting a savings plan, the Marshall family earned $81,994 more toward retirement than the Robinsons, who started their retirement account 19 years earlier than the Marshalls. Add to that the 11 fewer years that the Marshalls had to make mortgage payments, and you start to get a sense of why it's important to make your house your primary investment.

Remember, you're always better off earning interest than paying it.

Good investment #2: Rental properties

If you've ever rented an apartment or bought a home, you probably have all the experience you need to evaluate good rental real estate. Compare that with your ability to evaluate soybeans, stocks, or art, and you'll see why many people are drawn to rental properties as investment opportunities. The bottom line is that with real estate you have a better idea of what you're getting for your money.

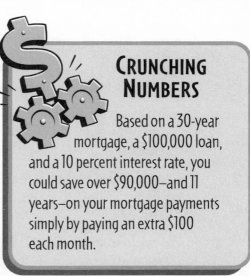

CRUNCHING NUMBERS

Based on a 30-year mortgage, a $100,000 loan, and a 10 percent interest rate, you could save over $90,000–and 11 years–on your mortgage payments simply by paying an extra $100 each month.

Another appealing aspect of this type of investment is that, unless you're renting property on Boardwalk or Park Place, you don't need a huge investment to get started. Even better is the fact that once you've made the investment and rented the property your tenants will pay off the mortgage for you in the form of their rent checks.

Good investment #3: Mutual funds

Mutual funds were designed to appeal to the average investor. Pooling the funds of a large number of investors to buy a broad range of stocks and other securities is a simple, but effective, way of spreading the risks.

Mutual funds are appealing for a few reasons. . .

1. Most funds allow small, incremental investments.

2. They provide professional investment management.

3. They allow tremendous flexibility through the shifting of funds between a variety of investments.

That's not to say you can invest in the first mutual fund offer that comes in the mail and then sit back and expect your dividends to come rolling in. As with all investments, you have to have a basic idea of what you're doing in order to be successful in the mutual fund market.

There are funds that perform well in good economies and then fold like a lawn chair during economic downturns. There are funds that hit the jackpot once but never duplicated their success. There are funds that charge outrageous administrative fees and reduce the return to their investors. And there are funds that have performed well for decades.

Even with the most successful funds, though, you have to be careful. Their success may be built on the expertise of a single manager. When that person leaves or retires, the fund—and its investors—may feel the effect.

If you have $10,000 or more to invest, you should subscribe to a good mutual fund newsletter so you can stay abreast of what's going on with the fund(s) you select.

Good investment #4: Insurance products

Generally speaking, insurance products such as annuities and whole-life policies have been among the safest—if not the highest earning—investments available. Policies that offer the dual benefit of insurance coverage and relatively high yields have become attractive products to many long-term investors.

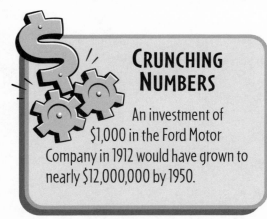

CRUNCHING NUMBERS

An investment of $1,000 in the Ford Motor Company in 1912 would have grown to nearly $12,000,000 by 1950.

Chapter 8 covers the topic of insurance in detail, so we won't get into specifics here. What we will do is issue the obligatory warning to do your homework before you invest.

While the insurance industry as a whole is very sound, several large companies have faltered recently due to poor investments. That's why it's important that you choose your insurer carefully and continue to monitor the company's financial health annually (at least), just as you would with any other investment.

Good investment #5: Company retirement plans

Though there's nothing special about the names of these plans—401(k), 403(b), TSA, HR-10, R-E-S-P-E-C-T (okay I made that one up)—there is something special about the features they offer.

First, there's the fact that the funds invested in these plans are tax deferred, meaning you don't have to pay taxes on them until you withdraw them—

presumably when you're old enough to qualify for a lower tax bracket.

Second, there's the matter of matching funds. Many companies offer to match their employees' retirement plan investments, up to a certain amount. You can't beat getting two investments for the price of one—unless you happen to work for one of the companies that provides 100 percent of its employees' retirement funds. You read that right: 100 percent.

Third, there's the wide array of investment options available to you. Depending on your company's plan and how it's administered, your options may include annuities, mutual funds, company stock, CDs, or any combination of these.

Good investment #6: Government-backed securities

Government-backed investments are considered absolutely secure by the experts who rate investment risk. Government-backed securities are the standard by which all other investments are measured.

Once you've saved enough to meet your investment goals—once the kids have graduated from college and you've retired comfortably—it seems like a logical move to shift your funds to government-backed investments, such as CDs, T-bills, and bonds. After all, why leave your money at risk when there's no longer any need to?

GLAD YOU ASKED

Where can I find a good financial advisor?

The best place to start your search is in your church. Ask your fellow church members if they have anyone they would recommend. From there, you can check the candidates' credentials with the National Association of Securities Dealers to make sure they are registered brokers. If you find that any of them have had their licenses suspended or revoked, cross them off your list.

One More Thing

Let's look at three final tips for investing.

1. *Start early*. Compound interest and dividends are beautiful things. The sooner you get your money working for you through investments, the more of it you'll have on your payroll when you really need it: later in life.

2. *Be consistent.* Setting aside money for investments when it occurs to you or when you have more than you know what to do with is not a sound financial plan. Discipline yourself to set aside a certain amount each month. It doesn't necessarily have to be a large amount (though it wouldn't hurt), but it should be consistent.

3. *Keep your eyes on your eventual goal, not on the peaks and valleys in between.* Don't panic in bad times or gloat in good times. Remember, you're in this for the long haul.

The Buck Stops Here

Think you're an expert on investing? Here's a quiz to see how much you know.

1. Which of the following is true when it comes to investing?
   a. Buying mutual funds is financially riskier than gambling in a casino.
   b. Investigating an investment opportunity before you jump in is a waste of time.
   c. Risk is not necessarily bad.
   d. If you're not willing to risk everything you have on a single investment, you shouldn't be in the market.

2. Which of the following is not a recommended method for reducing your investment risk?
   a. Don't get involved with things you don't understand.
   b. Don't risk money you can't afford to lose.
   c. Don't make a quick decision.
   d. Don't tell anyone what you're planning to do.

3. Why is diversification an important investment strategy?
   a. The more spread out your assets are, the less risk there is of losing everything in one bad market.
   b. Federal trade laws prohibit you from investing all of your money in one stock.

    c. If you try enough different investments, you're bound to strike it rich with at least one of them.

    d. It gives you the chance to impress people by casually using a six-syllable word in conversation.

4. Why are tax shelters considered a bad investment?
    a. The IRS is so lenient in enforcing tax laws anyhow that there's no need to try to avoid them.
    b. The only people who usually end up making money on them are salespeople, attorneys, and accountants.
    c. Most tax shelters are built with a cheap grade of lumber.
    d. Most tax shelters are located in bad areas of town.

5. Why is a home considered a good investment?
    a. Most investors have a soft spot in their heart for anything family-related.
    b. You can actually get use from it while its value appreciates.
    c. Most damage can be covered up with a coat of paint.
    d. It makes realtors feel important.

Answers: (1) c, (2) d, (3) a, (4) b, (5) b

CHAPTER 6

Putting the Gold in Your Golden Years

ACME HAMMOCK

SNAPSHOT

"We're here this afternoon to honor a man who has given this company 38 years of dedicated service. . . Jay Wrigley!" Mr. Campbell announced as he pointed to the gray-haired man sitting behind him on the stage.

The crowd of workers who had gathered in the assembly room, mostly because of the retirement party goodies, clapped politely.

Jay rose from his seat slightly and said, "I'd be happy to make it 40 years. I really would. I don't mind sticking around another couple of years."

The crowd roared with laughter.

"That's one of the things we'll miss most about you, Jay," Mr. Campbell said with a chuckle. "Your sense of humor."

"But I'm serious!" Jay pleaded. "I don't want to retire. I want to keep working. I'd. . ."

Mr. Campbell interrupted. "Jay, your coworkers all chipped in to buy you a present. On their behalf, it

SNEAK PREVIEW

1. Your ability to embrace and enjoy your retirement depends to some degree on your personality type.
2. It's better to view retirement as a slow-down period than as the end of your working days.
3. The best time to begin preparing financially for retirement is by age 40.

gives me great pleasure to present you with this $40 gift certificate to Brittany's Steak House."

The crowd responded with a halfhearted round of applause.

"Would it be possible to get the cash value for that certificate?" Jay grimaced as he said, "With my pension, I won't have enough money to buy groceries next month."

Mr. Campbell frowned, feeling a bit uncomfortable, and shook his head. "Always the kidder," he said.

"I'm not kidding," Jay said with a sigh. "I'm not ready to retire. I've got nothing in the bank."

"And finally, Jay," Mr. Campbell continued, virtually ignoring him, "the company would like to show you its appreciation by giving you this gold watch."

A hush fell over the crowd as Mr. Campbell handed the timepiece to Jay.

"Really, I'd rather stay. I'll take a pay cut. I just can't retire."

Still ignoring him, Mr. Campbell called out, "How about one more round of applause for Mr. Jay Wrigley!"

The crowd clapped politely and filed out the door.

Jay's head dropped and he stood looking at the gold watch. "I really would rather keep working," he said to no one in particular.

* * * * * * * * * * * * * *

Retirement Realities

A few years ago, a famous fast-food chain ran a commercial that showed the trials and tribulations of a "new kid" on the job as he struggled to learn how to take customer's orders, work the cash register, and prepare the food. The commercial ended with a heartwarming scene of the new kid's coworkers cheering his success and accepting him as one of their own.

What made this commercial stand out, though, is the fact that the "new kid" happened to be an elderly retiree.

It was one of those commercials that projected a warm feeling the first time you saw it. Whose heart wouldn't be warmed by the sight of a kindly old man being accepted in the workplace by kids 50 years younger than himself?

But there was an unsettling aspect to the commercial. You had to wonder, *What in the world is this septuagenarian doing slinging hamburgers with red-cheeked coworkers young enough to be his grandchildren? Is he enjoying his golden years?*

No one wants to picture somebody's grandma or grandpa having to slave away over a hot grill or getting splattered by onion ring oil—especially not for a minimum wage job. There's nothing heartwarming about that image. In fact, it's actually a little sad.

The one question you don't want to be forced to ask in your retirement years is, "Would you like fries with that?"

Of course, that's not everyone's retirement reality. Many people spend their golden years doing the things they've always wanted to do but never had a chance to when they were younger—things like traveling, golfing, and antiquing, mixed with a lot of volunteering, while enjoying life at their own pace.

One of the keys to successful retirement is preparation. Some people are prepared to retire; some people aren't. The purpose of this chapter is to assist you in your preparation.

Picture Yourself

Even if you're just starting out in the workplace, chances are you've already had some thoughts about retirement. (Monday mornings are an especially popular time for retirement fantasies.) When you think about your post-career years, where do you see yourself?

> ➤ On a golf course in Florida with a bunch of other senior citizens dressed in Bermuda shorts and multicolored hats?

> ➤ In a garden outside your house, on your hands and knees, nursing a sick hibiscus back to health?

➤ On the road in a Winnebago, helping to build a youth camp for underprivileged kids?

➤ Or, horror of horrors, in front of a TV, watching your third soap opera of the day while waiting for the next talk show to begin?

➤ On a lake with a fishing pole in one hand and a grandchild in your lap?

Nowhere does the phrase "Different strokes for different folks" apply more than to retirement plans.

PENNY FOR YOUR THOUGHTS

To live content with small means; to seek elegance rather than luxury…to be worthy… wealthy, not rich…This is to be my symphony.

–WILLIAM HENRY CHANNING

Living Longer

I'm not going to try to tell you which plans make good financial sense and which ones don't. Your plan for life after retirement is just that—*your* plan. I do encourage you to look at the big picture of retirement and take the necessary steps now to make your plan a reality in the future.

Before you start making plans, though, there is one thing you should know about your retirement years: Statistics indicate that there will be a few more of them—a decade's worth, to be precise. Since 1934, the average life expectancy of a man has increased *10 years*, from 63 to 73.

That means whatever you choose to do with your retirement years, you should make sure that it's something you can enjoy—and afford—for a long, long time. Remember, you've got an extra decade to fill!

The Retiring Type

Several years ago Harvard University conducted a study on 200 of its 65-year-old male graduates, 100 of whom had retired and 100 of whom had not. By age 75, seven out of every eight of the retirees had died. Only one out of every eight of the non-retirees had died.

After eliminating outside factors, such as illness, the conclusion the researchers reached was this: Most of the men died of terminal boredom.

Kind of makes you want to postpone your retirement party for a couple of decades, doesn't it?

In helping you look at the big picture of retirement, the first question to ask is this: Do you really want to stop working?

Even the question itself may come as a shock to many people who assume that retirement—the earlier the better—is not only the goal, but the right, of all workers. But as the Harvard study clearly indicates, retirement may not be your best course of action.

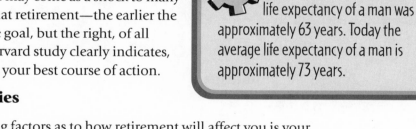

CRUNCHING NUMBERS

In 1934, the average life expectancy of a man was approximately 63 years. Today the average life expectancy of a man is approximately 73 years.

Type A Personalities

One of the determining factors as to how retirement will affect you is your temperament. The fact is, some people respond well to the change of pace that retirement brings; others go crazy after a week or so of down time.

Your chances of maintaining an enjoyable retirement may depend on whether you have a Type A personality or a Type B personality. To illustrate this, let's look at some of the characteristics of each type.

Type A people tend to. . .

➤ seek immediate challenges and results.

➤ make decisions easily, even if they're the wrong ones.

➤ hate the status quo and require a variety of tasks regularly.

➤ assume authority easily.

➤ manage a variety of tasks simultaneously.

➤ thrive on problems.

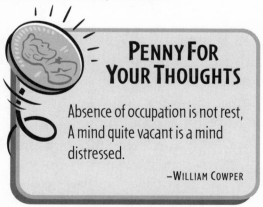

PENNY FOR YOUR THOUGHTS

Absence of occupation is not rest, A mind quite vacant is a mind distressed.

—WILLIAM COWPER

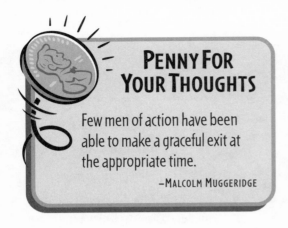

All of the traits that make Type A personalities good leaders in the workplace tend to work against them in retirement. Unless they have a variety of specific, challenging goals that keep them active in some type of work, they tend to become more introverted and easily irritated, even with their loved ones. (Pity the spouse of a retired Type A personality.)

As strange as it may seem, the leisure of retirement may cause too much internal stress for Type A personalities and result in all kinds of health problems—and, in some cases, early death.

Type B Personalities

Type B people tend to. . .

➤ accept circumstances that can't be changed.

➤ adjust to most situations.

➤ be more people-oriented than project-oriented.

➤ be "laid back" or "easygoing."

➤ find contentment in minor tasks, such as home maintenance or yard work.

➤ be passive about their finances.

Type B personalities are somewhat better suited for retirement than their Type A counterparts. However, if they're not careful, Type B people can have their retirement plans derailed by their passive approach to money. Instead of considering their post-career finances before they retire, they tend to take a wait-and-see approach. Unfortunately, most people who wait until retirement to consider their finances discover that they're too late to do anything about it.

This information is not to suggest that all Type A personalities should continue putting in 70-hour work weeks until they keel over on the job or that all Type B personalities should abandon the workplace at their earliest convenience. Fortunately, there are alternatives to a miserable post-career existence.

A Better Option

Rather than viewing retirement as an end to your working days, as many people do, it might be better to think of it as a sabbatical or a time for shifting your life into a lower gear.

The inescapable fact is that, unless you're like Dick Clark, age will catch up with you. Eventually it may even prevent you from performing your job responsibilities. Some jobs, such as ones that require intense physical labor, may be affected earlier than others. Ultimately, though, age will become a hindrance in most careers—if not in your opinion, certainly in the opinion of your employer. (Companies don't offer early retirement out of the goodness of their hearts.)

But just because you're no longer able to do what you're used to doing doesn't mean you can't do *anything*.

Many professional athletes become broadcasters when their careers are over. Some Hollywood actors make the transition to politics. If they can change careers, why can't you? Who's to say that you can't make the transition to another job later in life?

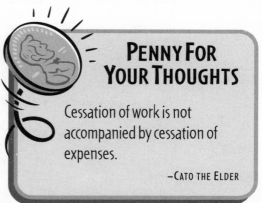

PENNY FOR YOUR THOUGHTS

Cessation of work is not accompanied by cessation of expenses.

—Cato the Elder

Not only will a post-career job keep you busy and perhaps even give you some fulfillment, it also will bring in some much needed extra cash. Living on a fixed income can be tough, especially when the cost of the things you're buying is anything but fixed.

If you're not careful—and even if you are careful—you may find yourself in the position of needing a job later in life to supplement your retirement benefits. Depending on your personality, you may see that as a problem or an opportunity. Either way, it will help to be prepared.

The Multitalented You

You can begin preparing for a post-career job even now by developing interests and skills apart from your normal work responsibilities. For example, remodeling your home or building a deck is a great way to improve your carpentry skills. With enough experience, you may be able to put those skills to use as a handyman when you retire.

If you have expertise in a certain technical area, you may want to consider hiring yourself out as a consultant in your post-career years. Not only do consultants pull down considerable dinero, they also have the freedom to set their own schedules.

Or maybe you'd prefer to pursue interests completely unrelated to your work experience. Chances are, you already have skills that can be applied to any number of jobs. The key is to expand your horizons and learn to "think outside the box" to discover what you're actually capable of.

Career Change Possibilities

For example, who's to say that . . .

> ➤ a factory worker couldn't become a museum tour guide?

> ➤ a postal worker couldn't become an artist, selling her creations at craft shows and fairs?

> ➤ an accountant couldn't become a church building manager?

The possibilities are limited only by your imagination (and your unwillingness to work).

The more versatile you are—the more useful and employable skills you have—the better chance you'll have of finding a second career (or even a part-time job) later in life that satisfies you and your budget.

The Retiree's Budget: Don't Leave Work Without It

If you're fortunate enough to avoid a major crisis, there is the possibility that you could stumble your way across the financial landscape of college and married life without a "map" or budget to guide you. It's not recommended, but it is possible.

Attempting a directionless journey through your retirement years, on the other hand, could be disastrous. The reason can be summed up in two words: fixed income. If you're collecting a salary, there's always the potential for a raise or a bonus to help you improve your financial picture. If you're drawing a pension (or some other form of retirement pay), what you see is what you get. There are no incentive bonuses for being a good retiree.

With a limited earning potential, it's absolutely necessary for you to be wise in allocating the money you have. So before you even consider retirement, you should have a workable budget, based on the most accurate income numbers you can get your hands on.

Find out what your monthly pension will be and apply that amount to your monthly expenses to see what you can expect from your retirement years. Will you have sufficient funds to cover the various budget categories? Will you need to scale back your living expenses? These are the questions you must answer before you say "Sayonara" to your regular income.

Having a budget may also help you rein in your spending before your fixed income takes effect. Many retirees make the mistake of continuing their normal spending habits on their reduced income.

When the bills come due, they discover that they no longer have the funds to cover them. The usual result of this predicament is debt. And while no time is a good time for debt, your retirement years would have to be considered the absolute worst time.

For more information on how to set up a budget that works for you, check out chapter 2. For more information on how to avoid debt, see chapter 1.

Separate Baskets for Your Retirement Eggs

In addition to creating a budget, you'll need to make sure that your post-career income is secure. What are you counting on to get you through your retirement years?

> ➤ A pension?

> ➤ An individual retirement account (IRA)?

➤ An investment portfolio?

➤ Income from property you own?

➤ Your children?

All of them are perfectly acceptable forms of income. But are they dependable? Consider the following facts.

➤ Many companies have jettisoned their employee pension funds—or simply declared bankruptcy—with little interference from the courts.

➤ One piece of legislation could affect the taxable status of IRAs and other similar funds.

➤ The stock market is vulnerable to the slightest winds of change in society. One news event or corporate announcement can send the value of your holdings plummeting.

➤ Property values can stagnate at any time.

➤ Your children are susceptible to the same financial downturns that you are.

Mistakes to Avoid

Obviously most of the factors that can affect your potential income are beyond your control. So the best strategy for minimizing your risk is to diversify your holdings. (English translation: Don't put all your retirement eggs in one basket.)

This is especially important to remember when you're faced with a "great investment opportunity." You may be tempted to invest most or all of your assets in a can't-miss venture, with the hopes of hitting it big. Resist the temptation.

One major financial mistake in your retirement years could affect the rest of your life. With a fixed income, you won't have the resources to correct the mistake. That's why the safest financial strategy is to invest your money in a diverse array of sources.

If you have your assets spread around, you won't have to worry about being completely devastated if one or more of your income sources dries up.

For more information on how to invest, take a look at chapter 5. For more information on how to invest for your retirement, check out chapter 7.

Prepping for Retirement

Assuming that you're not yet pushing retirement age, you may be wondering how soon you should start preparing for it. Obviously, a lot depends on your situation and your goals.

People who plan to divide their retirement years between the fairways of Pebble Beach and Augusta are going to need a considerably larger war chest than people who plan to catch up on their whittling. However, there are a couple of general principles that apply to almost everyone.

First, regardless of how ambitious your goals are for your golden years, the best time to start a retirement fund is around age 40. Some financial planners may disagree, though, suggesting that it's better to start saving at a very young age to allow the interest on your money to compound over a longer period of time.

Although that makes good financial sense, it's not very practical. For most young people, the temptation to withdraw that money for a new car, a new stereo, or some other must-have item is too great.

Second, your number one priority as a young adult should be to get yourself debt free. Not just free from credit card debts and personal loans but free from mortgage payments as well. Once you've cleared yourself of those financial burdens, you can focus your attention on retirement—and still have enough time to build the kind of funds you'll need.

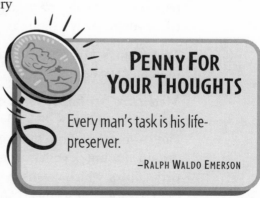

GLAD YOU ASKED

Will I be able to live on my Social Security benefits when I retire?

Don't bet on it. The future of the Social Security system lies in the hands of our elected officials. Because it's considered a sacred cow in political circles, it's unlikely that the system will be modified substantially any time soon. However, the reality is that Social Security as it exists now cannot continue to function. It simply can't generate the funds it needs to stay afloat. So even though you may receive Social Security checks when you retire, you should not count on them for your total income.

PENNY FOR YOUR THOUGHTS

Every man's task is his life-preserver.

–RALPH WALDO EMERSON

Cover Me

The double whammy of living on a fixed income while facing the reality of declining health makes insurance one of the primary concerns of most retirees. Add the enormous cost of medical care to the mix, and you can see why most senior citizens perk up when they hear TV commercials promising that "you can't be denied coverage for any reason."

Because insurance is such a hot topic for retirees, I would be remiss if I didn't include a section about in this chapter. However, since chapter 8 offers more information than you'll ever need to know about insurance, for the purposes of this chapter, I'll confine myself to a few specific things you should be aware of regarding retirement.

Don't bank on your company health plan.

The health insurance benefits that many companies offer for their retirees are slowly going the way of the dinosaur. And it's not hard to pinpoint the cause of their near extinction. Health care costs are skyrocketing.

The cost of providing health insurance as a retirement benefit is rapidly becoming too expensive for most companies to justify—especially for retirees who have access to Medicare. The companies that still offer the benefit will likely be trying to drop it like a hot potato in the next few years.

So even if you were lured to your present company by promises of health care retirement benefits, that's no guarantee that those benefits will still be around when you're ready to collect on them.

That means you're going to have to find other forms of health coverage for your retirement years.

Medicare probably isn't enough.

Medicare coverage is divided into two plans: Part A—hospitalization, and Part B—medical. Both plans have caps, which means they will pay only up to a certain amount of your hospitalization and medical bills. Both plans also have deductibles, which means that patients must kick in a certain amount of cash to help pay for their medical expenses.

That's why many retirees choose to purchase supplemental insurance, called medigap insurance, to cover what Medicare doesn't.

Medigap insurance makes sense, as long as it's not overdone. You don't need a policy that will cover every medical cost you ever have. You probably couldn't afford such a policy anyway. And even if you could, the expense wouldn't be worth it.

What you want is a policy that will cover the major expenses that can carpet-bomb your finances at a time when you're most vulnerable. Since the two Medicare plans cover most normal expenses, you want a policy that will cover the abnormal.

For example, Medicare Part B requires you to pay 20 percent of your medical costs yourself. Depending on your circumstances, that can be quite a chunk of change. Therefore, it might make sense to purchase a medigap policy that will pay 80 percent of your Part B deductible.

That's probably too many terms, letters, and figures to throw at you in one paragraph. So here's the bottom line: With a supplemental insurance policy, you would end up paying only about 4 percent of the medical expenses that Medicare doesn't.

When you're dealing with four-figure (or, in some cases, five-figure) medical bills, the extra coverage that supplemental policies provide can mean the difference between financial inconvenience and disaster.

Know your provider.

The tricky thing about buying insurance is that you never really know what you have until you need it most. Unfortunately, your policy is only as dependable as your insurer. Gibraltar Life & Casualty (est. 1856) is no better than Sneaky Pete's Medikle Inshurrence if it doesn't cough up the money when you need it most.

Maybe you've read horror stories of retirees who tried to file claims with their insurance carrier, only to learn that the company had declared bankruptcy six months earlier. As a result, these trusting souls found themselves faced with medical bills they couldn't possibly pay.

There are three things you can do to reduce your chances of being burned by an insurance (non)provider.

1. *Check the company's rating.* You can find annual reports that rate most insurance providers at your local library. Ideally you should verify a company's rating over a three- or four-year period. A company whose rating has declined steadily over that period may not be the best place to sink your premiums into.

2. *Write the insurance commissioner's office in the company's home state.* Ask about complaints against the company—especially ones involving failure to pay claims.

3. *Carefully review the specifics of your contract.* It may very well be the most boring thing you ever do, but someday you'll be glad you did it. Some insurance providers reserve the right to cancel your policy for excessive claims. If they have this right, your policy may be terminated just when you need it most.

You'll also want to check on the *renewal premium clause.* (Don't you think they could at least come up with more interesting names for these things?) If your insurance provider is allowed to increase your premiums based on how many claims you file, it can price you out of the market and leave you high and dry.

PENNY FOR YOUR THOUGHTS

It is necessary to work, if not from inclination, at least from despair. Everything considered, work is less boring than amusing oneself.

–CHARLES BAUDELAIRE

Due South... or West

Believe it or not, there is no federal law that requires all people over the age of 63 to move to Florida or Arizona. It only seems that way. When the time comes for you to retire, you'll need to decide whether to join the great exodus or go your own way.

Obviously there are a lot of personal and economic factors to consider when making your choice. As you think about your options, though, there are a few things you should not do.

1. *Don't act out of emotion.* When you're choosing the place where you'll likely live out the rest of your days, it's probably not a good idea to act on impulse. In fact, it may not even be a good idea to act on your desires or wants. The question you should probably start with is "All things considered, where is the best place for me to live out my retirement?"

2. *Don't pull the trigger too quickly.* You may be convinced that your friends in Florida are living in paradise. And maybe they are. But that doesn't mean it will be paradise for you. And if you rush into relocating there, you may not discover your mistake until it's too late to do anything about it. Ideally you should give yourself at least one year after retiring to decide where you will relocate.

3. *Don't look for an escape from the rest of the world.* Outside of heaven, there are pros and cons to every location. Life in retirement communities may be relatively "safer" than in other communities, but it's also much slower. And if you're not used to it, the pokey pace may get irritating fairly quickly. The idea of "getting away from it all" is an illusion. The truth is, it all comes with you. Or it's already where you want to go.

4. *Don't underestimate the strength of family ties.* Moving out of state or away from your children and grandchildren can take a serious toll on your emotional health. And if you're not prepared for the wallop, it may bring you home sooner—and more permanently—than you expect. Many retirees have moved out of state to enjoy their golden years, only to return home a year or so later to be with their family. And even though the reunion may be heartwarming, the cost of moving their possessions back and forth (not to mention the financial hits they may have taken in buying and selling their homes) is no cause for celebration.

5. *Don't lose sight of the job market.* At some point in your retired life, you may need to take a part-time job to supplement your benefits. If you relocate in an area crawling with retirees, you'll probably face stiff competition for a limited number of available openings. Your best bet for employment opportunities lies close to home, where you've established a lifetime's worth of relationships and contacts.

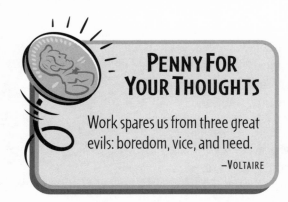

If you haven't retired yet, you have the luxury of putting some careful thought into where you will spend your post-career years. As you have the opportunity to travel and talk with people, pick their brains for nuggets of information that you can use when the time comes for you to make your post-retirement living arrangements.

Factors for Future Living Arrangements

Here are some questions you may want to ask.

➤ What is the weather like in your area?

➤ What are the utility rates like?

➤ How accessible and affordable are hospitals?

➤ Are there many geriatric physicians in the area?

➤ What are real estate taxes like?

➤ What about income taxes?

➤ What about personal property taxes?

If you get negative responses to any two or more of these questions, you may want to cross that region off your short list of retirement options.

Getting Rid of Your Leftovers

After you've enjoyed the fruits of your life's labor in your retirement years, you want to make sure that your family can do the same when you're gone. What you need is a will or trust.

Chapter 9 covers the basic points of how to draw up a will and establish a trust, so there's no need to go into that information here. Instead, here is a sobering statistic: Approximately 70 percent of all men die without leaving a valid will for their family members.

To put it another way, 70 percent of all families are forced to rely on the state to give them what's rightfully theirs. You see, if you die before you make a valid will (or trust), the state in which you lived will decide how the assets of your estate are distributed.

If that thought doesn't frighten you, you probably haven't had a lot of experience in dealing with government officials. The decisions they make regarding your estate may be completely contrary to where you wanted your assets to go. Unfortunately, you won't be able to do anything about the situation because, well, you'll be six feet underground. And lifeless.

The process of drawing up a will is relatively inexpensive and not terribly frightening. Once you've completed it, you can rest easy in the knowledge that your loved ones will receive your assets, just the way you want them to.

Think of it this way: A small amount of time and money invested in the will-drafting process now can result in a huge savings of time, money, and grief (for your loved ones) later.

One More Thing

With our ever-changing economy, it is nearly impossible to predict what society and life will be like when you retire. There's a good chance that much of the information in this chapter may be obsolete by then. But one timeless truth remains: The more time you give yourself to prepare for retirement—not only financially, but emotionally—the easier your transition into your golden years will be.

CRUNCHING NUMBERS

Seven out of every 10 men die without leaving a valid will for their family members.

GLAD YOU ASKED

Should I consider maintaining a second home in another state?

Only if you have quite a bit o' the green stuff stashed away. Many retirees who try to maintain two residences wind up in over their heads financially, unable to enjoy either one. The average cost of maintaining a second home, even one that is totally debt-free, runs anywhere from $3,000 to $6,000 a year.

The Buck Stops Here

Think you're an expert on preparing for retirement? Here's a quiz to see how much you know.

1. What did Harvard researchers conclude had killed 100 graduates who retired at age 65?
   a. The Yale bulldog mascot
   b. Their fed-up spouses
   c. An Ivy League virus
   d. Terminal boredom

2. What is it that makes a budget so important for retirees?
   a. The cost of buffet dining
   b. Twice-a-week Bingo nights
   c. Greedy grandkids
   d. Living on a fixed income

3. When is the best time to start preparing financially for retirement?
   a. Whenever the urge hits you
   b. As soon as your neighbor starts preparing for his retirement
   c. Around age 40
   d. The first time a store clerk calls you "Sir" or "Ma'am"

4. Which of the following will probably not help you reduce your risk of being burned by an insurance provider?
   a. Checking the company's rating
   b. Making threatening calls to your agent
   c. Writing the insurance commissioner's office in the company's home state
   d. Carefully reviewing the specifics of your contract

5. What do 70 percent of all men die before doing?
   a. Asking for directions
   b. Putting the toilet seat down
   c. Watching the Love Story movie
   d. Leaving a valid will for their families

Answers: (1) d, (2) d, (3) c, (4) b, (5) d

CHAPTER 7

Future Tense– or Relaxed?

SNAPSHOT

When Brian walked out of the study, Greta was waiting for him.

"Did you finish it?" she asked.

"Yep," Brian replied. "I did everything the financial counselor told us. First, I wrote down our retirement goals."

"You didn't include the one about wanting to be the first hardware store manager in space, did you?" Greta asked.

Brian gave her a wounded look. "No, I chose to sacrifice my lifelong desire for the sake of our financial health."

"Remind me to mail in your nomination for Husband of the Year," Greta replied. "So what did you do next?"

"I estimated how much it will cost to afford the

SNEAK PREVIEW

1. Between the ages of 20 and 40, your best investment strategy is to establish a reasonable lifestyle and control your spending to free up a monthly surplus of funds.

2. Between the ages of 40 and 60, your best investment strategy is to eliminate all debts, including your home mortgage, and invest in high growth areas.

3. After age 60, your best investment strategy is to settle on a retirement lifestyle and preserve your assets in reasonably secure investments.

retirement lifestyle we want," Brian said.

"And?"

"As far as I can tell," Brian explained, "there are three requirements to meeting our retirement goals. First, it will require commitment."

"Well, we're not in our 20s anymore," Greta reasoned. "I think we're mature enough to handle a little commitment."

"Second, it will require sacrifice," Brian continued.

"We've already talked about cutting back on our spending," Greta reminded her husband. "It may take a while, but I think we can do it. What's the third requirement?"

"A rip in the fabric of the space-time continuum, because we're going to need to travel back in time about 10 years in order to save enough money for retirement."

* * * * * * * * * * * * * * * *

If you believe you have a bright future ahead of you, you can justify just about anything, financially speaking.

➤ Looking for a new stereo system? Might as well buy top-of-the-line. After all, you should be able to pay off the debt when you get your next raise.

➤ Need a new car? Why not go for the special-edition SUV with GPS tracking, Internet access, and aromatherapy heating and air-conditioning options? After all, it's the kind of vehicle vice presidents drive—and sooner or later you're bound to become a vice president.

➤ In the market for a new home? You can't beat a golf course location. Years from now you'll be glad you shelled out the dough to live there.

There's really nothing wrong with this type of thinking. . . that a 180-degree turn won't fix.

Unfortunately, people who expect the future to take care of their present often discover too late that they were looking at things backwards. In reality, the present is the key to your financial future.

An Early Start

In chapter 6, it was suggested that the best time to start investing for retirement is 40. But that's not entirely accurate. The seeds of a saving and investing lifestyle are actually sown much earlier than that. In fact, the financial patterns and precedents you set as a young adult may very well determine how successful you are in investing for retirement when the time comes.

The first thing you need to understand is that there are three distinct periods—or "seasons"—of life that require different financial priorities and strategies:

➤ Season One—ages 20 to 40

➤ Season Two—ages 40 to 60

➤ Season Three—age 60 and up

Your best bet for securing your financial future is to adjust your priorities, goals, and strategy to fit the specifics of each season.

Obviously, the degree of success you enjoy will depend on the age at which you start preparing for your financial future. If you're in the early stages of the first season—between, say, 20 and 30 years of age—you'll have quite a head start on those who begin preparing in their late 30s and early 40s.

But even if you're. . . well-seasoned, you can still use the seasonal approach to finances to determine what to do with what you have.

Let's take a look at the specific strategies and priorities of each season.

Season One: The Frugal Years

If you're at the early end of this age spectrum, you probably already have plenty of financial thoughts taxing your gray matter. Among other things, you may be worried about. . .

PENNY FOR YOUR THOUGHTS

Whoever, in middle age, attempts to realize the wishes and hopes of his early youth, invariably deceives himself. Each ten years of a man's life has its own fortunes, its own hopes, its own desires.

–JOHANN WOLFGANG VON GOETHE

➤ affording your first home

➤ paying off your school loans

➤ finding the right job.

What you're probably *not* worried about is making the right investments so that you'll have enough to live on when you're 65. And that's okay. For now, at least, your focus should be on immediate things.

In Season One — when you're between the ages of 20 and 40 — your best financial strategy is to establish a reasonable lifestyle for you and your family and to control your spending so that you have a monthly surplus of funds to work with.

That's it. You don't have to worry about determining investment risk or establishing tax-deferment plans. All you have to do is figure out ways to set aside a few extra shekels here and there after your bills have been paid.

Obviously, the best way to do that is to cut back on your spending. Unless you just happened to open to this page, you know that this book — particularly chapter 1 — is chock-full of tips on saving money by reducing your spending.

So instead of getting into the gory details of what to look for when you're buying off-brands instead of name-brands at the grocery store, let's will focus on a few general areas that can help you start shaving money from your current budget for future investments.

Season One Insurance Strategies

Would you rather be insured against structural damage caused by termites when you're 25 years old or be able to travel for a month in Europe after you retire?

Chances are, that's a question you've never been asked before. And even though it may not make a lot of sense as an either-or proposition, it does illustrate the fact that the choices you make now—including those involving your insurance coverage—will have an effect on your future finances.

If you're an adult, you need insurance—no matter how carefully you try to live your life. At the very least, you must have liability on your car and home, in case of damage or injury to another person.

What you *don't* have to have is a deluxe insurance package. Keep in mind that each dollar not spent on unnecessary insurance is a dollar that can be saved toward your long-term goals, such as retirement, education for your kids, and debt reduction.

The better you understand your specific insurance needs, the better decisions you can make about what's right for you. Toward that end, let's take a look at some tips for trimming your insurance costs.

1. Raise the deductible!

Increasing your deductible (the amount you're responsible for in the event of an accident) from $100 to $500 can cut your premiums (the amount you pay for your policy) in half. So if you can afford to pay the first $500 in repairs on your car—if you ever do have an accident—you can save more than $150 a year.

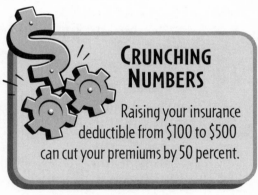

CRUNCHING NUMBERS

Raising your insurance deductible from $100 to $500 can cut your premiums by 50 percent.

If you want to get *really* optimistic, consider this: If you're able to save that amount each year in Season One—from the time you're 20 to the time you're 40—you'd be looking at more than $3,000, ready to be invested and start earning dividends for your future.

And that's just on your auto insurance. Imagine what you'd save if you were to raise the deductibles on your home insurance, health insurance, and any other applicable policies you may have.

2. You'd better shop around.

Have you ever compared the price of movie snacks with their counterparts in grocery stores? Some treats have a markup of 200 to 300 percent. Yet theater owners can get away with those prices because they know most moviegoers will choose what's most convenient for them instead of what's most economical.

This same principle—let's call it the Junior Mint Truism—applies to insurance. Depending on your policy and insurer, you may be paying 200 to 300 percent more for your insurance than you need to.

With a little investigation and comparative shopping, you may be able to cut the cost of your insurance bill in half—at least. One of the best resources available for this task is *Consumer Reports* magazine. Each year it evaluates different types of insurance and reports on the assets and liabilities of all major insurers. You probably can find the latest issue at your local library.

CRUNCHING NUMBERS

Insurance rates for comparable policies may vary by as much as 200 to 300 percent.

3. Don't forget, the more the merrier.
In the course of your shopping, you may find that one company offers the best price for auto insurance but another offers the best price for life or health insurance. You may be tempted to grab the best deals in each category and split your insurance among two or three companies.

Believe it or not, that may not be the wisest course of action. Many companies offer substantial savings for the privilege of taking care of all your insurance needs. Those savings usually offset the reduced prices offered by the various companies.

4. Say, "Thanks, but no thanks" to your mortgage lender.
When you buy a home, your lender will likely offer you all kinds of insurance options. Your wisest move is to politely decline. A good homeowner's policy—one that covers not only the house but contents, liability, jewelry, clothes, and temporary housing—purchased from a reputable company will likely cost less than a simple fire insurance policy sold through your lender.

This same principle applies to mortgage insurance, which guarantees that the lender gets its money in the event of your death. Most lenders require mortgage insurance, but that doesn't necessarily mean you have to buy it from them. You probably would save quite a bit of cash by buying your own life insurance and assigning the amount necessary to pay off the mortgage to the lender.

5. Choose the life for you.

First things first: if you're not married and you have no children, you probably don't need life insurance (except for burial costs). The only good reason to own life insurance is to provide for your dependents in the event of your death.

If you have dependents, at this stage in your life, you're probably better off with term insurance. The bad news is that term insurance accumulates no cash value and pays no dividends. The good news is that, at least for now, it costs a fraction of the price of your other insurance options.

To be a little more specific, a good, annual renewable (to age 100) insurance policy for people between the ages of 25 and 35 will cost less than one-tenth of an equivalent cash value policy at the same age.

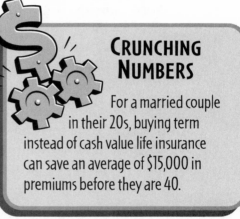

CRUNCHING NUMBERS

For a married couple in their 20s, buying term instead of cash value life insurance can save an average of $15,000 in premiums before they are 40.

However, saving and investing are the key words here.

To be even more specific, a young couple in their 20s can save an average of $15,000 in premiums before the age of 40 by buying term life insurance instead of cash value (or whole life) insurance. Invest that money wisely, and you could be looking at $200,000 by the time you're 65—all as a result of making the right insurance decision when you're young.

Season One Debt Management Strategies

In order to have money to invest later in life, you must learn to squeeze funds from your budget early in life. One of the best ways to make sure that there are funds to be squeezed is to control your debt—particularly in three areas: credit cards, automobile, and home loans.

Credit cards

Don't use them.

Ever.

That may be a lot to ask, but there's a lot to be gained in return. If, in Season One, you can establish a pattern of paying cash (or checks) for everything you buy, you won't be faced with the prospect of paying off your debt later in life. Instead, you can use the money to accomplish your life goals.

The best strategy for preventing credit card debt—aside from torching the cards themselves—is to do without anything you can't afford to pay cash for. (For more information on debt and credit cards, take a look at chapter 1.)

Automobile

Probably the best debt management advice for you regarding buying a car is to ignore your natural tendencies. Your ideal may be a sleek, sporty new car that will make you the envy of your friends; your budget's ideal is a dependable used car that you can pay cash for.

If paying cash is an impossibility, look for the least expensive way to finance your car. (Hint: Usually it won't be through the dealership.) If your parents have the resources to loan you the money for the purchase, consider that option first. If that's not possible, your next stop should be a credit union, if you belong to one. If not, compare the rates of various banks and lending institutions in your area.

What you're looking for is a simple-interest loan that you can pay off in two years or less. If you can't do it in that amount of time, find a cheaper car to buy.

Home loans

By financing your home over a shorter period of time—say, 15 years instead of 30—you can cut 1 percent or more off your annual interest rate. On a $100,000 mortgage, the 1 percent interest saved amounts to $1,000 in the first year alone.

There are also government programs available for first-time home buyers that offer preferred interest rates. Since these programs change frequently, you'll have to verify the details when you're ready to buy.

Season One Investment Goals

Becoming debt-free should be your first investment goal. Only after you've achieved that goal—including paying off your mortgage—should you start investing in other areas.

The only exception to this strategy is a company retirement account that offers matching company funds. If your employer is willing to match your deposits in your retirement account at no extra cost to you, the best way to show your appreciation for that generosity is to take maximum advantage of it. Invest as much as you can under the terms of the matching agreement so that you will *receive* as much as you can from your employer.

Later you can withdraw the proceeds from your retirement account—a large portion of which will have been paid by your employer—to get rid of your home mortgage.

Let's assume that by age 35 you manage to accomplish your first financial goal and pay off your mortgage. (Quit laughing—it's just an *assumption*.) Your next financial goal will likely be to pay for your children's college education.

If your kids have reached their teen years and are within five years of college, at least half of the funds you set aside for their education should be kept in investments that can be converted easily into cash as needed. In other words, you want to be able to get at your money as soon as possible. These investments include no-load mutual funds, short-term bonds, or liquid savings plans, such as money market funds and CDs.

If you already have enough socked away to meet your kids' college needs, those funds should be kept in relatively low-risk investments. You don't want to take any more chances than those that are necessary to meet your financial goals. After all, your kids' education and, quite possibly, their career paths are at risk.

If your funds are lacking, though, you'll have to take more risks with your money. I'm not suggesting that you go nuts and roll the financial dice on a prototype for a water-powered car or some such thing. Investing in high quality growth mutual funds is probably as risky as you want to get with your kids' college funds.

Keep in mind too that a small college fund is better than nothing. If you can accumulate only enough money to send your kids to a local community college, it's better than risking everything and not being able to send them at all.

PENNY FOR YOUR THOUGHTS

Future, n. That period of time in which our affairs prosper, our friends are true and our happiness is assured.

—AMBROSE BIERCE

Season One Savings Strategy

I've said it before and I'll say it again: The most important investment strategy for people between the ages of 20 and 40 is regular savings. Unfortunately, it's not as easy as it sounds.

If you manage to pay off your mortgage, you may find yourself tempted to kick up your spending level a few notches. You might even tell yourself it's a reward for being so financially diligent. Controlling these impulses and avoiding indulgences like a bigger house, a new car, or an expensive vacation are vital to your long-term plans.

If you manage to pay off your mortgage early, but waste the next few years spending your money on your heart's desires, you'll have nothing to show for your hard budgeting work.

That's why, as soon as you start to free up cash from your budget, it's a good idea to begin funneling it into some kind of interest-bearing account. Mutual funds are preferable for most people in Season One because they normally allow monthly payments of as little as $10 (or as much as you can afford).

You'll also want to keep a cash reserve on hand for emergencies, such as a job layoff, an illness, or an unplanned pregnancy. In specific terms, you should have approximately three months worth of income set aside to live on, if the need should arise.

If by the age of 40 you have. . .

➤ paid off your home mortgage,

➤ saved at least one-half of your first two children's college education expenses,

➤ begun a long-term investment plan,

. . . you will have accomplished more than 95 percent of the people in our country today.

And you'll be ready to move on to Season Two.

Season Two: The Risky Years

If, by the age of 40, you've achieved the goals outlined in Season One, you're ready to move on to the next stage of your financial life. If, however, you've been unable to become debt-free, including your home, you need to make that your top priority.

That doesn't mean, however, that you should panic and begin investing in every Internet start-up company that comes down the DSL. Don't let desperation cloud your good judgment—even if you're approaching your sixties. Rethink your strategy to accomplish your debt-free goals in this phase and adjust your retirement goals to later in life.

If you're facing the prospect of your children heading to college with no funds stashed away to cover their expenses, resist the urge to plunge further into debt by taking out a home equity loan, a government loan, or some other kind of loan.

Help your children to the best of your ability—without taking on more debt. It may be necessary for them to attend a local junior or community college for the first year or two of their education. They also may have to get a part-time job to help pay for tuition.

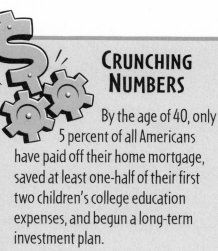

CRUNCHING NUMBERS

By the age of 40, only 5 percent of all Americans have paid off their home mortgage, saved at least one-half of their first two children's college education expenses, and begun a long-term investment plan.

PENNY FOR YOUR THOUGHTS

Tomorrow lurks in us, the latency to be all that was not achieved before.

—LOREN EISELEY

Season Two Housing Investments

By the age of 40 if you haven't settled into a consistent, fiscally responsible lifestyle, it's time to do so. Too often Season Two becomes the indulgent years when couples buy motor homes, large boats, second homes, or sports cars.

Granted, if you've paid off your kids' education, you may have some extra funds to spend. But moderation is the key. You don't want to derail your financial plans in midlife by trying to recapture your youth through acquisitions.

Couples in the 40 to 60 age group tend to gravitate toward one of two general lifestyle strategies. The first strategy is to go for broke and buy the house you always wanted but never could afford while your kids were at home.

The good news with this strategy is that it means your children have a place big enough to come back to all at once on holidays and vacations. The bad news is that it means the majority of your assets are sunk into your home.

If you opt for this strategy, you'll need to consider the possibility of having to sell your dream home before you retire, since so much of your net worth is invested in it. Unfortunately, many couples in this situation don't make the decision to sell until the costs of taxes, utilities, maintenance, and insurance overrun their retirement budget. The danger, then, is that you might be forced to sell in a down market and lose a large part of your net worth.

If the majority of your net worth is wrapped up in your home, you need to be realistic about when—or if—you can retire. If you know that company policy is going to push you out the door at age 65, you'll need to adopt a budget matching your retirement income at least five years before that to determine whether you can afford your home after you retire. If you decide that you can't, you'll need to allow yourself time to sell the house at market value.

The second lifestyle strategy for people between the ages 40 and 60 is to pare down as retirement approaches. Specifically, this involves moving into a smaller home, to free up money for investing and traveling during your leisure years.

This strategy requires some sacrifices—for example, a smaller house may mean that you're unable to host your entire family at one time. And since it's a decision that will affect everyone, it should be discussed with your family first. You'll find, however, that this lifestyle decision pays large financial dividends in the long run.

Season Two Insurance Strategies

Remember that term insurance that was so inexpensive in Season One? By now, it's probably not quite as cheap as you remember it. And you'll find that the longer you live, the more expensive it becomes. By the time you're 50, there's a good chance that your term life insurance will be too expensive for you to afford—unless you're a specimen of physical health and are able to qualify for a reduced rate.

Unfortunately, your life insurance alternatives narrow rapidly after age 50. In fact, you'll find that there are really only three options available to you:

1. You can continue to pay the high cost of term, if you can afford it.

2. You can reduce your premium by reducing the face value of your policy.

3. You can convert your term insurance to whole life, assuming your policy provides that option.

If your need for life insurance declines—that is, if your house is paid for, your children are grown, and you're regularly saving some of your earnings—reducing your coverage may be your best option. Of course, you'll still need *some* life insurance—at least until your spouse reaches age 62 and until your investments have matured enough to provide income for your dependents.

Since there are, literally, hundreds of different life insurance options available to you, your best bet is to find a good independent agent who can explain them to you. The right agent will be able to sell you what you need at a price you can afford.

Season Two Risk Strategies

If you have the itch to take a risk with your investments, Season Two is the best time to scratch it. Between the ages of 40 and 60, you should logically be able to absorb the highest degree of risk with your investments. If you're debt-free, have your children's college expenses taken care of, and can afford to venture beyond the safety of guaranteed returns with a portion of your money, now's the time to do it.

That's not to say you should risk your life savings in soybean futures. I'm not

GLAD YOU ASKED

How do I determine what's an okay risk and what's a foolish risk?

A good rule of thumb to keep in mind is that if your financial advisor gasps when you suggest an investment, it's probably too risky. Beyond that, the level of risk you can absorb depends on your income. In a nutshell, if you can't afford to lose it, you shouldn't risk it.

talking about taking foolish risks. I'm talking about looking for investments that multiply, as opposed to simply earning interest.

I should point out that there are some people for whom this risk option doesn't apply. First, there are those investors who can earn all the money they will ever need with "safe" investments. If you already have enough, there's no reason to risk it on the possibility of earning more. (Remember, greed is not an attractive character trait.)

The second group for whom this risk option doesn't apply includes widows, divorcees, and disabled people. Keep in mind that risk is not just a factor of age. Temperament, income, and the ability to replace funds that may be lost must also be considered.

For example, a widow in her early 40s with a lump sum from her husband's estate to invest should probably adopt the Season Three strategy of preserving her capital, instead of risking it on growth funds.

Season Two Retirement Account Strategies

If you have access to a retirement account, you'll find that your account is a useful vehicle for long-term investing. That's assuming, of course, that the people running the account have a good track record. If past history suggests that they don't know their Ginnie Maes from their IRAs, you may be better off paying the taxes and earning 10 percent on your own investment choices.

The most flexible retirement accounts available to you are individual retirement accounts (IRAs). Because of their flexibility, you should make good use of them in your financial planning.

First things first: IRAs are not investments themselves. They are retirement accounts that shelter income by deferring (delaying) the income taxes until the funds are withdrawn. Because your tax rate decreases as you get older, IRAs allow you to pay less tax on your investments. An IRA can contain mutual funds, stocks, bonds, CDs, treasury bills (T-bills), and any other type of investment available to the general public.

"Self-directed" IRAs allow you to place your money in a cash account, such as a money market fund, and then later inform the administrator of the fund in which you want the money invested.

Self-directed IRAs are available through selected banks. Most banks charge an annual administration fee that ranges from $10 to $50. Check with your bank about its fees and policies before you set up a self-directed IRA.

IRAs also give you the option of canceling one account and transferring the funds into another, provided you do so within the legal time period, without additional tax consequences. There are, however, limitations that allow you only one such transfer a year. Note: Roth IRAs require after-tax deposits but provide tax-free earnings even when withdrawn at retirement age.

The bottom line is, if you can use a tax-deferred retirement plan without sacrificing good investment strategy, you should go for it.

> **GLAD YOU ASKED**
>
> **What kind of investment opportunities do self-employed people have?**
>
> Self-employed people, and those who work for them, have access to several good retirement plans, including an HR-10 (Keogh) plan, a Self-Employed Pension (SEP) plan, and IRAs. The SEP is flexible and is offered by most insurance companies as an option. The funds are invested according to your personal choices and can be transferred, if necessary.

Season Two Financial Goals

What are your plans for the future? Would you like to. . .

➤ retire on 80 percent of your present income at age 62?

➤ retire on 50 percent of your present income at age 59 and supplement income from another source?

➤ continue working for as long as possible, while storing money away, in the event that you're unable to work at some point?

Whatever your goals, it's important that you define them as specifically as possible. It's also important that the goals you set are the result of a joint decision between you and your spouse. After all, you'll both have to live with the results.

At age 40 Fern set a goal to retire at 62—on at least 70 percent of her present income, which is $40,000 a year. After her retirement, Fern plans to work for a nonprofit organization 20 hours a week, earning at least an additional 10 percent of her salary. Based on current Social Security benefits, she can expect to receive approximately $15,000 a year in retirement benefits.

That means that in the next 22 years Fern will need to accumulate at least $150,000 in savings and investments. That amount, invested conservatively, could earn $14,000 a year to supplement Fern's income.

In order to reach her savings goal, Fern would need to set aside $3,000 a year until she reaches age 62—for a total contribution of $66,000 ($3,000 x 22). That money, invested in one or more quality mutual funds that average approximately 8 percent real growth a year, should help her reach her target of $150,000—and then some.

For instance, if Fern had invested in one of the 10 leading mutual funds over the past 20 years, her investment of $66,000 would have grown to nearly $200,000. Obviously, nothing guarantees that any investment plan will match past performance, but the point is that you should be able to achieve the return you need.

The concept of goal-setting is critical and deceptively simple. You need to know what you're trying to accomplish and then select the investments that will achieve those goals with the least risk possible.

Here's one more example. Just before his 50th birthday, Rodger managed to pay off his mortgage and become debt-free. As a result, he now has $400 a month to invest (after taxes). His goal is to retire at age 65 on at least 75 percent of his current income of $30,000 a year.

His Social Security retirement benefits will come out to about $12,000 per year. His monthly savings will total $72,000 ($400 x 12 months x 15 years) by the age of 65. His income needs above Social Security will be about $10,500 a year. In order for Rodger to provide that amount from his retirement account it would have to grow at least $150,000 by age 65.

If Rodger had the entire $72,000 to invest at age 50, that would be no problem. At 8 percent interest his money would double every nine years. Even after taxes he would have the amount he needed by the time he retired.

Unfortunately, he doesn't have all $72,000 to invest at once. What he has is $400 per month. That means Rodger will need to average about 15 percent a year on his investment to meet his goal.

That figure is not out of the ballpark, by any means. Many investments have earned 15 percent or more over the past decade. However, again it's important to note that you can't fully judge an investment based on its history.

You also can't park your money in one or more investment funds and forget about it. You'll need to keep a close eye on your investments and move funds when necessary. In Rodger's case any investment that averaged less than the necessary 15 percent over any five-year period would need to be changed.

The strategy for people in the 40-to-60 age range is to come out of this season debt-free, with your goals clearly in mind and the majority of your needed funds in well-performing investments.

It really doesn't matter whether you select mutual funds, stocks, annuities, real estate, or antique cars, as long as you stay on track with your goals. The more funds you have available, the more you can and should diversify.

Season Three: The Preservation Years

If, by age 60, you've achieved your goals from the previous two stages of life, you've earned the right to give your financial advice to young whippersnappers everywhere, regardless of whether they want it or not. You're also allowed to tell complete strangers about how difficult your life has been and how you managed to overcome.

Okay, maybe not.

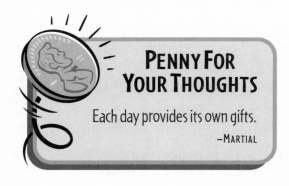

PENNY FOR YOUR THOUGHTS

Each day provides its own gifts.

—MARTIAL

Actually, accomplishing your financial goals by the time you're 60 means that you're ready to enter the "preservation" phase of life. After you've worked so hard to achieve financial health, you want to make sure that you maintain it so that you have the funds you need when you need them most.

If you *haven't* achieved your financial goals by the time you're 60, you'll need to. . .

➤ delay your retirement plans

➤ work to become debt-free

➤ accumulate the supplemental funds you and your spouse will need to live on

➤ adopt a very conservative lifestyle.

Unfortunately, it's a very common mistake to retire without adequate financial preparation. People assume that 62 or 65 represents the mandatory retirement age from the workforce, regardless of their situation.

Two points need to be made here.

1. *There is no mandatory retirement age.* People can and do remain productive in the workforce long into their 70s and 80s. They may not be able to work as hard as they once did, but they've learned to work smarter.

2. *You can't take a 50 percent (or more) cut in income and expect to enjoy your retirement years.* Unless you adjust to your projected retirement income at least three years before you retire, you're fooling yourself if you believe you can "make do" with that much less than you're used to.

Often the people who retire without adequately preparing for it soon find themselves trying to reenter the job market, only to find that they can't earn anywhere near the salary level they left.

You should be aware of the fact that current laws prohibit mandatory retirement, except in age-critical professions, such as airline pilot. So retirement is an option, not a requirement.

If you can't adjust to the income you expect to receive after retirement at least three years before that time—stay at your job. Reset your retirement goals to 65, 68, or 70, but don't become a poverty statistic.

Season Three Alternate Income

A marketable skill is the most dependable retirement plan you can have. As long as you're reasonably healthy and have skills that people need, you won't have to worry about earning money. If you don't have a marketable skill, develop one. Sign up for night classes at a good vocational school and learn a trade that suits your abilities.

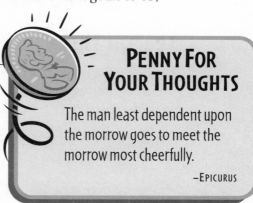

PENNY FOR YOUR THOUGHTS

The man least dependent upon the morrow goes to meet the morrow most cheerfully.

—EPICURUS

Season Three Retirement Strategy

If you've met your financial goals—if you're debt free and have enough investment savings for the rest of your life—it's time to make some adjustments in your financial strategy. Specifically, it's time to develop a more conservative long-range outlook. Your principal objectives now are protection and conservation, instead of growth.

That doesn't mean you have to shift all of your assets into Treasury bills. Your strategy may be as simple as shifting from high-growth mutual funds to income funds.

Most mutual fund companies offer a wide range of investment pools or mixes, each with a different objective. By requesting a company prospectus, you can determine which of the plans best fits your age and desired strategy.

Adopting a more conservative strategy may mean that you'll miss out on some major stock market

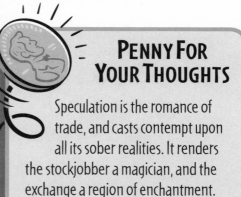

PENNY FOR YOUR THOUGHTS

Speculation is the romance of trade, and casts contempt upon all its sober realities. It renders the stockjobber a magician, and the exchange a region of enchantment.

—WASHINGTON IRVING

rallies, not to mention those "can't-miss" investment opportunities your friends and family members pitch to you. Such is life. If you want to retire with some degree of financial security, you'll need to make such sacrifices. The whole object from age 60 on is to try to avoid the financial disasters that can wipe you out.

Season Three Investment Strategy

The obvious question is, How do you make the necessary financial adjustments to a more conservative approach? To help illustrate, here is a chart that shows how your funds may have been allocated up to this point.

SECURE FUNDS (money funds, CDs)	20 percent
LONG-TERM FUNDS (Treasury bills, bonds)	0 percent
GROWTH FUNDS (growth mutual funds, real estate)	25 percent
SPECULATION FUNDS (international funds)	50 percent
RISK FUNDS (gold, silver)	5 percent

You'll notice that the majority (nearly 80 percent) of the investments are geared toward more aggressive funds. During your 40s and 50s, the only funds you needed in the conservative realm were those used to pay for your kids' college educations as they came due.

During your 60s, 70s, and beyond, you'll need to shift most of your assets into conservative funds, as illustrated by the following chart.

SECURE FUNDS (money funds)	10 percent
LONG-TERM FUNDS (bonds)	50 percent
GROWTH FUNDS (growth mutual funds)	25 percent
SPECULATION FUNDS (international funds)	10 percent
RISK FUNDS (gold, silver)	5 percent

You'll need to keep about six months' salary in a cash reserve account, in case of emergency. As you receive your regular dividend income, you can deposit it into this account. Once the account accumulates more than eight months' reserve, you can shift it to a longer-term cash reserve account, such as a CD, to earn more interest.

Your goal should be to maintain a spendable income of approximately $2,500 per month after retirement—including Social Security, investment earnings, and some generated income.

One More Thing

Planning for retirement requires you to order your priorities. In a sense, you must determine that your immediate wants and desires are secondary in importance to your future financial health. That's a tough thing to convince yourself of, especially when the future seems so far off.

Obviously, the younger you are the more tempted you'll be to postpone getting serious about saving and investing for your retirement. Resist that temptation. Take advantage of the time you have. Start your financial planning immediately.

 ## The Buck Stops Here

Think you're an expert on planning for your future? Here's a quiz to see how much you know.

1. What is the best financial strategy for people between the ages of 20 and 40?
   a. Establish a reasonable lifestyle and control your spending to free up a monthly surplus of funds.
   b. Spend the majority of your money while you're still young enough to enjoy it.
   c. Keep your money in a simple savings account until you have the life experience necessary to know what to do with it.
   d. Always follow your gut instincts.

2. Which of the following is not a recommended insurance strategy for people ages 20 to 40?
   a. Raise your deductible.
   b. Claim to be 65.
   c. Shop around.
   d. Use one insurer.

3. What is the best financial strategy for people between the ages of 40 and 60?
   a. Don't let your kids know that you have surplus funds.
   b. Include in your budget planning funds for a new red sports car when the inevitable midlife crisis hits.
   c. Resist the urge to invest in anything riskier than T-bills.
   d. Eliminate all debts, including your home mortgage, and invest in high growth areas.

4. Which of the following is not true of an IRA?
   a. It was originally known as an ERA until financial advisors began confusing it with the baseball statistic for a pitcher's earned run average.
   b. It is the most flexible retirement account available.
   c. It is a tax shelter, not an investment.
   d. It may contain mutual funds, stocks, bonds, CDs, T-bills, and any other type of investment available to the general public.

5. What is the best financial strategy for people over the age of 60?
   a. Pass your money on to your kids and let the government take care of you for the rest of your life.
   b. Transfer at least 75 percent of your investments to speculation and risk funds.
   c. Settle on a retirement lifestyle and preserve your assets in reasonably secure investments.
   d. Spend like there's no tomorrow.

Answers: (1) a, (2) b, (3) d, (4) a, (5) c

CHAPTER 8

Like a Good Neighbor with a Piece of the Rock in Your Hands

SNAPSHOT

"It's that time of year," Pam said as she tossed the insurance folder on the desk.

Stan looked up from his computer and grimaced. "Have I ever mentioned how much I dislike reviewing our insurance policies?"

"Yeah, my heart goes out to you," Pam said as she pored over the life insurance policy. "So do you want to stick with our term life insurance or switch over to a universal policy?"

"Definitely universal," Stan said without hesitating.

Pam looked up in surprise. "You seem pretty sure about that. Why universal?"

"It's bigger," Stan replied. "Why settle for just earthly insurance when you can have universal?"

"I should have known you weren't going to be serious about this," Pam said. "You never are."

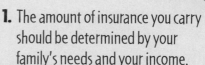

SNEAK PREVIEW

1. The amount of insurance you carry should be determined by your family's needs and your income.
2. Insurance should be considered a supplement, not the primary source of income, after the wage earner's death.
3. Even though your need for health insurance will increase as you get older, your need for life insurance will decrease.

"Come on," Stan said. "Why don't we just have our agent tell us what we need?"

"Oh, that's a good idea," Pam replied. "Then after that we can go to a car dealership and have a salesperson tell us how much we should spend for a car."

"Okay, okay," Stan said, holding up his hands. "You're right. We should do it ourselves. Let's talk some more about life insurance."

Pam stared at the policy in front of her. "Have I ever mentioned how much I dislike reviewing our insurance policies?" she asked.

* * * * * * * * * * * * * * *

➤ Charting glacier movement

➤ Judging the qualifying rounds of the World Solitaire Championship

➤ Watching mime practice

➤ Writing legal disclaimers at the bottom of contest entries

➤ Training goldfish

This is just a partial list of things that are more exciting than reading about insurance.

Unfortunately, in order to have a complete understanding of your finances, you have to know about insurance. And the more you know, the better decisions you can make about what's best for you and your family.

Unless you work in the industry, you probably don't want to read any more than you have to about insurance. That's why we've included only the essentials in this chapter. You'll find the information you need to make an informed decision regarding your insurance options and not much more.

Load up on caffeine. Splash cold water on your face. Take a brisk jog around the block. Do whatever you need to do to keep your eyes from glazing over, because once you understand what you need and don't need in your insurance policies you'll be able to free up some serious cash in your budget.

Insurance 101

In its basic form, insurance is simply a plan for using a portion of your current income to offset a future potential loss usually related to death, health, accident, theft, or natural disaster.

Taken to its extreme, insurance becomes a vehicle for protecting anyone against anything that could possibly go wrong.

Are you worried about...

➤ your dishwasher malfunctioning in the middle of the rinse cycle?

➤ termites gnawing through the load-bearing beams of your home someday?

➤ a computer virus destroying your hard drive?

For better or worse, you can buy insurance policies to cover these and other potential damages and losses. Some Hollywood stars have even gone so far as to insure specific parts of their bodies against disfigurement or weight gain. It's safe to say that if there's something you really want to protect, whether it's a baseball card collection or a pet iguana, you can find an agent to sell a policy for it.

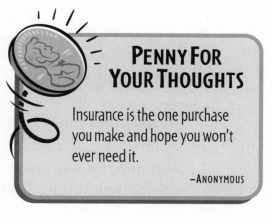

PENNY FOR YOUR THOUGHTS

Insurance is the one purchase you make and hope you won't ever need it.

—ANONYMOUS

With a limitless array of insurance options available to you, choosing what's right for you and your family can be tricky. There's a Goldilocks-like dilemma of deciding how much insurance is too much, how much is not enough, and how much is just right.

In order to make that decision, though, you must be familiar with the many legitimate options that are available to you.

F.Y.I.

Before we get into the specific types of insurance you have to choose from, there are a few basic terms you should be aware of. You've probably heard most of these words before and may even have a pretty good idea of what they mean. But for the sake of establishing a common frame of reference, here are basic definitions.

Policy: This is the contract between you and your insurance provider that details what you will pay and what protection and reimbursement you will receive in return.

Coverage: This is the specific protection that your insurance policy includes. Generally, the more coverage you have the more expensive your policy will be.

Premium: This is the amount you pay for an insurance policy—usually in the form of a bill that you write a check for and mail in. Most premiums are paid annually (every 12 months) or semiannually (every six months).

Claim: This is the request for reimbursement that you file with your insurance company when you experience a loss, an accident, or a medical need.

Deductible: This is the amount you copay with your insurance provider in the event of an accident or a medical need. Generally, the higher your deductible is (meaning, the more of the damages or bill you pay) the lower your premium will be (meaning, the less you will pay for your policy).

Beneficiary: This is the person or persons who will receive the payout from your insurance provider, specifically in the event of your death.

With that out of the way, we can introduce the main characters in the insurance saga and get you acquainted with each one. In no particular order, they are life insurance, health insurance, homeowner's insurance, and automobile insurance.

The Pros and Cons of Life Insurance

The purpose of any life insurance policy is to provide for your loved ones—the people under your care after your death. If you knew exactly when you were going to die, you might be able to set aside the necessary funds on your own. But since none of us are born with an expiration date stamped on our bodies, we must rely on insurance to do the job for us.

As with most everything else in life, there are benefits and liabilities associated with insurance. The key to making wise decisions is being able to properly weigh the benefits against the liabilities before choosing a course of action.

The primary benefit of having life insurance is knowing that your family's needs will be provided after you're gone. The obvious liability of life insurance is that, like everything else in your budget, it costs money. You have to divert funds from your current finances to pay for future protection. And although insurance costs vary wildly, you can count on spending a hefty chunk of change for your coverage.

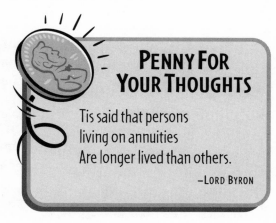

PENNY FOR YOUR THOUGHTS

Tis said that persons living on annuities Are longer lived than others.

–LORD BYRON

Your Life Insurance Needs

Most wage earners (who typically are men but include a growing number of women) need the greatest amount of life insurance when they're young because they have a spouse and children at home who may not be able to support themselves in the event of the wage earner's death. So insurance is used to supply the needed income. The insurance becomes a substitute, financially speaking, for the wage earner.

Unfortunately, you can't just walk into an insurance agency and say, "I would like one life insurance policy to go, please." It's not that simple. That would be like walking into McDonald's and saying, "I would like something to eat, please." You have to be more specific, a lot more specific.

Let's take a look at the different life insurance options you have to choose from. Depending on your unique circumstances, some options will work better for you than others.

The Least You Should Know About Term Life Insurance

Term insurance, as its name implies, is sold for a specific number of years. Most term policies don't accumulate any cash reserves, meaning that the premiums you pay aren't saved in an account for you to use later. And you won't collect any interest or receive any dividends from them.

GLAD YOU ASKED

Should my spouse and children have life insurance?

If your family is dependent on your spouse's salary, yes, you probably should insure him or her. First, though, you must determine whether you can afford two policies. If your funds are limited, insure the primary wage earner first. The only logical reason to have insurance on your children is to cover potential burial expenses.

In fact, the only way you can collect on what you pay into the insurance is to, well, die. The death benefits will be paid only if you pass away while the policy is still in effect.

What term life insurance does offer is the largest immediate death protection for your premium dollar. If taking care of your family's needs is your only reason for having life insurance, term life may be your best option.

For term life insurance, your insurance provider will determine the amount of your premium based on your age. The older you get—more specifically, the closer to death you get—the more the cost goes up. When you get into your 50s and 60s, the premiums for term life insurance will be significantly more expensive than they are in your 20s and 30s.

A term life insurance policy can be guaranteed renewable and convertible. That means you can continue your insurance coverage at the end of each term, without a medical examination, simply by paying the increased premium. Renewable term policies can be continued until a certain age—70, 80, or even 100—when all coverage stops. Convertible term life insurance allows you to switch to a whole life policy to continue your coverage. (We'll discuss whole life insurance later in the chapter.)

There are two basic types of term life insurance: decreasing and level. *Decreasing term* premiums remain the same, but the face value (or face benefit) of the policy decreases according to a certain time line. That means the benefits your family stands to gain after your death will decrease every year (or every five years, 10 years, or whatever period of time your insurer prefers) you pay on the policy.

With *level term* insurance, the premium increases but the face value of the policy stays the same. Both decreasing and level term insurance can be purchased for periods ranging from one to 30 years, or until you reach age 65.

If you anticipate that the amount of insurance you need will decrease as your kids get older and move out of the house, leaving you with fewer people to support, you may want to opt for decreasing term policy. If you don't anticipate your insurance needs decreasing at a predictable rate, a level term policy may be best for you.

The other major factor you'll need to consider is your budget. Can you afford to pay an increase in your premium every year or so? If not, a decreasing term policy may be your less-than-ideal necessary choice.

Along those same lines, you should know that term life insurance policies are sold in two basic forms: *guaranteed premiums* and *current assumption*. Guaranteed premiums will not increase for the term of the policy, so you don't have to worry about your rates going up. Current assumption policies usually guarantee premiums for a certain number of years, after which they may be increased or decreased as the insurance company deems necessary.

Is it necessary to tell you that guaranteed premium policies are more expensive than current assumption policies? Rest assured that any insurance benefit your provider offers will eventually come out of your pocket—even that chintzy little desk calendar they send you every Christmas.

Okay, now you're ready to pass a term life insurance vocabulary test. Let's move on to the stuff you really want to know.

Before You Buy Term Life Insurance. . .

Here are four tips to keep in mind if and when you decide to purchase term life insurance.

1. Buy only what you need.

2. Make sure you buy a renewable policy that cannot be canceled due to bad health.

3. Make sure you buy a policy that is renewable to at least age 100. (If your loved ones aren't able to support themselves after that, tough luck.)

GLAD YOU ASKED

Should a single person buy life insurance?

If you're single and have no financial dependents, you probably don't need life insurance. Remember, the purpose of life insurance is to provide for someone after your death for whom you are providing while you're alive.

4. Make sure you compare the cost of term life insurance for a 20-year period to other kinds of insurance, such as whole life.

If you determine that term insurance will best fit your budget and your family's needs (and, unfortunately, to make an informed decision, you have to read about the other types of insurance too), ask an insurance agent you trust to explain to you the pros and cons of various policies.

You also should do a bit research yourself. *Consumer Reports* publishes a yearly comparison of insurance companies that may prove to be helpful to you. You may also want to call A.M. Best, a respected rating firm that evaluates insurance providers and passes that information on to consumers. You can contact A.M. Best at 908-439-2200. The call will cost about $2.50 a minute, but when you consider how much you can save on insurance premiums you'll find that the expense is well worth it.

The Least You Should Know About Cash Value Insurance

Fortunately, or unfortunately, term life is not your only life insurance option. There are also policies known as *cash value life insurance* policies. If that name doesn't ring a bell, maybe one of these does: whole life, universal life, variable life, ordinary life, or permanent insurance. They are all forms of cash value life insurance.

Cash value life insurance is usually purchased for an individual's lifetime at a flat rate for the life of the policy. Unlike a term life policy, a cash value policy accumulates a cash reserve from the premiums that are paid.

As the policy accumulates a cash value, it begins to earn interest. In many cases, the insurance provider will pay dividends (cash returns) to policy holders, which can be used to offset the cost of insurance.

The annual cost of cash value life insurance starts at a higher rate than term insurance, but the premiums never increase. For a young family with limited funds, cash value life insurance may not be a wise purchase. In fact, the insurance can be so costly that, to afford it, you may be forced to buy inadequate amounts of coverage just when your need is the greatest.

A cash value life policy, like a term policy, may include what's called a waiver of premium disability benefit and/or an accidental death benefit. Because these are extras, your premium rate will be higher if you include them in your coverage.

Under the waiver of premiums benefit, if you become permanently disabled and are unable to pay your insurance premiums, your provider will make your payments for you. In case you're wondering, the disability usually must last for at least six months before it's considered permanent.

The accidental death benefit guarantees that your beneficiaries will receive double the face value of your policy if your death occurs by accidental means. That's why the accidental death benefit is often called double indemnity.

The Least You Should Know About Universal Life Insurance

Universal life, sometimes called complete or total life insurance, is a combination of term insurance and a tax-deferred savings account that pays a flexible interest rate. The interest rate usually reflects current market rates and is much higher than that guaranteed by other policies. It's a policy that's broken down into three parts: death benefit, administrative costs, and savings.

Premiums may be paid at any time and for any amount above a certain minimum. Premium amounts may be flexible or level. Eventually, premiums may not be required at all if you accumulate enough money in the savings portion of your policy to pay the death benefit and administrative costs for your life expectancy (according to the calculations of your insurance provider).

A universal life insurance policy is normally sold by agents on the basis of how much you will accumulate by age 65 in the savings portion. This tactic emphasizes life insurance as an investment and not as a means of providing for your dependents at your death.

If you know you'll need life insurance in your 70s and 80s, a universal life policy might make more sense than term insurance. To be blunt, though, the need for insurance after age 70 is usually due to poor planning or a lack of discipline while you're young. If you have enough time to build a nest egg for yourself and your dependents, you shouldn't have to worry about life insurance as a septuagenarian.

If you're considering a universal policy, keep in mind that you will not be eligible for the return on your policy until you've been paying on it for approximately 15 to 20 years. If you decide to cancel the policy before that time, it will cost you dearly, compared to the alternative of purchasing term life insurance and investing the difference in some other kind of tax-deferred account.

The Least You Should Know About Credit or Mortgage Life Insurance

If you have a credit card or a mortgage, chances are you receive periodic offers for this type of insurance. A credit or mortgage life insurance policy is decreasing term life insurance sold in connection with home loans, auto loans, or other forms of credit. This type of policy is designed to relieve survivors of some of their economic strain by paying off the deceased's outstanding loan balance. (Credit disability insurance covers monthly payments if you are disabled.)

The next time you start to toss one of these offers in the garbage, stop yourself and consider how that coverage might benefit you. Then go ahead and throw it away. Rather than buying several of these small, relatively expensive policies, it would be wiser to incorporate these needs into your overall life and disability insurance planning and purchase a single policy.

Forced Savings: Good Idea or Not?

Many people use cash value insurance policies as a means of forcing them to set aside money for savings. But is an insurance policy the best place for your savings to go?

Keep in mind that when you borrow or withdraw the cash value of your policy your death benefits are reduced. The end result is that your family may be left without enough provision after your death. That's not the kind of thing you want to happen with a life insurance policy.

On top of that, there are a few things you need to know about using a cash value life insurance policy as a savings account.

1. There are two components to a cash value policy's interest rate or earnings: the actual guaranteed rate and the projected rate—or dividend. The guaranteed earnings are typically between 3 and 5 percent.

2. The quoted interest rate is probably calculated before administrative fees and commissions are subtracted. Therefore, your net earnings will be reduced.

3. Interest rates are adjusted annually, if not more frequently. So what you think you're getting when you sign up for the policy may not be what you end up getting.

As for whether it's a good idea, forcing yourself to save reflects a lack of discipline. Your better option is to learn to set aside the funds you'll need for emergencies and future needs. As a short-term investment, the savings in most insurance policies draw less than half the interest that could be earned elsewhere. That's a high price to pay for a lack of discipline.

Glad You Asked

What happens if I fail to make my premium payment on time?

You have a grace period of 30 days during which time you may make your premium payment without penalty. If you don't make the payment during the grace period, your policy is considered lapsed. To reinstate your policy after it has lapsed, you must again qualify as an acceptable risk and pay your overdue premiums, as well as the interest you owe.

How Much Is Enough?

The amount of life insurance you carry will be determined by a number of variables. For example, you must take into account your family income, the age of your children, the ability of your spouse to earn an income, your existing debts, your family's current lifestyle, your Social Security status, and any other sources of after-death income you may have besides life insurance.

You must also consider the standard of living that you want to continue for your family in the event of your death. Some people may prefer to supply enough insurance proceeds for their families to live off the interest income alone. Others may prefer to provide enough for their families to live on for a specific number of years. Obviously these are decisions that should be made by you and your spouse together.

A typical family's life insurance needs begin when the first child is conceived and reach a maximum when the last child is conceived. The need for insurance increases again when the children are grown and out of the home and before the non-wage-earning spouse reaches the age of 62.

With proper planning, your insurance needs drop to zero at retirement age when you and your spouse have accumulated debt-free assets, investments, and adequate retirement savings. Therefore, your life insurance policy should provide a maximum amount of protection while your family is growing and taper off as your family gets older and smaller.

Budgeting for Insurance

The next obvious question is, "How much insurance can you afford?" From a budgeting standpoint, insurance costs should make up approximately 5 percent of your Net Spending Income—your take-home pay after tithes are taken out.

The 5 percent figure excludes home or automobile insurance and includes life insurance, health, disability, and any other types of insurance you have. The figure also assumes that your health insurance is part of a group plan, most likely one offered by your employer.

If you're not part of a group health insurance plan, this percentage of your budget will increase, and you'll have to be extra choosy about your life and health insurance. Remember, if you increase the insurance category of your budget from 5 to 10 percent, you have no alternative but to decrease another area of your budget in order to make it balance. (For more information on budgeting your income, check out chapter 2.)

Watch Out

If you're not careful, you can be talked into buying life insurance coverage that you don't need. You're especially vulnerable if you don't know what kind of sales pitches to ignore.

Here are three things to keep in mind when you buy life insurance.

1. Avoid the double indemnity clause. Most people don't die by accident. Besides, you should have the amount of insurance your family needs without having to depend on your dying in an accident.

2. Forget the premium waiver. Although it may seem like a good idea to have your insurance provider pay for your premium if you become permanently disabled, it is a large expense for a small benefit.

3. Don't be sold insurance. Learn to buy what you need rather than what someone else wants you to have.

Tips for Policy Holders

If you already have a life insurance policy, here are some tips on what you can do to become a more responsible policy holder. (That is one of your life's goals, isn't it?)

1. Keep your insurance company informed of your address. If you move, let your insurance provider know about it. Otherwise, you may risk accidentally allowing your policy to lapse.

2. Read your life insurance policy. Your agent should be willing to walk you through every section of your policy. When he or she does, don't do the vacant nodding routine. Make sure that you understand all of the basic provisions and benefits. If you don't

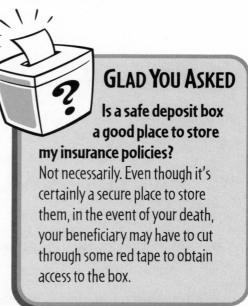

GLAD YOU ASKED

Is a safe deposit box a good place to store my insurance policies?
Not necessarily. Even though it's certainly a secure place to store them, in the event of your death, your beneficiary may have to cut through some red tape to obtain access to the box.

understand something, ask for a clear explanation.

3. Keep your policy in a safe place. You can get a duplicate if your policy is lost or destroyed by fire but not without some inconvenience and delay. As an additional safeguard, keep a separate record of your policies. Be sure that your beneficiary knows where a copy of your policy is kept. Generally, policies must be sent to the insurance provider when your beneficiary files for benefits.

4. Discuss your insurance program with your family or other beneficiaries. Get their input before you make decisions that will affect their lives.

5. Review your life insurance program with your agent once a year or when a major event, such as a birth, death, marriage, or divorce occurs. Your insurance needs are constantly changing. You need to make sure that your policy reflects those changes.

The Bottom Line on Life Insurance

When you talk about selecting the right kind of life insurance, you must consider not only the current annual cost but its cost during the next 20 years. Shop for the policy that best fits your individual needs at the lowest cost. You can probably get the best value by purchasing term insurance and saving the difference in a deferred or tax-free investment.

In reality, though, most people don't save the difference; they spend it. When they get to be 50 or older, their term insurance can become too expensive for them to afford. So buy term life insurance if you can't afford cash value insurance, but if by the age of 35 you have not been able to save the difference that the cash value policy would have cost, then convert to a whole life plan.

Your Health Insurance Needs

In our society health insurance is an absolute necessity. Few families can afford the cost of a single hospital stay, let alone a major operation or an extended illness. Your best strategy for assuring that you and your family will receive the care you need when you need it is to find quality health insurance at a reasonable rate.

However, in order to determine what type of health insurance is best for you,

you have to know at least a little about the different coverages that are available. To make this as simple as possible, we'll divide health insurance into two general types: basic coverage and major medical.

The Least You Should Know About Basic Health Coverage

Basic health coverage includes hospitalization, surgical, and general medical expenses.

Hospitalization provides coverage for daily and miscellaneous expenses when a person is in the hospital. Daily expenses include room and board and nursing charges. Miscellaneous expenses cover services such as X-rays, drugs, lab examinations, dressings, and physical therapy.

CRUNCHING NUMBERS

Insurance costs should make up approximately 5 percent of your Net Spending Income (your gross income minus taxes and tithe). That 5 percent figure includes all insurance costs except home and auto. The figure also assumes that your health insurance is part of a group plan.

Surgical provides coverage for operations performed in or out of the hospital. Some policies pay only up to a maximum amount for surgical fees; those aren't the kind you want. Surgeons charge different rates for their services. Your policy should cover the rates charged in your community.

General medical provides coverage for any doctor's visits in or out of the hospital that do not involve surgery. Diagnostic and laboratory tests may also be included. Most general medical policies have distinct limitations. That's why it's important for you to find out how much your policy pays per visit, how many visits it will allow, and whether the policy covers house calls and office visits.

The Least You Should Know About Major Medical Health Coverage

Major medical insurance, also known as catastrophic coverage, includes hospital, surgical, and other medical treatment not covered by basic health insurance policies. A major medical policy normally covers 75 to 80 percent of all expenses above your deductible (the amount of the bill you must pay before your insurance provider starts paying).

In addition to your deductible, that leaves you with the remaining 20 to 25 percent of the expenses. This type of coverage is commonly called coinsurance, because you share the burden of the medical bill with your insurance company. Coinsurance is a way of encouraging people to keep their medical costs low.

CRUNCHING NUMBERS

If your health insurance is not part of a group plan, you will need to increase the insurance budget category from 5 percent of your total Net Spending Income to 10 percent.

Your deductible may be any amount from $1 to $10,000. The higher your deductible is, the less you pay in premiums. If you can't afford the health insurance you like, it would be wise to purchase a major medical policy with a high deductible. This would cover you in case of a serious illness or accident. The money you save in premiums could be used for minor health care.

A major medical policy may include a stop-loss provision that limits the amount you have to pay. For example, your policy may state that after you've paid $1,500 of your own (out-of-pocket) money, the insurer will pay the rest of your medical expenses.

The Least You Should Know About Disability Insurance

Disability insurance provides you with income in the event you are disabled and unable to work. Before you consider purchasing a policy, though, you should consider how much disability protection you already have.

If you pay Social Security taxes, you already have some disability coverage. These disability benefit payments are based on your level of earnings over a period of years. However, these benefits pay only if your disability is expected to last for more than 12 months.

It's worth mentioning, though, that Social Security has been determined by the United States Supreme Court not to be an insurance plan but social welfare provided by the government. So your decision to accept Social Security disability coverage will depend on your convictions regarding government welfare.

Many employers provide a form of disability protection through their employee group insurance plan. Check around to see if your employer is among them. Normally, disability benefits are paid as a percentage of your regular gross income. Most policies require total disability before benefits are paid, but in some cases you can collect on partial disability.

When it comes time to review a disability policy, make sure that you find a clear explanation of what constitutes disability. The best definition would be one that states that you are unable to perform the main duties of your occupation. The worst definition would be one that states that you are unable to perform the main duties of any occupation.

When the time comes to collect on your insurance, you don't want to be denied because of a technicality in the wording of the policy.

Other disability coverage options include a provision for payments to begin after a set waiting period (30 days, 60 days, or more) following the beginning of disability. The longer the waiting period, the lower your premiums will be.

You also will have to choose whether the benefits will be paid for one year, two years, five years, or until age 65. The shorter the period of your disability coverage, the lower your premiums will be.

Stand Alone or Join the Crowd?

Health insurance policies may be purchased through a group plan or on an individual basis from an insurance company. Many employers offer group health insurance coverage to their employees as a fringe benefit. Premiums for a group plan are usually lower than those for individual coverage. The employer may pay all or part of the premium.

Individual health insurance policies are those you buy yourself through an agent. The good thing about the do-it-yourself approach is that you get to choose the benefits you want. Your premiums will be based on your age, sex, and physical condition, as well as the amount of coverage you choose.

If you decide to go the individual route, make sure you do plenty of shopping around for quotes. You will find that costs for virtually identical health insurance policies may vary as much as 50 percent from one major insurance company to another.

The Least You Should Know About HMOs

In America we tend to use doctors and hospitals primarily as firefighters. We wait until we have an emergency and then call someone to save us. We don't take good care of ourselves. We don't eat right. We don't get enough exercise. We're under so much stress that our bodies eventually give out on us. So we go to the doctor and ask for a pill to get over it.

Health maintenance organizations (HMOs) have developed as a result of this fix-me-up mentality. HMOs negotiate with major employers to take care of all their health care needs, from obstetrics to surgery to minor care, as long as the employees use the HMO's doctors, hospitals, and clinics.

The employer (or individual) enrolls as a member by paying a fee that covers all medical expenses, from office visits to long-term hospitalization. The reasoning is that since the premiums are so low, members will seek medical care before major treatment is needed.

The negative side of HMOs is that if you want to use a health provider outside the group you pay the bill!

GLAD YOU ASKED

Is nursing home insurance recommended?

The cost of nursing home insurance must be weighed against your ability to pay the premiums and the probability of need for such insurance. Before you invest in such insurance, consider the alternatives, particularly the possibility of caring for older family members yourself.

The Least You Should Know About Medicaid

Medicaid is a government-sponsored program that pays medical bills for low-income people who can't afford the costs of health care. You can get a copy of the guidelines for eligibility, which are very strict, from your local public health or welfare office.

Before you look into this type of health insurance, though, you need to think about your convictions concerning government welfare. You also will need to consider the marginal treatment that many Medicaid patients receive.

Because of the high cost of medical care, many Medicaid patients are pressured to leave the hospital before they are well. When their benefits run out, the government puts the medical staff under a lot of pressure to move these patients out of the hospital. It's still medicine, but it's also an example of getting what you pay for.

The Least You Should Know About Medicare and Medigap

Medicare is the government sponsored health insurance program for most people 65 and older and for some people who are disabled.

The Medicare system is actually a two-part program. Part A provides hospital benefits for short-term illness and some benefits for care in a skilled nursing facility or at home. People who are not automatically eligible for coverage pay a monthly premium that is adjusted every year.

Part B is optional medical insurance that is available for a small fee each month. You may have the premium automatically deducted from your Social Security benefit check, if you receive one. This coverage pays most of your medical and surgical fees. Part B is an excellent value because it is inexpensive and gives you at least some help with doctor's fees and other medical costs.

Even with both parts of Medicare, though, you'll still be faced with medical expenses. That's where Medicare supplemental insurance comes in. Medicare supplemental insurance, also known as *medigap*, is designed to take up where Medicare leaves off.

Medigap insurance is relatively inexpensive for the amount of coverage it provides. For instance, let's say you needed heart bypass surgery. The total cost could run more than $50,000. If Medicare picked up 80 percent of the tab, that would still leave you with a bill of more than $10,000!

Instead of having to use your life savings to pay your hospital bills, it might be better to shell out $50 or so every month ($600 per year) to provide for that contingency.

The Bottom Line on Health Insurance

When you start to plan your health insurance program, make sure that your coverage fits your needs and your budget. Examine your policy carefully. Know which expenses are covered by your insurance and which are not.

It's also important that you do not duplicate coverage. Some insurance providers will not pay if another policy is in effect for the same coverage.

Look over your policy every few years to make sure it fits your family's current needs. Make sure you're covered against major expenses when your funds are limited.

And don't forget to compare policies and costs. Remember, rates vary greatly from one company to another.

Your Homeowner's Insurance Needs

Comprehensive homeowner's insurance covers everything that could happen to your home and its contents: fire, theft, water, hail, wind damage. It also provides liability coverage in case someone is injured in or around your house.

When you purchase homeowner's insurance, you need to be aware of the difference between *actual cash value insurance* and *guaranteed (true) replacement value* on your contents or structure. Actual cash value refers to the depreciated value of your belongings, taking into account their age and condition. Guaranteed replacement means your contents and structure will be replaced at 100 percent of their value.

Obviously guaranteed replacement value insurance is more expensive than actual cash value insurance. Even so, a guaranteed replacement value policy is worth considering, if you can afford it.

The Least You Should Know About Renter's Insurance

Even if you don't own a home, you'll most likely need insurance for your dwelling. Aside from the fact that your landlord probably requires it, there are three reasons to have renter's insurance.

1. It covers the value of your furniture for replacement.

2. It covers the liability if someone is hurt as a result of your negligence or the negligence of your children; for example, if someone trips on a toy or falls on ice outside your apartment.

3. It protects you against a suit from the landlord's insurance provider for damage to the property.

Like all insurance needs, your decision on renter's insurance should be weighed on a need-versus-cost basis. If you can afford to replace all of your household furniture or cover a liability suit resulting from fire or water damage or from negligence, you don't need renter's insurance. But if you can't, renter's insurance represents wise planning, because it involves spending a small amount to avoid a large possible liability.

The Least You Should Know About Private Mortgage Insurance

If you've already purchased a home, you probably already know about PMI (private mortgage insurance). If you haven't yet purchased a home, you'll find out for yourself soon enough. Banks and other institutions that lend money for homes require private mortgage insurance for their loans that equal or exceed 80 percent of the purchase price.

Don't be confused about who's protected under this insurance. It's not you. Private mortgage insurance is designed to protect your lender in case you ever default on your loan. But even though your lender is the one being protected, you are the one who pays for the insurance.

The premium for private mortgage insurance is usually a percentage of the loan value, broken down into monthly increments. The amount is determined by the insurance company's loss experience ratio, which is based on its history with defaulting borrowers.

The Least You Should Know About Umbrella Liability Insurance

An umbrella liability policy provides coverage over and above the liability limits on your auto or homeowner's insurance policies.

Statistically speaking, few homeowners will ever face a million-dollar lawsuit.

But if you're wealthy and your occupation gives you a lot of public exposure, it may be wise to cover yourself in our sue-happy society.

You can usually purchase a million-dollar limit policy for less than the annual premium on your homeowner's insurance. To qualify, you're normally required to increase your auto and homeowner's liability limits first. If you have a lot of assets and don't want to risk them, this premium is not too high a price to pay for a million dollar's worth of coverage.

Your Auto Insurance Needs

Auto insurance is no longer a matter of choice; it's a law. You must carry liability insurance on your car or face legal consequences. If a police officer pulls you over for a moving offense, he or she will probably ask to see your driver's license and proof of insurance. So the question is not whether you should have auto coverage but what kind of coverage you should have.

Liability insurance, the minimum legal requirement, will cover the cost of an accident to other people and their vehicles. Usually the cost of liability insurance is relatively small, especially when you consider the alternative. Even one at-fault accident without insurance can send you into debt spiral that you may never pull out of.

If you want maximum protection for you and your car, though, liability insurance is merely a drop in a bucket. Let's look at some of the other types of coverage that are available to you.

The Least You Should Know About Full Coverage Auto Insurance

If liability insurance is the minimum, full coverage on your vehicle is the maximum. Full coverage includes protection against bodily injury, liability, property damage, medical payments, collision, comprehensive, and uninsured motorists. If you have a new car, you should seriously consider carrying full coverage.

If the cost of full coverage is a little pricey for you or if your car just isn't worth insuring to the hilt, there are countless other options you can choose.

Let's take a look at some of the specific coverages that are available.

Bodily injury liability

This type of insurance pays for injuries or deaths to passengers in other vehicles, passengers in your car, or pedestrians as the result of an accident involving your car for which you are legally liable whether you're driving or another person is driving your vehicle with your permission.

Coverage under this type of policy is referred to in terms of 15/30, with the first number being the amount (in thousands) that the policy will pay for one person and the second number being the total amount (in thousands) that it will pay for all persons involved in an accident.

Personal injury protection

This type of insurance pays benefits to injured people for medical expenses, lost wages, and death, no matter whose fault the accident was. This protection remains in effect whether a person is riding in your vehicle, getting in or out of it, or is struck by it as a pedestrian.

Property damage liability

As you may have guessed from its name, this insurance covers damage to property, houses, buildings, fences, livestock, or any other property belonging to someone else caused by your car. The terms of the coverage are expressed as 15/30/10. That means the insurance company will pay a maximum of the amount indicated (in thousands) for (1) each person injured, (2) each accident, and (3) property damage.

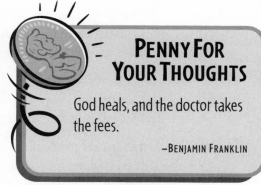

PENNY FOR YOUR THOUGHTS

God heals, and the doctor takes the fees.

—BENJAMIN FRANKLIN

Medical payments

Medical payments coverage applies to medical expenses resulting from accidental injury to anyone riding in your automobile or struck as a pedestrian.

Collision insurance

This type of insurance pays for damages to your vehicle, but not the other person's, when you are involved in an accident. Usually with this coverage your insurance provider will pay only the market value of your car in case of an accident.

For example, let's say your four-year-old compact car sustains $2,500 in damages in an accident, according to an adjuster. If the car's market value is only $500, you will receive $500, minus your deductible. That's why, if your vehicle is older than three years, you can save money on your auto insurance by dropping the collision coverage.

If you can afford to pay for damages to your vehicle, you can self-insure your car. Since collision insurance is relatively expensive, you can put aside the value of the car into an interest-bearing savings account to be used in the event that your car is damaged. However, if you can't afford to save money to repair your vehicle, you'll need collision insurance.

Comprehensive physical damage insurance

This type of insurance provides for the replacement of glass and other damages and losses that result from anything except collision. This would include fire, theft, vandalism, and hail.

The premiums are relatively inexpensive, and generally the things that are covered are the same regardless of your car's age. You'll need to make the decision about this type of insurance with a little help from your spouse and your budget. If the cost is too high for your income, you should carry liability only.

But before you drop your comprehensive or collision insurance, keep in mind that simply by shopping around for the lowest rate of insurance you may be able to save enough money to pay for extra coverage.

Uninsured motorists

This type of insurance pays for injuries to you and your family caused by a hit-and-run driver or one who doesn't have liability auto insurance.

Other coverage

If more coverage is what you're looking for, try death and dismemberment insurance, which provides benefits to you or your family in the event of a death or loss of limb as the result of an automobile accident. Towing insurance pays part or all of the towing charges if your car breaks down. Rental car reimbursement provides you with a vehicle to drive while yours is being repaired.

The Least You Should Know About Auto Insurance for Teens

Your insurance costs will change dramatically when your children reach driving age. And if you think that change will be for the better, wake up and smell the burning rubber. Insurance providers know that as soon as your children turn 16, you'll likely start letting them drive your car. Unfortunately, they also know how most teenagers drive.

You'll find that it's much cheaper for you to add your teenagers to your insurance policy than to purchase a separate policy for them. Limiting your kids to a small percentage of the total use of the family car may lower your rates slightly, but you'll still see quite a jump in your premiums.

Tips for Saving on Auto Insurance

Your best bet for reducing your auto insurance cost is to make sure your teenagers qualify for existing discounts.

For example, most insurance providers offer discounts for. . .

1. good students with a B average or above

2. drivers who have successfully completed a driver's education course

3. people who car pool

4. multicar families

5. students away at college

6. cars with air bags

7. cars with antitheft devices

8. senior citizens

9. farmers

10. defensive drivers

11. nonsmokers and nondrinkers

12. females, age 30 to 64, who are the sole drivers in their households

Check with your insurance agent to see if you qualify for any of these discounts.

You can also save money by avoiding traffic violations. Drunk driving, speeding, or other moving violations puts points on your driving record and adds dollars to your premiums.

The type of vehicle you drive also determines your premium. Sporty or expensive cars usually have higher premiums than family wagons.

It's important to let your agent know immediately when circumstances change in your family—when your child leaves for college, for example. It's also important to review your coverage annually to make sure that it still fits your needs.

Play Fair

Before we wrap up this chapter, let's take a look at one more insurance issue that may affect you.

Consider what you would do in the following situations.

Your doctor tells you that you need some diagnostic tests run and suggests that you have them done as a hospital outpatient because it will be less expensive. However, if you can get admitted to the hospital for at least two days, insurance will pick up the tab. You don't need to be admitted, but your doctor will do it if you want.

You return home from a trip to find that your car has been severely damaged in the airport parking lot. There's no note on your car, so you realize it was a hit-and-run. Because you don't carry collision insurance, you are responsible for the repairs. However, as you're driving home from the airport, you're involved in a multicar accident that's not your fault. The actual damage to your car from the accident is slight, but the adjuster assumes the damage from the hit-and-run was part of the accident and writes up a generous settlement.

What would you do?

Cheating your insurance provider can be a tempting proposition, especially if you allow your reasoning to guide you. After all . . .

➤ if the situation were reversed, you can bet that your insurance provider would try to cheat you. If you've ever been burned by an insurance company, you know what we're talking about.

➤ big corporations can afford to pay. Who doesn't want to see large, impersonal businesses brought to their knees occasionally? Besides, if you're not acquainted with anyone there, it's not like you're cheating a flesh-and-blood person.

➤ you pay enough for coverage. What's wrong with getting your money's worth, even if the situation is a little beyond the parameters of your policy?

Although these reasons may seem logical, there are also a few reasons to resist the temptation. For example...

➤ you and your fellow insureds will eventually pay for your cheating in the form of increased rates. You don't get something for nothing when it comes to insurance.

➤ you might be expecting too much from insurance. You can't legitimately expect your provider to protect you from every loss. That's not the way things work.

➤ lying and cheating are morally wrong. Why compromise your principles for the sake of a few (hundred) dollars?

The Buck Stops Here

Think you're an expert on insurance? Here's a quiz to see how much you know.

1. Which of the following is not a basic insurance term?
   a. Conscription
   b. Deductible
   c. Beneficiary
   d. Premium

2. Which of the following is not good advice when it comes to buying term life insurance?
   a. Storm out of your agent's office if he quotes a price that is too high.
   b. Buy only what you need.
   c. Make sure that it cannot be canceled because of bad health.
   d. Make sure it is renewable to at least age 100.

3. Which of the following tips should you not keep in mind when planning your health insurance program?
   a. Make sure the coverage fits your needs.
   b. Know which expenses are covered by your policy and which aren't.
   c. Don't waste your time shopping around, since all insurance companies have the same rates.
   d. Don't duplicate coverage.

4. What group of people should seriously consider umbrella liability homeowner's insurance?
   a. The poor
   b. The clumsy
   c. The superstitious
   d. The wealthy

5. Which of the following does not qualify you for a discount on your auto insurance?
   a. Car pooling
   b. Driving a sports car
   c. Owning more than one vehicle
   d. Successfully completing a driver's education course

Answers: (1) a, (2) a, (3) c, (4) d, (5) b

CHAPTER 9

Estate of Confusion (How to Avoid It)

SNAPSHOT

"**Y**ou need to make a will," Kay announced as she walked into the living room. Earl dropped the remote control and turned to look at her, the color slowly draining from his face. "Why?" he asked. "Did the doctor call about my checkup? What did he say?"

Kay waved her hand at her husband. "No," she replied, "I just read an obituary of a 41-year-old man who died of a heart attack while playing basketball at church."

Earl let out a deep sigh and put his hand on his chest. "I know of a 37-year-old man who just had some pretty strong heart palpitations of his own," he muttered.

"Don't you think it would be a good idea for us to get all of our possessions and financial instructions down on paper before you. . . well, you know," Kay continued.

"Sure, I guess so," Earl admitted. "But I've never

SNEAK PREVIEW

1. Your will is the key to your family's financial future.
2. A few strategic financial moves can prevent the loss of most of your assets to taxes after your death.
3. A carefully chosen trust will allow you to disburse your assets to your beneficiaries both before and after your death.

considered myself the type of guy who needs a will. I mean, besides my CD collection and my Mickey Mantle-autographed baseball, what would I put in a will?"

"Well, you've got your pension and your life insurance, for starters," Kay reminded him. "And that stock we bought a couple of years ago. Those are important things to protect if. . . something were to happen to you."

"Stop talking like that!" Earl pleaded. "You're really starting to give me the creeps." He picked up the cup sitting next to him and sniffed inside.

"What are you doing?" Kay asked.

"I'm making sure you didn't put anything in my root beer," Earl replied with a grin.

Kay rolled her eyes as she walked out of the room. "Do you really think I would go to all the trouble of poisoning you for a baseball signed by a cartoon mouse?"

"That's a Mickey *Mantle* autograph!" Earl called after her. "Not Mickey Mouse!"

* * * * * * * * * * * * * * *

When you think of a will, do you picture an eccentric old man leaving his fortune to the heir who. . .

> ➤ spends the night in a haunted mansion?

> ➤ convinces a complete stranger to marry him?

> ➤ successfully completes a wacky treasure hunt?

When you think of a trust fund, do you picture that person in college who drove a BMW, wore tennis clothes all the time, and went to Aspen for Christmas vacation and the Bahamas for spring break?

One of our goals in this chapter is to tear down these and other stereotypes associated with inheritances. You don't have to be a crazy, rich septuagenarian to write a will. And you don't need a name like Biff or Muffy to be concerned about a trust fund.

In fact, if you've accumulated anything of value in your lifetime and want to make sure that it goes to your loved ones after you. . . cash in your chips, you need a will or a trust. It's not a matter of being too young or too poor to have one; it's a matter of being too concerned about your family's future not to.

Where There's a Will, There Are... Lots of People Looking for Money

Before throwing around complicated legal terms like a lawyer trying to impress someone at a dinner party, let's cover the basics of what a will is and why you should care.

A *will* is a legal document that specifies where you want your money and possessions to go after you... take a dirt bath. Your will can be as general ("I leave everything I own to my wife") or as specific ("I leave three sticks of Juicy Fruit chewing gum to my nephew Timmy") as you desire.

Right now you may be saying, "My spouse and kids already know where I want my stuff to go after I... breathe my last. There's no need to write it down." And that certainly makes sense. But there's one family member you may be forgetting: your Uncle Sam.

If you... give up the ghost without leaving a will, you leave the door open for the state government to decide what will happen to your possessions. Think about it. Without a will, your family may be at the mercy of the state to receive what is rightfully theirs. How's *that* for a wake-up call?

I'm not suggesting that the state is waiting greedily for you to... expire, so that it can snatch your belongings away from your family. I'm merely pointing out that there's no reason for government officials to be involved in the first place in distributing your

GLAD YOU ASKED

What's a good age to start thinking about estate planning?

The obvious answer is, the earlier the better. However, estate planning can't really be considered a pressing matter until your estate is, well, worth making plans for. If you have a steady income, a few shekels in the bank, some investments, a pension plan, or even just a life insurance policy, you might want to consider your different options. If you have a family, though, you really need to get serious about estate planning.

money and possessions after your... expiration date. This is a situation in which "If you want something done right, you have to do it yourself" definitely applies. All you need to do to keep the state's hands off your money is to write a will.

PENNY FOR YOUR THOUGHTS

A son can bear with composure the death of his father, but the loss of his inheritance might drive him to despair.

—Niccolo Machiavelli

You can include just about anything in your will. (Hey, it's your last earthly statement. Why not make the most of it?) But what matters most to your family's financial well-being are your instructions regarding your *estate*. That's right, *you* have an estate. Before you start getting all cocky, though, you should know that *estate* is simply a legal term meaning everything you own. Your estate includes your house, car(s), furniture, electronic equipment, antiques, books, compact discs—not to mention your retirement benefits and life insurance. Some estates are worth billions; others are worth hundreds, but everyone has one of some size and value.

Before your will can be considered valid, it has to meet a few legal state requirements. These requirements vary from state to state, but there are some general guidelines you should be aware of.

➤ You should have your will prepared in the state in which you live.

➤ Your will should be in writing.

➤ You must be legally competent to sign your will.

➤ You must sign your will in the presence of at least two—and often three—witnesses.

The process of determining whether a will is valid or not is called *probate*. Because this process generally takes place after you've... checked out, it's important for your will to meet your state's legal requirements before that time. If it doesn't, it may be declared invalid, and your family will suffer the consequences.

When the time comes to put your will into effect, obviously you won't be around to make sure that everything goes where you want it to. So you need to choose someone to oversee the process of distributing your possessions for you. That person is called an *executor*.

The executor of your estate will be responsible for. . .

➤ locating your will and studying it carefully

➤ meeting with the attorney who helped you establish the will

➤ contacting the people who witnessed your signing of the will

➤ notifying creditors of your. . . passing

➤ locating all of your property

➤ inspecting your real estate contracts, leases, and mortgages

➤ filing your income and estate tax returns.

Many people choose their spouses to be executor of their wills. Others, not wanting to burden their loved ones with additional responsibilities during their time of mourning, choose their lawyers, accountants, or other financial professionals. Either way, it's important for your executor to know as much about you and your will as possible. Your goal is to make the inheritance process as smooth and problem free as possible for your loved ones.

Now that it's clear who's who and what's what in Willsville, let's talk about the steps you need to take to create your own will.

A Will of Your Own

The process of preparing a will can be tedious and complicated. But that doesn't mean the explanation of it has to be. Behold—a simple seven-step guide to securing your family's financial future after your. . . earthly citizenship is revoked.

1. Find a lawyer.
If you already have an attorney, perhaps one who helped you with the sale or purchase of your house or some past legal matter, you've already completed one-seventh of the will-drafting process. If you don't, you'll need to find one. (And although there may be plenty of good jokes that begin, "Where's the best place to

find a lawyer?" I'll take the high road right now and just give you the information you need.)

The best place to start your lawyer search is among your family and friends. Chances are, at least a few of your loved ones have worked with attorneys—perhaps even in drafting their own wills—whom they can recommend to you. If not, expand your search to include your church. Unless your congregation is very small, you probably can find a few (or more) attorneys among your fellow church members simply by asking around (again, we'll refrain from any jokes about lawyers in church).

Once you find an attorney that you're comfortable with, he or she will give you the necessary information about getting started on your will. Don't be afraid to ask up front how much you will be billed for the service.

2. Talk to your loved ones.

Before you start randomly assigning possessions in your will, talk things over with your loved ones. If you think it's appropriate, ask your family members whether there are any particular items that have special meaning to them. Your old photo albums, yearbooks, records, lockets, and knickknacks may have much more significance to your children than you imagine. Make a note of who requests what, and then do everything possible to accommodate your family's desires in your will.

Contrary to the popular media portrayal of heirs and heiresses as greedy, back-stabbing weasels, you'll probably find that your family members prefer possessions with tremendous sentimental value and relatively small monetary worth.

3. Take an inventory.

In order to assign everything you own to your loved ones in your will, first you must know how much you have to assign. Finding that out may require a little

GLAD YOU ASKED

Do I really need to get a lawyer involved? Couldn't I just draft my own will?

You could, but usually you shouldn't. Remember, your family's financial future is at stake. If you draft your own will, you increase the chances of it being declared invalid. Regardless of what you think of lawyers, you have to admit that they are less likely to make a disastrous mistake on your will than you are.

research and investigation on your part.

Some assets are pretty obvious—your house, car(s), furniture, collections, and savings account, to name a few. Others may not pop into your head right away. For example, what kind of insurance coverage do you have through your employer? Did you ever start a 401(k) account? Do you have any IRAs? Have you ever purchased any stock?

You can't be expected to remember every little investment you've made in your life. That's where financial statements and transaction records come in handy. Even if you can't recall a particular investment, chances are you have records of it some place. Dig through your files—not just your recent ones, but also records from years ago. If you find something—anything—include it in your inventory. Don't dismiss anything as being too small or insignificant unless your lawyer tells you to.

4. Choose an executor.

Selecting a person to oversee your legal and financial matters immediately, after you. . . go the way of all flesh, is not a decision to be taken lightly. Look back at the list of tasks an executor has to perform (on page 191). The position carries with it a tremendous amount of responsibility. So if you select someone who folds like a card table in the face of responsibility, you'll be doing your loved ones a great disservice.

If you don't name an executor in your will, or if the person you select fails to carry out the responsibilities, the court that is overseeing your case will appoint someone to fill the position. And with all due respect to the fine courts in our land, you don't want that to happen. If you choose your executor wisely, you will keep the decision-making process out of the court's hands.

Your spouse is probably your best bet to fill the role. Who else knows more about your finances or holds your family's interests in higher regard? Keep in mind, though, that in the wake of your. . . well, *wake*, your spouse may not be physically or emotionally up to the task of working out the details of nagging financial and legal issues.

That's why it's a good idea to name an alternate executor who can take over if your spouse is unable to serve. This alternate could be another family member, your accountant, or an attorney who's familiar with your circumstances and assets and knows where you keep important documents.

You may even want to select a second alternate, just to be safe. You might consider a major bank with an estate or trust department to serve as this alternate. You may be charged a fee for the privilege, but at least you could rest assured that your will would be administered in a professional manner.

Before you name anyone executor of your will, make sure the person knows exactly what will be expected of him or her and is comfortable with those expectations. You may even want to read through the list of responsibilities on page 191 very slowly and dramatically, while looking for telltale signs of brow sweat or nervous laughter from your potential candidate.

Once you've selected an executor, it's a good idea to stay in touch with that person (especially if it's your spouse) and periodically make sure that he or she is still willing and able to do the job.

5. Make it legal.
After you've talked with your family, identified your assets, and chosen an executor, it's time to finish the job and put your will in writing. A simple call to your attorney to schedule an appointment is all it takes to get the ball rolling. Your attorney will tell you what documents you need to bring to your appointment. At the meeting, he or she will guide you through your part of the drafting process.

You may be tempted to put off the initial call to your attorney for one reason or another. It's important that you resist that temptation. We're not going to resort to scare tactics or sadly ironic stories of people who died the day before they completed their will. We will remind you, however, that no one knows what the future holds. When your family's future is at stake, today is much more preferable than tomorrow for completing your will.

6. Find a safe place to store your will.
Before a court will probate a will, it must have the *original* document in its possession. To make that possible, you will need to find a secure place to store

your will in the meantime—a place where it will be safe from fire, flood, theft, and disgruntled potential heirs.

Many people prefer to keep the original copy of their will in their lawyer's office, along with their other important documents. Other people choose to keep their original will in a safe-deposit box.

If you opt for the latter option, you should investigate your state's laws regarding safe-deposit boxes. Some states allow bank officers to open the safe-deposit boxes of the recently deceased to search for wills. Other states require you to authorize another person to open your safe-deposit box after your. . . dying breath has been exhaled.

If you fail to authorize someone to open your safe-deposit box, say hello to government involvement again. A court order may be needed to open the box, resulting in unnecessary delays in the probate process. (You've probably noticed that the will-drafting process is full of little details like this. Unfortunately, if you don't take care of these details, you may be putting your will in jeopardy.)

Wherever you choose to store your will, make sure that your loved ones, your executor, and your lawyer know how to locate it. Leave a note in your home files that explains where the original copy is stored. You also should keep a copy of the will for yourself for future reference.

7. Keep your will updated.

Change is inevitable. A year from now, you will not be the same person you are at this moment. Your financial situation will be different—perhaps significantly different—than it is right now. Even your family may be different. Depending on your age and circumstances, you may have a new spouse, child, or grandchild within the next twelve months. Your will should reflect these changes.

That's why it's a good idea to review your will on a regular basis—perhaps even once a year—to make sure that it continues to reflect your preferences and your circumstances. You'll also need to ask your attorney to keep you updated on any new federal or state laws that might affect your will.

The good news is that even if it becomes necessary to change parts of your will, you don't have to rewrite the entire thing. Instead, you can make the changes through a *codicil*, which is just legal jargon for an addition or supplement to your will. All codicils must pass the same rigorous legal tests that wills do, so it's best to treat them as mini-wills. For example, only an original codicil is valid in court, so make sure that you attach the original version to your will.

Deep in the Heart of Taxes

Your will is finished and your family's future has been provided for. Now all you have to worry about is the government stepping in and walking away with a significant part of the assets you worked your entire life to accumulate.

Huh?

It doesn't seem possible, but it's true. Under certain circumstances, the government can take more of your estate's value in taxes than your family receives in inheritance! For many families, the loss of a loved one and the resulting loss of the majority of the estate is a one-two punch that they never recover from.

Of course, being hit with a 55 percent tax rate is only one scenario. There's also the possibility that your estate won't be taxed at all.

Say what?

Welcome to the wacky world of estate taxes, where your friendly federal government can take as much as 55 percent of your assets in taxes or as little as, well, nothing.

Originally this paragraph was going to contain an in-depth examination of estate taxes in 21st-century America, focusing specifically on their political, economic, and social ramifications. Serious terms like *unified credit exemption equivalent* and *illiquid assets* were going to be sprinkled throughout the text. It was going to be one of the most complex and impressive paragraphs in the entire book. But writing it got really, really boring.

You see, the finer points of the tax code could be debated until the accountants come home, but the only question that really matters right now is this: *What can you do to make sure that your beneficiaries pay as little as the law will allow in estate and inheritance taxes?*

A simple question deserves a simple answer. The most effective thing you can do to protect your loved ones from extreme taxation is to leave your entire estate to your spouse. Doing so qualifies you for something called the *unlimited marital deduction*, which means your spouse won't owe a penny of estate tax after you... climb that final hill.

CRUNCHING NUMBERS

Estate taxes can run as high as 55 percent of the value of your assets.

If you aren't married (or if your spouse isn't alive), currently you're allowed to pass up to $600,000 to your beneficiaries without federal estate taxes. That sounds like a lot of money, and it is; but when you're talking about an estate—the grand result of a lifetime of saving, investing, and acquiring—you'll find that that $600,000 limit affects more than just "rich" people.

The solution is so obvious that many people fail to recognize it. Instead of waiting until you're... six feet under to give money to your loved ones, do it while you're still alive, so that you can enjoy the gift-giving process as well. The tax law includes something called an *annual gift tax exclusion*, which currently allows you to give up to $10,000 annually to each of your beneficiaries, tax-free.

The more you give away before your... passing, the less you'll have to worry about that $600,000 limit later.

CRUNCHING NUMBERS

The maximum amount that may be passed to a beneficiary without federal estate taxes being deducted is currently $600,000.

CRUNCHING NUMBERS

The annual gift tax exclusion allows a person to give up to $10,000 annually to each of his or her beneficiaries, tax-free.

A Matter of Trust

Many people assume that a *trust* is just another name for a will. That's understandable. Trusts are often established as part of a will, so the two terms are frequently used together. But they are not the same thing.

A trust is a vehicle for owning and managing assets. Got that?

For those of you who don't speak Accountant-ese, here's another way to look at it. If you tossed a will, a checking account, and an allowance into a blender, the result would look something like a trust.

Like a will, a trust involves a person transferring assets to beneficiaries. Like a checking account, a trust involves deposits and withdrawals. Like an allowance, a trust involves distributing funds at regular intervals.

For our purposes, let's say that a trust is a financial arrangement that allows you to provide for your beneficiaries in very specific ways but helps you to avoid major taxes on your assets.

Here's how the process works. You set up a trust (preferably with the help of an attorney), transfer assets into it, and choose a *trustee* to manage the assets and distribute them to your beneficiaries.

Okay, it's a little more complicated than that. You see, there are many different types of trusts to choose from. (Get your pencil and notepad ready. I'm going to throw out a few technical-sounding words that you can use later to impress your friends and family.) A *living trust* is one that is set up and put into action while the *trustor* (the person giving away his or her assets) is still alive. A *testamentary trust* is one that is set up to begin after the trustor's... departure from planet Earth.

A *revocable trust* is one that the trustor can change or even cancel after it's been established. Assets can be added or subtracted from the trust for as long as the trustor is alive. An *irrevocable trust* is one that cannot be changed after it's established. That means once an asset has been placed in the trust, it stays there.

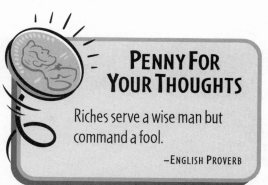

PENNY FOR YOUR THOUGHTS

Riches serve a wise man but command a fool.

—ENGLISH PROVERB

Go ahead, ask the obvious question: If it's a choice between being able to change your trust and not being able to, who would ever choose to set up an irrevocable trust? Answer: Someone who prefers not to have his or her trust funds taxed.

The assets in a revocable trust are counted as part of the trustor's estate at death. That means they could be taxed if they push the total value of the estate over that $600,000 mark we mentioned earlier. The assets in an irrevocable trust, on the other hand, are not counted as part of an estate. Can you say "tax-free"?

Here's a practical example of how an irrevocable trust could be used. Remember that $10,000 annual gift tax exclusion we mentioned a few pages back? Let's say you have three kids, and you want to set aside $10,000 a year, tax-free, for each of them. If you set up a trust and put that money in it each year, not only would those funds be tax-free, but so would the earnings that come from investing those trust funds over the years. So even if the trust doubled or tripled in value, none of it would be counted in the estate tax.

Even after you've decided between a living or testamentary trust and between a revocable or irrevocable one, you're left with a variety of trust options. Call it the Baskin-Robbins approach to estate planning—a flavor for everyone.

Regardless of your purpose for starting a trust, you'll probably find a specific type to meet your needs. For example, if you want to set aside money for your child's college education, you'll probably be interested in the 2503(c) trust, which allows you to make periodic tax-free gifts to the trust. Then when your child reaches college age, the trustee disburses the money to cover the cost of his or her education.

Or let's say you want to take care of your spouse with a trust, but aren't crazy

about your distant kin getting the money after your spouse dies. All you have to do is reach for a QTIP (no, it isn't in the medicine cabinet—that's a *qualified terminable interest property trust*). According to the stipulations of the trust, your spouse would be taken care of until his or her death. After that, the money would go to a designated beneficiary, including your favorite charity.

Or let's say you want to give most of your assets to your favorite charity but still want to collect income for yourself from the funds you set aside. A *charitable remainder trust* will allow you to do just that.

So the question isn't, "What can a trust do for you?" The question is, "What *can't* a trust do for you?"

The Trusty Trustee

Compared to a trustee, the executor of a will has a cushy job. For the most part, an executor's responsibilities are over as soon as the person's estate has been distributed to his or her beneficiaries. A trustee's responsibilities, however, may continue indefinitely.

Most trusts are intended to handle and distribute assets for a long period of time. Throughout that time, there is occasional accounting to be done and tax reports to be prepared. Your trustee should be skilled in both of those areas.

Additionally, as manager of the trust fund, the trustee may be given the power to buy and sell trust assets or make any number of other business transactions in the name of the trust. The duties of the trustee should be spelled out clearly in the trust document.

Obviously, reliability is an important characteristic to look for in a potential trustee—not only a personal reliability, but a professional one too. You want someone you can trust to carry out your instructions when you're gone, but you also want someone who's not going to ruin the trust through careless decision making and unwise investing.

If you have a financial counselor, get his or her advice on choosing a trustee. If not, talk to your lawyer or a representative from your bank to see what services they offer and what rates they charge.

A Few Words of Advice

It's one thing to know the basics about wills and trusts; it's quite another thing to put that knowledge to work in your financial life. Here are a few final tips to get you started.

Anticrastinate.

Don't bother checking the dictionary for that subhead. The word was created to suggest the opposite of procrastinate. If this were a TV commercial, this is where you would hear the pitch, "Call now! Operators are standing by."

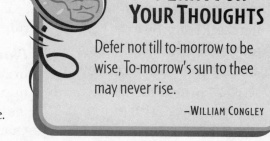

PENNY FOR YOUR THOUGHTS

Defer not till to-morrow to be wise, To-morrow's sun to thee may never rise.

—WILLIAM CONGLEY

Don't put off your estate planning to wait for a more convenient time. That time will never come. The quicker you get it done, the sooner you'll be able to take comfort in the fact that your family's financial future is secure.

Scare tactics are acceptable if they will spur you into action. If you die without a will, your family will be put through a very difficult process. They may even be forced to hire lawyers to protect what's rightfully theirs. All because you waited too long to do what you knew needed to be done. That's not the kind of legacy you want to leave.

Don't split heirs.

The news that you are making a will may stir up some anxieties and unpleasant thoughts of mortality that a lot of people would rather not deal with. Avoiding the issue may be a natural reaction. But if your beneficiaries, particularly your children, are old enough to understand the concept of a will, they should have at least a small role in the will-making process.

It was mentioned earlier that you should give your loved ones a chance to lay claim to possessions that were especially precious to them. If, however, some of your loved ones start jockeying for big-ticket items, or if there's any dispute about your possessions, you will need to be prepared to make the final decision as to who receives what and why.

GLAD YOU ASKED

My daughter can't seem to control her spending. I'm afraid that if I leave her money in my will, it will be gone before the ink on the check is dry. How can I provide for her future without actually giving her the money? Set up a trust to regulate her inheritance. Appoint a trustee to control the fund and then place some limits on how the money can be spent. That way, your daughter can still receive your money, but there will be a measure of accountability attached to it.

So, as you write your will, keep your family informed of the decisions you're making and your reasons for them. In cases where you can't accommodate a loved one's request, explain why and try to help him or her understand.

If you talk about these things with your family and friends before your... expiration date, you might spare them some conflict, jealousy, and other nasty surprises when the time comes to read your will.

Plan ahead.

In addition to making a will and perhaps setting up a trust, there are a lot of little things you can do to ease the burden on your loved ones when you're gone. One of the most helpful things you can do is to make a list of all your important papers and files and where they can be found. The more specific you can be in your directions, the better. Don't assume that your spouse or loved ones will know where your insurance files are located or what your will looks like.

The next thing to consider is a list of instructions and things to do in the event of your... unfortunate passing. Obviously, what you include on your list will depend on your family's circumstances. The purpose of the list is to assist your spouse or executor in settling your estate as quickly and painlessly as possible.

Here are some common responsibilities that your spouse or executor should be aware of.

➤ Get certified copies of the death certificate to use in filing life insurance claims, applying for Social Security, settling banking and legal matters, and transferring the name on property titles.

➤ Locate all life insurance policies, including health insurance policies that offer life benefits. Write each company and ask for a claims form and a summary of the information you need to have your claim processed.

➤ Contact the Social Security office. Ask what benefits you can expect to receive and what you need to do to file a claim.

➤ Contact the Veteran's Administration and ask for information on the benefits that are due you.

➤ Convert property titles to your own name.

➤ Organize your bills according to their due dates so that you don't fall behind on payments.

➤ Locate important documents, such as insurance policies, business contracts, bank books, loan agreements, securities, deeds, tax records, automobile titles, and birth and marriage certificates.

Any phone numbers you can provide for the companies and agencies on your to-do list would be welcome additions.

One more time: *sooner is better than later when it comes to making your will. Your family's financial future is at stake.*

The Buck Stops Here

Think you're an expert on estate planning? Here's a quiz to see how much you know.

1. What is the main purpose of a will?
   a. To give probate court workers something to do
   b. To see how far your loved ones are willing to go to get their hands on your money
   c. To make sure your assets go where you want them to go after you die
   d. To make your heirs realize that you weren't as bad as they thought you were

2. Which of the following is not a responsibility of an executor?
   a. Studying your will carefully
   b. Contacting the witnesses to your signing of the will
   c. Filing your income tax returns
   d. Counseling death row inmates

3. What's your best protection against estate taxes?
   a. A menacing appearance
   b. Your spouse
   c. A false identity
   d. Luck

4. Which of the following is true of a trust?
   a. You need to appoint a trustee to run it.
   b. Your options are extremely limited.
   c. There's no guarantee that the money you set aside will ever reach your beneficiaries.
   d. Most people find it insulting to be named a beneficiary.

5. If you're thinking about establishing a will, what should you keep in mind?
   a. Most beneficiaries prefer to compete in outrageous contests to earn their inheritance.
   b. If detective shows have taught us anything, it's that people with wills are always in danger of being knocked off by greedy relatives.
   c. The best way to avoid taxes is to spend everything you have before you die.
   d. The sooner you make your will, the better.

Answers: (1) c, (2) d, (3) b, (4) a, (5) d

Family Issues

For Richer or Poorer

SNAPSHOT

"**S**teve, do you promise to love, honor, and cherish Sue for as long as you both shall live?"

Steve beamed with pride as he stared at his bride. "I do," he answered in a firm, confident voice.

"And do you promise to include Sue in your financial decision making?" the minister continued.

Steve paused for a moment. *Financial decision making?* he asked himself. *I don't remember that part from the rehearsal yesterday.* Then it occurred to him that Sue must have rewritten the vows at the last minute.

"I do," he said.

"And do you promise to scale back your monthly entertainment expenses when you get married?"

Steve gave the minister a questioning look, but the minister just smiled back at him as though he had

SNEAK PREVIEW

1. Preparation for marriage must include many intensive discussions of each person's financial history, tendency, and philosophy.
2. Maintaining successful marital finances requires mutual sacrifice and commitment.
3. The benefits of maintaining a two-career family must be carefully weighed against the drawbacks.

recited the same vows hundreds of times before. Steve glanced around the church to see if anyone else seemed to notice anything unusual. No one did. Finally he looked at Sue, who was smiling expectantly at him from beneath her veil.

"Uh, I do," he said after a moment or two.

"And do you promise to start a college fund for your future kids with your next paycheck?"

"What?" Steve asked. "Start a college fund? What kind of vows are these?"

"Do you promise to. . . " the minister repeated.

"Yes!" Steve said. "Yes, I promise!"

"Do you promise to open a Roth IRA with your next bonus check?" the minister read.

"Oh, come on!" Steve shouted as the church began to spin around him. "I didn't expect this kind of stuff!"

Steve sat up in bed, his heart tap dancing in his chest. He grabbed the phone next to him and frantically punched in the numbers.

"Hello?" a groggy voice answered.

"Sue, do you want me to start a college fund for our kids?" Steve asked.

"Steve?" Sue asked, her voice still thick with sleep. "What are you talking about? A college fund? We don't even know if we'll have kids."

Steve smiled and breathed a sigh of relief. "You're right," he said. "I just had a bad dream. I'm sorry for waking you. Go back to sleep. I'll see you at the church tomorrow."

"Steve, wait," Sue said. "As long as we're on the subject of finances, maybe we can talk about some last-minute changes I made to our vows. . . . Steve? . . . Are you there? . . . Hello?"

* * * * * * * * * * * * * *

Don't let the chapter title fool you. You're not going to find anything in here about the ups and downs of romance, the secrets of keeping the flame burning through good times and bad, or any other topic suitable for a Hallmark card.

The focus of this chapter is money—cash, currency, greenbacks—stuff that seems relatively unimportant to most starry-eyed couples until, oh, about the first day of their honeymoon.

Specifically, let's think about how a married (or nearly married) couple can work together as a team, complement each other's strengths and weaknesses, become wise stewards of their finances, and have some fun along the way.

Uh Oh, It's That C-Word Again

Communication is the key to successful marital finances. But you knew that already, didn't you? If you've ever sat through a premarital counseling session, read any books on relationships, or watched even five minutes of *Oprah*, you know that communication is the key to *everything*.

➤ Trying to improve your relationship with your parents? Communication will do the trick.

➤ Feel a midlife crisis coming on? Communication is what you really need.

➤ Changing the fan belt on a '93 Honda Civic? Communication is the key.

Okay, maybe that last one didn't come from Oprah, but you get the idea.

In light of the endless parade of relationship experts yammering on and on about *communication*, you can be forgiven for occasionally rolling your eyes when you see or hear the word.

Just make sure you remember this one thing: Communication really is the key to successful marital finances.

Let's take a look at why that's so.

CRUNCHING NUMBERS

Ten percent of all couples who undergo rigorous premarital counseling decide to postpone or cancel their wedding.

Yours, Mine, and Ours

When you get married, the term *my money* should cease to have any relevance to you. In fact, the quicker you phase out words like *mine* and *yours* (in relation to your spouse) from your vocabulary, the easier it will be for you to apply the principles of healthy finances.

In practical terms, what this means is that you can't buy things like the newest video game or a set of Calphalon cookware on a whim anymore. Remember, it's not *your* money to spend; it's money that belongs to you and your spouse (or spouse to be). Every purchase and every financial decision affects both of you. It only makes sense, then, that both of you should have a say in where your money goes.

And if you don't think that talking to your spouse (to be) about every significant purchase will start to seem restrictive after a while, think again.

This is especially true if you've lived on your own for a while and are used to answering to no one but yourself about what you do with your money. Suddenly having to run your financial decisions past another person may trigger some intense flashbacks of your teenage years. You may start to view your spouse less as a partner for life and more as a killjoy who reminds you more and more of your parents every day.

This Could Happen to You

Now is the time when the more chivalrous and optimistic among you start rushing to the defense of your spouse (to be), saying, "No way that would never happen with my Snuggle Bunny. We agree on everything."

Uh huh.

What most couples find is that things change—sometimes dramatically—after marriage. The qualities you once admired (or at least put up with) in your loved one start to become irksome.

For example, your loved one's impulsiveness and spontaneity, which made life so exciting when you first began dating, may start to seem like flakiness and instability as you get older. Or your sweetheart's careful, calculated approach to life, which seemed kind of quirky and endearing at first, may start to feel like a straitjacket after a few years (months) of marriage.

Don't misunderstand. No one's asking you and your spouse (to be) to iron out your personality quirks or to become the same person. The fact is, couples with opposite personalities and tendencies can live together in harmony and even complement each other, if given the chance.

The secret is communi. . .

Oh, you know what the secret is. (If you don't, ask Oprah.)

No Time Like the Present

The earlier you start communicating with your spouse (to be) about money matters, the less likely you are to experience severe conflict over them later. If you don't learn to mesh your financial approach with your spouse's before you get married, you're in for a bumpy ride down Matrimony Highway.

> **GLAD YOU ASKED**
>
> **When is the best time to start talking about finances with a person you're dating?**
> Giving someone a financial compatibility test on your first date may be rushing things a bit. But when you start thinking the person you're with could be the one you'll be with forever (and when you start to sense similar feelings from him or her), it's probably time to start talking about money—in general terms at first and later in more detail.

After you get married, there are a lot of things you have to learn—things that unmarried couples tend to take for granted.

Among other things, you have to learn to. . .

> ➤ adjust to each other's schedules. This can be a problem if you and your spouse work two different shifts or if one of you is a night owl and the other is an early riser.

> ➤ cook and eat meals together. This can be a challenge if one of you is used to chicken cordon bleu and the other is used to microwave burritos or if one

of you prefers candlelight and fine china and the other likes standing in front of the TV with a paper plate.

➤ share the same space together. This can be a challenge if one or both of you are used to living alone, because having someone else around day and night, even if you're married to that person, can take some getting used to.

The point is, with so many other pressures to deal with, you may not have time to hash out your differences over finances. And the longer you let the discussion go, the more of a problem your finances will likely become.

CRUNCHING NUMBERS

Couples who marry for the first time face a 50 percent chance of divorce. Couples with children who marry a second time face a 65 percent divorce rate.

Full Disclosure

I don't mean to make these financial discussions with your spouse seem more formal than they need to be. There's no reason to reserve a conference room at your local Hyatt Regency to talk about money matters with your spouse (to be).

In fact, just by listening between the lines during unrelated conversations with your spouse (to be), you may be able to pick up some clues as to his or her thoughts and feelings about financial matters.

You may even be able to determine—with a fair amount of accuracy—where on the spectrum he or she stands on such core values as...

➤ selfishness versus cooperation

➤ pride versus humility

➤ self-control versus impulsiveness

➤ greed versus generosity

➤ sacrifice versus immediate gratification

➤ planning versus spontaneity.

The Heart of the Matter

But regardless of how adept you are at picking up verbal clues from your spouse (to be), there is no substitute for direct, purposeful conversations about financial issues. That's where you'll find out what's in each other's hearts.

In these conversations, your best bet is to take a warts-and-all approach. Don't try to sugarcoat your attitude about finances. Don't try to anticipate what your spouse (to be) wants to hear and say that. Be honest, even if the truth reflects badly on you or goes against everything your spouse (to be) stands for. In time, you'll both be glad you did.

Knowing exactly what the other person is bringing to the table, financially speaking, will help you and your spouse (to be) create a spirit of teamwork in your relationship. By examining your financial strengths, weaknesses, tendencies, and characteristics, you'll be able to determine in which areas you and your spouse (to be) complement each other and in which areas you can expect, well, more discussion.

Your talks should include not only your financial attitudes but your financial history as well. Nobody wants to find out a week into a marriage that his or her spouse is carrying a debt the size of Nebraska. Ditto for a bad credit rating, child support payments, or any other financial surprises.

Two Extremes

What you'll soon find in your discussions is that you and your spouse (to be) have obvious leanings or tendencies toward one of two financial extremes: hoarding or overspending. But don't let that bother you. Most people tend to lean toward one direction or the other.

Let's take a look at these two extremes to see how they might affect your marital financial picture.

Hoarding is the extreme form of saving. People

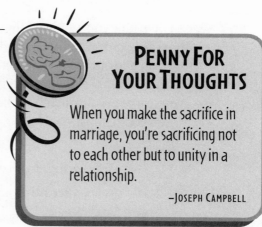

PENNY FOR YOUR THOUGHTS

When you make the sacrifice in marriage, you're sacrificing not to each other but to unity in a relationship.

—JOSEPH CAMPBELL

PENNY FOR YOUR THOUGHTS

The sum which two married people owe to one another defies calculation. It is an infinite debt, which can only be discharged through all eternity.

–Johann Goethe

who are prone to hoard devote themselves to accumulating as much as they possibly can—and way more than they ever will need.

On the surface, that may not seem like an unhealthy devotion. After all, what's wrong with having a bit of money tucked away? Unfortunately, though, the compulsion to save often causes hoarders to overlook or neglect their family's legitimate needs.

Overspending lies at the opposite end of the financial spectrum. People who are prone to overspend regularly run up bills that their budget and income can't afford.

Most overspenders suffer from "I gotta have it." That is, when they see the latest computer gadget, fashion trend, or status symbol, they feel compelled to buy it right away. That eagerness makes them vulnerable to all kinds of advertising and marketing strategies.

What About You?

You probably already know whether you lean more toward being a hoarder or an overspender. What you may not know is how extreme your mindset is in that direction.

To help give you an idea, following is a compiled list of 50 statements—25 for hoarders and 25 for overspenders. Read through the list in the category that best fits you and circle the statements that apply to you. The more statements you circle, the more extreme your position is. (If you want to make sure which way you lean, read through both lists and see which one has more circled statements when you're finished.)

Hoarding

1. I set aside savings from each paycheck.

2. If I use a credit card, I pay the full balance each month.

3. I know exactly how my money is spent.

4. I pay all my bills on time.

5. I usually put off buying something and think about it for a while.

6. I have money set aside for future expenses, such as taxes or car repairs.

7. I never borrow money except to buy a house or a car.

8. I follow an established plan for saving money.

9. I balance my checkbook with my monthly bank statement without any major problems.

10. I am very careful to control my spending.

11. I live on a budget.

12. I try not to buy unnecessary items if I can help it.

13. My family and friends would say that I am a saver.

14. I believe most people could get by if they would learn to live on what they make.

15. It makes me feel good to save money.

16. I save before I spend.

17. I save because money provides security.

18. It's very important for me to have money.

19. Saving money is more important than living comfortably.

20. I never write checks unless I have sufficient funds in my account.

21. Staying out of debt is more important than having a new car, a lot of clothes, and a nice house.

22. I tend to lean more toward being stingy with my money than being generous with it.

23. I have a strong desire to be wealthy.

24. As a young person I had my own savings account and regularly put aside money from my own earnings.

25. When I graduated from high school and started college, I had some of my own money set aside for my education.

Overspending

1. I rarely set aside money from my paycheck for savings.
2. I usually carry a balance on my credit card bills each month.
3. I have a hard time figuring out where all my money goes.
4. I am sometimes late in paying my bills.
5. When I see something I really want, I usually just reach for my credit card and buy it.
6. I usually have to cover unexpected expenses with my credit cards and then make payments to get rid of the debt.
7. I sometimes borrow money from friends and relatives to get by.
8. It takes everything I earn to maintain my current standard of living.
9. I often have a hard time balancing my checkbook with my monthly bank statements.
10. If I have money available, I usually have something already selected to spend it on.
11. I don't make enough money—or I make too much money—to worry about budgeting.
12. I tend to buy things because they are on sale, even though I don't really need them.
13. My family and friends would say that I am a spender.
14. I believe that if I just made more money, I could get by.
15. It makes me feel good to buy something new.
16. I save only what I have left over after I spend.
17. I plan to start a savings program in the future, when my financial situation improves.
18. I don't care about having a lot of money.
19. Living comfortably is more important than saving money.
20. I sometimes pay a charge for being overdrawn in my checking account.

21. Having a new car, a lot of clothes, and a nice house is more important than staying out of debt.

22. I tend to lean more toward being generous with my money than being stingy with it.

23. I don't worry about how much money I have.

24. As a young person I usually spent what I earned and did not save much of my income at all.

25. When I graduated from high school and started college, I had no money for education set aside from my personal earnings.

The purpose of this exercise is not to show you what a financial freak you are. Remember, most people have a clear tendency toward one extreme or the other— so that puts you in the majority.

The purpose of this exercise is to help you understand the underlying values you and your spouse (to be) bring to money management. Once you understand those values, you can begin to see the unique perspective and contributions you can bring to your marital financial lifestyle.

Let's take a closer look at the attitudes and perspectives of hoarders and overspenders.

That's a Hoarder

Hoarders (also known as tightwads, misers, cheapskates, and other less polite names) are as compulsive about saving as overspenders are about spending. Hoarders are often driven by the fear of not having enough money. As a result, they try to hang on to every cent they earn.

Most hoarders follow unrealistic financial plans of setting aside as much money as possible for savings,

GLAD YOU ASKED

Are prenuptial agreements a good idea or not?
Though many financial experts will tell you that asset protection is always a good idea, there's no getting around the fact that bringing a prenuptial agreement into your relationship is like planning to fail. Your marriage must be built on trust. If you can't trust your partner before marriage, how can you trust him or her afterward?

even to the point of neglecting other basic budget areas, such as groceries and entertainment. It's not unusual for hoarders to become obsessed with finding the absolute best bargain for an item before they purchase it, even if it means comparing prices from a half-dozen (or more) stores.

If you're trying to come to grips with life with a hoarder, here's the most important thing you need to know: Most hoarders have a difficult time relaxing their rigid saving and investing standards.

Understanding Overspending

Overspenders, on the other hand, generally don't put a lot of thought into their financial standards or goals. As a result, they rarely have a clear plan of action when it comes to their finances. Instead, they prefer to be spontaneous and impulsive.

What often happens is that overspenders get caught up in a purchase/worry cycle. The "high" they experience when they buy something is quickly replaced by the "low" of figuring out a way to pay for the purchase. The low usually lasts until the next purchase is made. Thus, the cycle is continued.

Overspenders also tend to overestimate how far their money will go. They often think in terms of immediate payment (such as an installment plan) and fail to consider the long-term cost of their purchases.

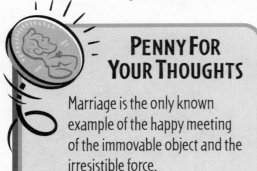

PENNY FOR YOUR THOUGHTS

Marriage is the only known example of the happy meeting of the immovable object and the irresistible force.

—OGDEN NASH

If you're trying to come to grips with life with an overspender, here's the most important thing you need to know: Most overspenders have a hard time structuring their finances and living with restrictions on their buying habits.

What Does It All Mean?

You might think that a marriage between a hoarder and an overspender would have to be sanctioned by the WWF, but that's not necessarily the case. Many couples with opposing financial philosophies and tendencies have learned how to resolve their differences and become a team, without letting their disagreements drive a wedge between them.

You too can learn how to mesh your attitudes and tendencies with those of your spouse (to be) and function as a financial team.

Introducing...the Budget

Believe it or not, the best strategy for developing a financial partnership with your spouse (to be) is to work on a budget together. Creating a guideline for your monthly expenditures can go a long way toward bringing balance and compromise to your family finances.

For better or worse, a budget is an equal opportunity "restrictor." For overspenders, a budget can help you control your urge to splurge and avoid the miseries of debt. If you commit to following a budget and base your financial decisions on it, you won't have the funds for impulse purchases.

For hoarders, a budget can breathe some flexibility into your family's spending and generally make life more comfortable for everyone involved. If you commit to a budget and allow it to govern your financial decisions, you won't be able to overload your savings account at the expense of other budget categories.

Chapters 2 and 3 cover the topic of budgeting in detail, so there's no need for us to deal with specifics like budget categories and guideline percentages in this chapter.

What should be emphasized is the importance of working closely with your spouse (to be) not only to create a budget for your family, but to evaluate and discuss it on a regular basis.

Scheduled Time

The ideal would be to schedule a time at the end of each month for you and your spouse to review the month's finances. Together you can determine which categories came in under budget and which ones went over budget. You can prioritize your outstanding debts and bills. You can discuss your spending habits for the month and identify areas for improvement. You can talk about strategies for shaping your finances in the future.

In addition to giving you an excuse to spend some quality time together, meeting regularly to discuss your budget will help you gradually develop a shared financial vision. It also will help you ensure that your finances bind you together instead of driving you apart.

Just the One of You

Even though it will take both you and your spouse, working as a team, to develop a successful financial strategy for your family, it will take only one of you to do the dirty work of bill paying and record keeping.

It doesn't matter which one of you it is, as long as that person takes the responsibility seriously and can be counted on to stay on top of your family's financial situation.

The primary responsibilities include. . .

➤ writing checks for bills

➤ keeping track of the budget

➤ balancing the checkbook.

GLAD YOU ASKED

Is it okay for spouses to keep separate checking accounts?

It depends on motives, but usually having separate accounts is no more logical than living in separate houses. If you and your spouse (to be) are unwilling to join all of your assets and bank accounts after marriage, it's safe to say that you have some unresolved trust issues still lingering in your relationship. Those issues must be resolved before you can expect to achieve real intimacy.

What you probably will discover as you and your spouse (to be) learn more about each other is that one of you is more naturally equipped to handle the job than the other one is. The person who is more analytical or detail oriented is probably the better candidate.

If both you and your spouse have a burning desire to mail bills, work a calculator, or make little check marks in your account register, try rotating the responsibilities every six months or so. Just make sure that only one of you at a time is responsible for the job.

The Only Way to Live?

Beyond budgeting, you and your spouse (to be) have to make some basic choices about how you will live, financially speaking. You have three choices: living *within* your means, living *at* your means, and living *above* your means. Let's take a look at what each one might mean for you.

Living *within* your means requires you to spend less money than you make. If your monthly Net Spending Income (which is your take-home pay minus your tithe) is $2,000, your monthly expenditures must be $1,999.99 or less. (Of course, most people who choose this lifestyle prefer to have more than a penny left over at the end of the month.)

This lifestyle requires you and your spouse (to be) to have the self-discipline to control your spending and to keep your needs, wants, and desires in their proper relationship. It also means you can't rely on credit or borrowed money to take care of your normal living expenses.

Living *at* your means is a polite way of saying spending every dime you earn. On the surface, that may not seem like a bad lifestyle choice—especially if you're meeting your budget each month.

GLAD YOU ASKED

My spouse and I are planning to share all household responsibilities. Why shouldn't that include keeping our financial books?

To paraphrase a common saying, Too many bookkeepers spoil the budget. If more than one person is responsible for paying bills or minding the details of your budget, there is an increased risk of things falling between the cracks because each person assumed the other would take care of it. However, both of you must work on the budget together!

The downside of this choice, though, is that it doesn't account for emergencies. Car problems, an unplanned pregnancy, and unexpected medical bills are just three possible scenarios that can sabotage your strategy of simply making ends meet each month.

The Most Dangerous Lifestyle

Living *above* your means is the most common, the most tempting, and the most dangerous of the three lifestyle options. This is serious debt territory, since it involves habitually spending more than you earn.

This is a lifestyle fueled by credit and borrowing, and it's an exciting way to live. . . until the bills come due.

Unfortunately, everything that's borrowed must ultimately be repaid, and that's when the stress begins. If you can't pay what you owe, your only real option is debt, and that's when stress really kicks in.

The high life of buying what you want when you want it is replaced by a life of ducking creditors and figuring out how to make minimum monthly payments on your credit card bills. And with that life change comes a lot of bickering and blaming. The stress and damage that living above your means ultimately causes in a marriage can be intense—and sometimes permanent.

Of course, if all you had to do was *choose* a lifestyle, everyone would be living within their budgets. Once you choose a lifestyle option (and may I recommend living within your budget?), you must gear your spending habits and approach to finances to fit that lifestyle.

Two Incomes or One?

Before wrapping up this chapter, I need to address one more issue that affects most married couples— that is, whether both spouses should pursue careers (or jobs) outside the home, particularly after you have children.

GLAD YOU ASKED

Is divorce a legitimate option for couples who can't mesh their financial attitudes and tendencies?

No, it's not. The best thing a couple can do for their relationship is to throw the word divorce out of their vocabularies. In their wedding vows, couples pledge themselves to one another through all circumstances—better or worse, sickness or health, richer or poorer—until they are parted by death. If that's the case, divorce should not even be considered as an option.

If this book had been written several years ago, the subhead above probably would have read, "Women in the Workplace?" But in recent years, the phenomenon of the stay-at-home dad has changed the breadwinning landscape. Now the issue is not whether women should work outside the home but whether a family needs more than one paycheck (no matter which spouse earns it) to survive.

If you're looking for a firm yes or no answer regarding two-income families, you won't find it here. What you will find are four questions you and your spouse (to be) should consider carefully together as you evaluate your career decisions and your future.

The four questions are. . .

➤ What is your motivation for maintaining two careers?

➤ What are your priorities?

➤ How do the benefits of two careers measure against the drawbacks?

➤ What makes the best sense for your family?

What is your motivation for maintaining two careers?

The reasons most people give for pursuing a career outside the home can be boiled down to three: money, prestige, and fulfillment.

Money

Many two-career families will tell you that one income just isn't enough for them, that they wouldn't be able to survive without two sets of paychecks each month. And in some cases, that's true.

Often, though, the problem isn't a lack of money; it's an excessive lifestyle. If your family requires two sets of paychecks to pay all of your bills each month, it's possible that you're living above your means. Perhaps you bought too much house, or you bought a car that's more expensive than you can

PENNY FOR YOUR THOUGHTS

Marriage is the greatest adventure of all.

—McCall's

really afford. Whatever the problem is, an extra income may not be the best solution. Instead, downsizing and learning to live with less may be the answer.

Some couples view the two-career track as a temporary measure. One of the spouses may be working until a child is born or until the down payment for a home has been safely tucked away.

And although that strategy certainly makes sense, it's important to think it through completely. With a house, you want to make sure that once you have a down payment, you can afford to live in that house on one income later. Otherwise, you may find yourself stuck in a job for a lot longer than you'd expected just to afford the mortgage payments.

Prestige

Many people find identity in their careers. You may enjoy being recognized and even respected for what you do. You may like the perks, both financial and non-financial, that come with your job.

You may view being a stay-at-home mom or dad as a step down in the eyes of your peers. You may not want to give up the excitement, pressure, and rewards of the workplace. If you're a college graduate, you may even worry that you're wasting your education by staying at home with kids.

Keep in mind, though, that "the hand that rocks the cradle rules the world." And although world domination may not be on your agenda, the point is valid. No other job is as prestigious or will make more of a difference in the world than the parenting of children.

Fulfillment

Many people work because they truly enjoy it and find fulfillment in it. You may believe you were given specific gifts, talents, and abilities to use in the workplace. Furthermore, you may believe that giving up your career is akin to wasting those gifts.

But don't underestimate the fulfillment that comes from interacting with your children throughout the day, observing their physical and emotional growth, teaching them life skills, and guiding their development. Most stay-at-home parents will tell you that having a front row seat for their kids' daily lives is the greatest job perk of them all.

What are your priorities?

While you're listing your priorities, go ahead and put the top five or so in order, if you would. Then answer this question: Which is your higher priority—your children or your job?

And if you wouldn't mind answering one more question, try this one: Does your lifestyle reflect your priorities?

Many people will tell you that their families are a higher priority to them than their jobs, and they believe it. But the evidence may not support the statement. If you're spending most of your waking hours away from your children when it's really not necessary, it's tough to say that your children are more important to you than your job.

Of course, there's always the argument that you work to benefit your family, which means that you have your kids' best interests at heart. But if that's your position, you have to determine whether your children benefit more from the money you bring in or from the time you could be spending with them.

How do the benefits of two careers measure against the cost?

With the enormous cost of professional child care today, many two-career families find themselves in the odd position of having one spouse bring home just enough to pay for their kids to be taken care of during the day. Society tells us that this is true. Just look around at the results of parentless kids.

And unless there are other circumstances that factor into the decision, that lifestyle choice doesn't seem to make much sense. Why pay for someone else to watch your kids when you could do it yourself with very little change in your financial bottom line?

Even if you have relatives watching your kids for free, though, you need to weigh the pros and cons of maintaining a second career outside the home. To put it bluntly, what does it take to justify entrusting your kids to other people for most of the day and missing out on so much quality time with them?

I'm not necessarily packing your bags for a guilt trip here. Many two-career families have few other options available to them. However, you should consider the *entire* cost before you make your decision.

What makes the best sense for your family?

This is the question that no one can answer for you. Only you and your spouse (to be) know the specific effects that maintaining two careers will have on your family life. Only the two of you can determine whether the benefits of two incomes outweigh the costs of both of you being away from home all day.

I do suggest that you put a lot of thought into your answer. This isn't a choice to be taken lightly. No matter what you decide, it will have a tremendous effect on your family. If you give up one income, you will have to change your lifestyle. If you choose to work, you'll have to make the best possible arrangements for your children.

Choose wisely.

One More Thing

You and your spouse (to be) have had a lifetime to develop your financial habits and attitudes, so you can't expect to change them overnight. Learning to compromise and mesh your financial styles takes time and effort. It's a trial-and-error process, so you'll have to be prepared to learn from your mistakes.

The good news is that it is possible to become financial partners, no matter how different your financial styles are. As long as you remain committed to doing what's best for your family, you will succeed.

GLAD YOU ASKED

Should my spouse and I accept money from my family?
You betcha—if it's a wedding, birthday, or Christmas present. But if it's needed to "get on your feet" or to bail you out of a jam, your response should be, "Thanks, but no thanks." As a married couple, you need to cut the financial strings to your parents and learn to stand on your own. If you know Mumsie and Popsie will funnel cash your way anytime you need it, what incentive do you have to live within your means?

The Buck Stops Here

Think you're an expert on family finances? Here's a quiz to see how much you know.

1. What is the key to successful marital finances?
   a. Not talking about them with your spouse
   b. Good budgeting software
   c. Separate bank accounts for each spouse
   d. Communication

2. What is the best approach to discussing finances with your spouse (to be)?
   a. Changing the subject as often as possible
   b. Discussing only the positive aspects of your budget and keeping the negative stuff to yourself
   c. Being completely open and honest
   d. Being completely deceitful and misleading

3. Most people may be categorized as leaning toward one of what two financial extremes?
   a. Bulls and bears
   b. Hoarders and overspenders
   c. Odds and evens
   d. Rookies and veterans

4. Which of the following is true of a budget?
   a. It restricts both hoarders and overspenders.
   b. It's not necessarily important to follow, as long as you have one.
   c. It only works for rich people.
   d. It's wildly overrated as a financial help.

5. Which of the following is not one of the questions you and your spouse (to be) should consider when discussing whether or not you should both work outside the home?
   a. What does "casual Friday" attire really mean in your office?
   b. What are your priorities?
   c. What is your motivation?
   d. What makes the best sense for your family?

Answers: (1) d, (2) c, (3) b, (4) a, (5) a

Single Living
The Cost of a Solo Flight

SNAPSHOT

The Sorensen family was sitting quietly in the living room when Erik dropped the bomb.

"Mom, Dad, I've decided to move out," he announced.

Erik's mother let her magazine fall to her lap. "But you just graduated a couple months ago," she said. "Isn't this kind of sudden?"

"No," Erik said. "All of my friends from college already have their own apartments, and it's time I did too."

"But your father and I really don't mind if you stay longer," his mother coaxed. "Do we, Cliff?"

"Mmm hmmm," came the distracted reply from behind the newspaper. "Say, here's a one-bedroom in Park Forest for $525 a month."

"Cliff, what are you doing?" Erik's mother asked.

"I'm trying to tell Erik that as far as we're concerned,

> ### SNEAK PREVIEW
>
> 1. Living on your own may give you the personal freedom you're looking for, but it is likely it will restrict your financial freedom.
> 2. Taking on a roommate may solve the problem of paying your rent, but it also can create a whole new set of problems for you to deal with.
> 3. The fact that you are single and living alone gives you budgeting opportunities that other people cannot take advantage of.

he can stay here as long as he likes. Isn't that true?"

"Huh? Oh, yeah, you bet," his father replied without looking up from the paper. "Erik, you have our permission to stay here until—hey, a studio apartment in Rosemont for $475."

"Cliff!" Erik's mother exclaimed. "If you keep reading those ads, Erik is going to think we're anxious for him to move out."

"June, that's ridiculous," Cliff answered, still perusing the classifieds. "Erik knows how much we...wow, look at this: 'Roommate wanted to split $675 rent for two-bedroom condo in Arlington Heights.'"

"Cliff!" Erik's mother shrieked.

Erik smiled. "It's okay, Mom," he assured her. "I know I'm welcome to stay here with you guys. But I also know it's time for me to go."

"Well, it's your decision, Son," Erik's father acknowledged, his face still shielded by the paper, "as long as you know you're welcome. . .hey, a townhouse in Bensenville for $650!"

* * * * * * * * * * * * * * * *

A Less Than Ideal Situation

Do any of the following scenarios sound familiar?

➤ One of your college friends invites you over to check out his new apartment. As he's showing you his brand new oak bedroom set, it suddenly dawns on you that you've been sleeping on the same bed since you were in the eighth grade.

➤ When your mother asks you to take out the garbage before you leave for work, you roll your eyes and complain, just like you did in junior high.

➤ When people ask you where you live, you describe your home as "a bed-and-breakfast run by an older couple."

Living with your parents after college is a great way to save money. When you don't pay rent (at least, not the kind of rent that non-parental landlords charge), you're left with more funds for other areas of your budget.

But the arrangement is far from ideal. First, there's the issue of authority. If you and your parents are all adults, who's in charge? Second, there's the problem of embarrassment. Do you know any people your age who are proud of the fact that they still live with their parents? Third, there's the issue of development and growth. Sooner or later, you will need to be able to support and take care of yourself—and perhaps even a family. If you don't learn the skills you need now, when will you?

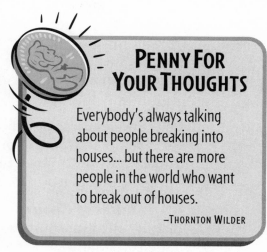

PENNY FOR YOUR THOUGHTS

Everybody's always talking about people breaking into houses... but there are more people in the world who want to break out of houses.

–THORNTON WILDER

Time for You to Fly?

You probably wouldn't be reading this chapter if you didn't already have the urge to bolt your family's home. But is now the right time for you to strike out on your own?

If you want your living alone experiment to last more than a month, you'll need to make some preparations before you move. If you're not equipped to handle life on your own, you may find that it won't take long before your checking account is as empty as your kitchen cabinets. Here are some steps you can take to keep that from happening.

Get a handle on your spending habits.
The more you spend on a place to live, the less you have to spend on yourself. The concept is so simple, many people don't think about it when they take their first steps toward independence.

On the average, how long would you say your paychecks last? A month? Two weeks? One week? The duration of the trip from the bank to the mall? The faster you typically burn through your paycheck, the more difficult life on your own will be—at least until you change your spending habits.

If you're used to buying what you want when you want it, then moving into your own place (and into a new set of expenses) is going to seem like anything but freedom. Instead of buying that great leather jacket you saw at Von Zaur, you'll be spending your hard-earned money on electricity. Rather than picking up that new outfit (and shoes to match), you'll be funneling your earnings straight to the gas company.

Don't underestimate the difficulty you're going to have accepting these realities. You're going to have to pay for things like water and cable that you've been getting free all these years. Accept it and deal with it, because the alternatives aren't pretty when you're on your own.

It's a Matter of Choice

Let's say you let your frustrations get the best of you and you buy the jacket instead of paying your electric bill. Even though it may seem like a harmless, one-time mistake, the consequences can be pretty far-reaching. The next month your electric bill will come again—only this time it will be for two months' worth of service, plus a penalty fee and a warning about your service being terminated if you don't pay. If your budget is already tight, an electric bill that is twice the normal amount could break it. That's usually where your credit card debt starts.

You don't want to wait until you've signed a lease to know whether you can handle such a severe spending cutback. If you're considering a move to a place of your own, stop your spending for at least two months first. This is not about cutting back; it's about stopping—cold turkey. No new speakers. No clothes. No compact discs. No movies.

This may seem like a radical suggestion, but actually it's not too far removed from the reality of life in a first apartment. If you are on a limited budget, and you want to live on your own, you will have to decide between buying the things you want or paying for the things you need.

The sooner you learn to make the tough decisions you have to make, the better chance you have of making it to the end of your lease without having to run back home for help from your parents.

Learn to budget.

You might want to grab a highlighter and mark the next sentence in this book; it's that important. *Before you leave home,* you must learn to live on what you will earn each month.

It's not enough to say, "I know how to budget my money." That's like saying, "I know how to drive" just before you start a cross-country road trip by yourself. You may genuinely believe you have the knowledge you need to complete the journey; but, if you've never actually been behind the wheel of a car, if you've never learned how to make the little corrections that prevent major crashes, there's a good chance your trip will end in disaster.

The same holds true for living on your own. Unless you have experience living on a budget, unless you've actually set aside portions of your money each month to cover rent, utilities, car payments, credit card bills, school loans, and entertainment expenses, there's a good chance your first solo adventure will end with a financial crash.

Talk to your friends who have apartments similar to what you're looking for. See if you can get a list of their average monthly expenses. The list should include the costs of rent, electricity, water, phone, cable, renter's insurance, and groceries. Add to that any other expenses you might have, such as car payments, auto insurance, school loans, and credit card payments. And don't forget to set aside money for entertainment, car maintenance, and savings. (For more information on what your budget should include, see chapters 2 and 3.)

Practice Saving

Once you have as complete a list as possible of expenses, practice setting aside that money each month while you're still living at home. Take the necessary amount from each paycheck, stick it in your savings account, and see what you have left.

Don't touch the money you set aside. Remember, if you were supporting yourself, it would be gone. If you can't live on what's left, you can't afford to live on your own. Your options, then, would be to continue living with your parents and saving money

CRUNCHING NUMBERS

Your monthly Housing expenses (rent, utility bills, insurance) should take up no more than 38 percent of your Net Spending Income—your take-home pay minus your Tithe.

until you can afford to move out or to find a roommate. (We'll talk more about this later in the chapter.)

If you can stay on budget for three months in a row, you just might be ready for the big leap into your own place.

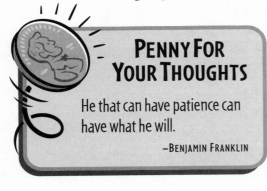

PENNY FOR YOUR THOUGHTS

He that can have patience can have what he will.

–BENJAMIN FRANKLIN

Talk to your parents.

Before you start chatting with landlords, let your parents know what you're considering and ask for their input. That doesn't necessarily mean you have to follow their advice to the letter (especially if your mom keeps calling you her little baby and tells you she never wants you to leave), but you should listen to what they have to say.

Who knows more about running a household than your parents? Who has more experience at paying bills, buying furniture, dealing with creditors, and finding bargains than your mom and dad?

If your parents are like most couples, they've tasted their share of financial struggles. As a result, they know the kinds of decisions that lead to trouble and the kind that lead to stability. They may be able to help you avoid some of the mistakes that tripped them up.

Most importantly, though, your parents can teach you the skills you need to live on your own. Remember, now you're the one who will be doing the cooking, cleaning, shopping, banking, (minor) repairing, and household managing.

Skills from Your Parents

Below you'll find a list of skills you'll need to develop before you leave home. You've probably mastered some, if not most, of them. Target the ones you're not familiar or comfortable with, and ask your parents for help in learning to do them.

➤ Living on a budget

➤ Saving money for future expenses

➤ Writing checks

➤ Balancing a checkbook

➤ Doing laundry without mixing colors and whites

➤ Cooking several different meals

➤ Paying bills promptly and in full

➤ Cleaning kitchen appliances and bathroom fixtures

➤ Cleaning sink drains

➤ Changing light bulbs

➤ Keeping your bedroom clean

➤ Shopping for groceries

➤ Recognizing and taking advantage of bargains

➤ Keeping track of household needs

➤ Scheduling doctor and dentist appointments

➤ Managing a schedule

Remember, practice makes perfect. Before you're forced to do these things for yourself, try them several times in the safety of your parents' home until you're comfortable with your ability to do them right.

A Place of Your Own

It's a go. You've checked your budget, weighed the pros and cons, learned the skills you need to know, and reached a decision you feel good about. It's time for you to become. . . Independent Single Person.

The first step in your transition is to find an independent place to live.

You know the kind of place we're talking about: an address in the center of the hippest, most bustling part of the city; a stately, well-kept building that shows its age only in a classic sense. An apartment unit the size of a small house with

PENNY FOR YOUR THOUGHTS

Home is the place where,
when you have to go there,
They have to take you in.

—Robert Frost

cathedral ceilings, impossibly spacious rooms, and enormous windows that offer a breathtaking view of the city's most notable features (perhaps a view of the lake). Rent that is affordable, even on a starting salary. Quirky neighbors across the hall who drop in unannounced and always seem to get you mixed up in some kind of wacky misadventure.

That's the kind of place for Independent Single Person to live. Right?

The good news is that apartments such as these are surprisingly easy to find. The bad news is that it costs $10 to even get a tour of them... because they're all located on Hollywood soundstages.

Waking Up to Reality

The kind of living spaces you see on the countless TV shows about the lives of young professionals are so far removed from reality that they should be considered special effects.

The truth is, few things in life can wipe a smile off your face faster than your first glimpse of an apartment you can afford. You won't know whether to laugh about the lime-green shag carpet in the hallway or cry about the lime-green mold on the bathroom fixtures.

Don't get me wrong. Not every apartment you can afford will be ugly or disgusting. No, some of them may be quite attractive, both inside and outside... though you probably won't be able to see much of the exterior through the smoke from the iron smelting plant next door. Others may be attractive *and* well situated ... and minuscule—the kind of places where you have to go outside to unfold a beach towel.

The point is, if you're serious about finding a place of your own, you might want to lower your expectations before you start your search. Accept the fact that you probably won't find the place of your dreams, and look for a place that meets your basic needs.

Of course, beggars can't be choosers, so we'll need to whittle down your list of basic needs to three: safety, proximity, and peace of mind.

Safety

You can find affordable housing, if price is your only concern. More than likely, though, you will find yourself in an undesirable neighborhood. If you're desperate or foolhardy enough, you might convince yourself that a risky location is a small price to pay for independence. Don't make that mistake.

You don't want to commit yourself to a 12-month lease and then find out two weeks later that you need body armor to walk to your mailbox. You don't want to have to wonder all day whether your TV, VCR, and stereo will still be there when you get home. You don't want to be in a place where the neighborhood welcoming committee flashes gang signs.

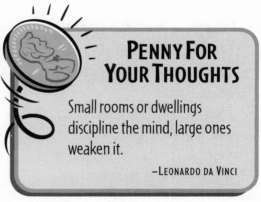

PENNY FOR YOUR THOUGHTS

Small rooms or dwellings discipline the mind, large ones weaken it.

—LEONARDO DA VINCI

If the only apartments you can afford to rent are in undesirable parts of town, save your money for a year or so, until you can find a safer place to live.

Proximity

Ideally your apartment should be centrally located among the places you spend the most time. The closer you are to work (or public transportation that gets you close to work), the less of a commute you will have and the more money you will save in gas and car maintenance. The closer you are to your family, the more free meals you can sponge off—er, share—with them. The closer you are to church, the easier it will be for you to participate in Bible studies or social gatherings. The closer you are to your friends, the more likely it is you'll spend time hanging out at each other's places—saving money on entertainment in the process.

Choosing an affordable apartment in an out-of-the-way location may end up costing you money in the long run, if you have to do a lot of driving back and forth. You'll need to take that into consideration before you make a final decision on where you're going to live.

Peace of mind

No, this isn't a rehash of the safety issue. We're talking about the peace of mind that comes from knowing your place isn't going to fall apart like something out of a Three Stooges routine the week after you sign your lease.

Sometimes all it takes is close observation to tell the condition of an apartment. Ask yourself the following questions.

➤ Do you see any stains on the walls or floor that might suggest the place is prone to flooding?

➤ Are there any funny smells coming from the carpet?

➤ Do the appliances appear to be well kept and in good working condition?

➤ Are there any holes in the walls or doors?

➤ In general, does the place—not just the apartment, but the entire complex—seem well cared for?

Some Practical Checkups

Don't be afraid to run a few tests as you look around. Crank up the oven to make sure that it works. Turn on the stove to make sure that all of the burners are okay. Run cold water, then hot water from every faucet in the place. Fire up the heating unit; then blast the air conditioning. Bring a night light with you to check the wall sockets in each room. Put on a white glove and run your finger across every surface in the place, checking for dust. (Okay, skip that last one.)

If something doesn't seem right, ask the landlord about it. The reaction you get may give you a clue as to whether the place falls into the "strong possibility" or the "don't bother" category. If the landlord seems hesitant to answer or is perturbed

GLAD YOU ASKED

Are classified ads the best place to find an apartment?

Probably not. Many landlords don't advertise in newspapers because they don't want to have to deal with hundreds of calls and inquiries. Instead, they prefer to find tenants through word of mouth or with a small "For Rent" sign in the window. If you have friends who live in an apartment complex or building that they think highly of, ask them to drop your name to the landlord so that when an apartment becomes vacant, you'll have a shot at it.

by your questions, he or she may be hiding something. If the landlord seems uninterested in your concerns, that's probably the reaction you'll get when something has gone wrong in the apartment and you need it fixed. Keep looking.

If you can't get a reading from the landlord, check with some of the other tenants. Find at least two people who are willing to talk to you. Explain that you're thinking of renting an apartment in the building and that you'd like to ask a few questions. If they agree to talk to you, choose three or four questions (per person) from the following list to ask. (Don't run through the entire list with each person you talk to. People will think you're a telemarketer and will try to discourage you from moving into their building.)

Questioning the Landlord

Choose from this list of questions.

> ➤ Does the landlord respond quickly when repair problems are reported?

> ➤ Has the landlord completed promised repairs for you or anyone else you know in the building?

> ➤ What happens if your rent check is late?

> ➤ Are common areas, such as sidewalks and laundry rooms, kept in good condition?

> ➤ Are there any major repair problems in the building, such as malfunctioning heating or air conditioning, faulty plumbing, leaky roofs, or overloaded electrical circuits?

> ➤ Are there any problems with cockroaches or mice?

> ➤ Are there any safety or noise problems in the area?

GLAD YOU ASKED

What is a security deposit?

It's money that you pay to your landlord before you move in to your apartment to guarantee that you won't trash the place like a rock star in a hotel room. Depending on the state you live in, the deposit can be as little as half your monthly rent or as much as two months' rent. When you move out, your landlord will inspect your apartment. If any damage is found, your landlord will keep some or all of your deposit to cover the cost of repairing it. The rest gets mailed back to you eventually.

The people you talk to probably will be glad to give you the real scoop on the condition of the apartment complex, especially if they've been burned by the landlord before. A 10-minute conversation with them could save you 12 months of misery in a lease you can't get out of.

Making a List and Checking It Twice

Rent and utilities aren't the only expenses you have to think about if you're seriously considering flying solo. Unless you move into a furnished apartment or swear off all earthly possessions, you'll also have to think about furniture. Worse yet, you'll have to buy it.

You may be able to move some things from your parents' house (while your father stands guard over the big screen TV to keep you from getting any ideas), but it probably won't be enough to furnish your place. So you'll have to buy the rest.

And you'll have to find a way to do it that won't vaporize your budget.

First things first: ease those credit cards back into their holsters. They'll only get you in trouble here. If you can't afford to pay for something with cash, wait until you can. If you have to delay your move a few more months while you save the money, so be it.

When you're ready to make some purchases, your best bet for getting the most for your money is to buy used. Come on, it's your first apartment. No one expects it to look like something out of *In Style* magazine. It's more important for you to get what you need than to please an interior designer.

Garage sales and thrift shops are the first places to look. Get up early on Saturday morning, with the rest of the bargain hunters, and check out all of the garage sales you can find. You'll find household items galore, many of them in decent condition with reasonable asking prices. If you can pick up a vacuum cleaner for, say, $10, you'll have more money to spend on other necessities.

For couches, tables and chairs, coffee tables, and dressers, head to your friendly neighborhood thrift shop. If you can't find what you're looking for there, try the free "buy and sell" periodicals you find in grocery stores or the classified ads of your local newspaper. Someone somewhere is selling what you're looking for. Keep searching long enough and you're bound to find it.

The one thing you shouldn't buy used, though, is a bed. In case you've just eaten, we won't go into a lot of disgusting details about why you shouldn't. Let's just say that old beds are often full of nasty little microscopic critters that do bad things to mattresses, pillows, and sheets. The situation is probably bad enough in the bed you've been sleeping in since you were a kid. You don't need a stranger's microorganisms giving you grief.

The same principle applies to couches too. It's okay to buy a used couch—as long as it's not a *used* used couch. Here's how to tell the difference between the two. If the first sound out of your mouth when you see the couch is "Ewww!" it's a used used couch. Don't buy it. Whatever the price, it's not worth it.

When you do find furniture you like, make sure you thoroughly clean and vacuum each piece before you bring it into the apartment. There's no sense in giving dirt a head start in your new place.

In addition to buying used, a good strategy for saving money on home furnishings is buying early. If your plan is to move out of your parents' house within the next six months, start stocking up on the things you're going to need by buying a little at a time, as your budget allows.

Necessary Furnishings

If you've never lived on your own before, the obvious question is, what do you need to buy?

The answer can be found in the following list of basic furniture items and furnishings.

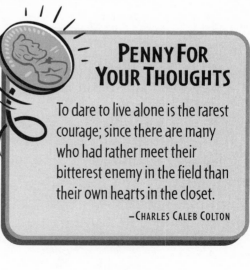

PENNY FOR YOUR THOUGHTS

To dare to live alone is the rarest courage; since there are many who had rather meet their bitterest enemy in the field than their own hearts in the closet.

–Charles Caleb Colton

Bedroom

- ☐ bed
- ☐ pillow
- ☐ pillowcases

- ☐ sheets
- ☐ blankets
- ☐ comforter

- ☐ mattress cover
- ☐ dresser
- ☐ bedside lamp

Bedroom (continued)

- ☐ mirror
- ☐ desk
- ☐ desk lamp
- ☐ computer
- ☐ alarm clock
- ☐ waste basket
- ☐ clothes hangers
- ☐ iron
- ☐ ironing board
- ☐ laundry hamper or basket
- ☐ suitcase

Kitchen

- ☐ plates
- ☐ bowls
- ☐ glasses
- ☐ cups
- ☐ mugs
- ☐ forks
- ☐ spoons
- ☐ knives
- ☐ cutting board
- ☐ kitchen knives
- ☐ serving spoons
- ☐ frying pan
- ☐ cooking pots
- ☐ mixing bowl
- ☐ measuring cups and spoons
- ☐ spatula (the pancake flipper)
- ☐ toaster
- ☐ microwave oven
- ☐ coffee maker (for your guests, if you don't drink coffee)
- ☐ can opener
- ☐ dishcloths
- ☐ dish towels
- ☐ dish rack (where you put dishes to dry after you wash and rinse them)
- ☐ oven mitt
- ☐ garbage can
- ☐ salt and pepper shakers
- ☐ rug
- ☐ popcorn maker (optional)
- ☐ cleaning products
- ☐ plastic bags

Dining area

- ☐ table
- ☐ chairs
- ☐ hot pads
- ☐ placemats or tablecloth

Supply closet

- [ ] broom
- [ ] dustpan
- [ ] mop
- [ ] vacuum cleaner
- [ ] paper towels
- [ ] light bulbs
- [ ] flashlight
- [ ] batteries
- [ ] candles
- [ ] matches
- [ ] pliers
- [ ] multihead screwdriver
- [ ] hammer, nails
- [ ] trash bags

Living room

- [ ] couch
- [ ] armchair
- [ ] curtains
- [ ] television
- [ ] VCR
- [ ] television stand
- [ ] bookshelf
- [ ] coffee table
- [ ] rug
- [ ] lamps
- [ ] stereo
- [ ] phone
- [ ] answering machine
- [ ] pictures (for walls)

Bathroom

- [ ] shower curtain
- [ ] bathtub mat
- [ ] bath towels
- [ ] hand towels
- [ ] washcloths
- [ ] laundry basket
- [ ] first-aid kit
- [ ] wastebasket
- [ ] plunger
- [ ] cleaning products

Don't let the size of this list discourage you. Many of the things on it aren't very expensive. Remind yourself that each item you check off your list brings you one step closer to independence. And remember that if you can't afford to pay cash, you probably can't afford it.

Roomies

All right, you seem like a nice person, so here's a little secret. All those expenses I've been telling you about? the ones that make it hard to live on your own? Did you know that you could cut them in *half*? What if, instead of saving for, say, a year to move out of your parents' house, you could do it in six months? Would you be interested?

What if it meant you had to share your place with someone else? Would you still be interested?

Imagine the possibilities. You and, say, your best friend split the cost of a really decent apartment (since there are two of you paying, you probably can afford a better place). Each of you pays for half of the security deposit, insurance, rent, utilities, and groceries. Both of you enjoy the freedom of living in your own apartment and host really cool parties for the rest of your friends, who wish they had a place like yours. Seems like a perfect solution, doesn't it?

Well, not quite.

Considering a Roommate

If you've ever lived in a college dorm, you know that getting paired with the wrong roommate can be a serious drag. It's not a pleasant feeling to dread going back to your own place because you can't stand the other person living there. You don't want that same dynamic spoiling life in your first apartment.

And, believe it or not, sharing a dwelling with someone you know—even your best friend—is no guarantee that it won't happen. You don't know what someone is really like until you live with that person.

There are a lot of "what ifs" to consider.

➤ What if your roommate isn't used to living on a budget and buys a new pair of skis instead of paying his or her half of the rent?

➤ What if your roommate constantly eats your food when you're gone but never chips in for groceries?

GLAD YOU ASKED

What are "move-in" costs and how much will they set me back?

Move-in costs are those nagging little expenses that usually go unaccounted for until it's time to pay them. If you're not careful, they can wreck your budget before you get your boxes unpacked. They include things like phone connection fees, cable connection fees, and moving costs (even it's just pizza and pop for your friends). Rates for these services vary greatly, but you could be looking at a couple hundred bucks—on top of your security deposit—for everything.

➤ What if your roommate decides to bolt for good, leaving you with all of the bills?

Choosing a roommate is not a decision to take lightly, because it will affect every day of your life for the next year (or however long your lease is for). Obviously you can't read a person's mind or see what's in his or her heart. But if you spend some time talking with the person about everyday routines and personal preferences, you might get a sense as to whether the two of you would be compatible.

CRUNCHING NUMBERS

Living with one roommate will save you 50 percent of your apartment costs — not only on rent and food, but on the security deposit, utilities, insurance, and furniture expenses.

The questions you ask will depend on the circumstances and the person you're talking to. Your goal is to determine whether he or she would be a good roommate or a bad one. Let's take a look at some of the differences between the two so that you'll know what kind of questions to ask.

A good roommate...

asks you how you would like to furnish the apartment, explains his or her own preferences, and then volunteers to go with you to flea markets and garage sales to find furniture that you both can live with.

A bad roommate...

shows up on moving day with a threadbare green-and-orange plaid easy chair, plops it down in the middle of your living room, and says, "Hope we have room for your stuff too."

A good roommate...

asks for your okay and checks the terms of your rental agreement before inviting a friend or family member to spend the night in your apartment.

A bad roommate...

Has more people crashing at your place than at the Indianapolis 500.

A good roommate...

is always conscious of safety and security issues and is careful not to do anything that would jeopardize you, your possessions, or your apartment.

GLAD YOU ASKED

Is it a mistake to rent an apartment with a friend?

It certainly can be. The frustrations that come from sharing an apartment with someone day in and day out can drive a wedge between even the closest of friends. No matter how compatible you think you are with a person, you will always find little habits, quirks, and personality traits that drive you nuts after a month or so. Lack of separation is the problem. When you get tired of each other, there's no place to go to be alone.

A bad roommate...
makes copies of your house key for friends, family members, people at the office, and random passersby.

A good roommate...
respects your privacy, recognizes when you need time alone, and learns to accommodate your moods.

A bad roommate...
thinks looking in your diary is a good way to get to know you and wakes you up every morning by asking, "What are we going to do today?"

A good roommate...
knows your schedule—when you go to bed, when you need to get work done, when you prefer to sleep in—and makes an effort not to disturb you.

A bad roommate...
believes the best kind of parties are the ones that begin after 1 A.M. . . . on weeknights.

A good roommate...
recognizes when the apartment needs to be cleaned and is willing to take turns with you on the really nasty jobs, like scrubbing the toilets or cleaning the bathtubs.

A bad roommate...
sprays a little air freshener in each room and says, "Ah, good as new!"

A good roommate...
is willing to sit down and talk about any problems the two of you may be experiencing.

A bad roommate...
curls up in a fetal position and moans any time he or she senses conflict.

No matter how much preparation and interviewing you do, you have no guarantee that the roommate you get will be the roommate you expect. Some people can talk a good game and convince you that they're something they're not.

The Need for a Written Agreement

That's why it makes sense to protect yourself, financially at least, with a written agreement before you move in. You may feel uncomfortable about asking someone—especially a friend—to sign such a document, but if problems arise later you'll be glad you did.

Your "co-renter's agreement" should specify that one of you (most likely you, since you're the one writing the agreement) will be responsible for collecting money for rent and utilities and then paying those bills on time. In return, the other person (or persons, if you have more than one roommate) will agree to faithfully and punctually pay for his or her share of all bills.

The agreement should also address food-related concerns (who shops for it, who pays for it, who's allowed to eat what), household duties (complete with a schedule for chores like shopping, cooking, cleaning, and washing dishes), house rules (noise levels, phone use, protocol for guests), and early departure contingencies (how much notice must be given, what happens to the furniture that was purchased jointly).

A Credit to You

Finding a place to live isn't the only financial challenge you'll face as a young adult. You'll also need to make some important decisions about credit cards, automobiles, and insurance. Let's take a look at these areas.

If you were to open this book to a random page, there's a good chance you'd see a warning against credit cards there. Call it a running theme throughout the book.

The same warning applies here. Knowing how to

PENNY FOR YOUR THOUGHTS

You are a king by your own fireside, as much as any monarch in his throne.

—CERVANTES

use a credit card can be like knowing how to hot-wire a car. In the right situation, it can be handy; in the wrong situation, it can get you into *el trouble grande*.

On the Plus Side

Let's look at some of the privileges of membership (as the good people at American Express might say)—the benefits of having a credit card.

Instant access

A credit card provides not only a line of credit—usually $500 to begin with—but instant access to it. Instead of carrying a lot of money around—and being forced to race back to the bank whenever you need more—credit cards allow you the convenience of carrying just one small piece of plastic.

Safety

The people who carry large amounts of cash around are tempting pickpockets and armed robbers. If you lose $300 in the mall—whether it's lost or stolen—you're out $300. If you lose a credit card in the mall, you can call an 800 number and report it missing. The company will either put a hold on the card or cancel it altogether and issue you a new one. So you don't have to worry about someone running up purchases that can cause you a lot of grief.

Debit cards are safer still. If you lose a debit card, anyone who finds it will be unable to use it without your secret PIN number. (Although, from a mathematical standpoint, if theives are really committed to discovering your number, they might try each one of the 10,000 possible variations until hitting on the right one.)

Insurance and disaster coverage

Many credit card companies offer thirty to ninety days of insurance coverage on purchases made with their credit card. So if you buy a watch or a set of luggage and it's stolen, lost, or damaged within that period, you can call another 1-800 number to report it. After verifying your purchase, the company will reimburse you for the item. All in all, it's not a bad protection to have.

Points and gift certificates

Most credit card companies award "points" when you use your card. This reward system typically funnels about 1 percent of the amount of all your credit card purchases back to you.

Some companies offer that amount in cash or balance reduction. Others require you to cash in your points for gift certificates at participating stores. That's great if the participating stores sell something of interest to you; if not, too bad. Many cards also offer frequent flyer miles redeemable at sponsoring airlines.

Credit rating

Some people use a credit card to establish a credit rating. If it's on record that you borrowed money and paid it back on time, you will be considered a "good risk." That may not mean much to you now, but when the time comes for you to apply for a larger loan—say, for a house—you'll be much more likely to qualify with the words "good risk" next to your name.

Disclaimer: The following paragraph should not be mistaken for an endorsement of using credit cards to pay emergency expenses. If you don't have sufficient funds to cover emergency expenses, you need to change your spending or living habits. You need to be able to put away a little money each month to cover emergency situations.

Supplemental funds

If you're new to the world of budgeting and finances, there's a good chance your savings account lacks, well, savings. If you find yourself living paycheck to paycheck, with little or no funds left over at the end of the month, one unexpected expense or financial "hiccup" could be disastrous. Without the cash to pay what you owe, you're only other option is credit—namely, a credit card.

On the Minus Side

For every legitimate reason to carry a credit card, there's a legitimate reason not to. Here are just a few of the drawbacks you should consider.

Even one misuse of a credit card can be dangerous.

One misstep with a credit card can produce serious long-term effects. This is especially true for credit card rookies. When you sign your name to the back of your first credit card, you may get the itch to put your plastic to work on a new stereo or new TV or a new microwave—or any combination thereof.

If you're not prepared to pay the resulting bill—in full—you will have debt. And you don't want debt in your life, because debt has a way of growing.

If you do go overboard with credit card purchases, it's not too farfetched to assume that you will find yourself still trying to pay off those purchases two or three years later—not to mention all the interest that grew up around the original amount.

There are no "do-overs" when you make a mistake with plastic. You can't plead ignorance. You're just stuck with the consequences.

Credit cards encourage spur-of-the-moment spending.

Credit cards fuel the "gotta have it" instinct in most people. The primary reason is that credit cards give you a sense of being wealthier than you are. Remember, the fact that you have a $2,000 limit on your credit card doesn't mean that you have $2,000 to spend. The amount you have budgeted for purchases is the amount you have to spend. When you exceed that amount, you invite debt into your financial picture.

Credit cards decrease the satisfaction of ownership.

People tend not to appreciate things that come quickly or easily to them. This principle applies especially to possessions. Before credit cards were the rage, people saved for months—even years—for the items they wanted. And when they were finally able to afford those items, they appreciated them because of all that went into saving for them.

Today, if you can get your name on a piece of plastic with the words VISA, MasterCard, or Discover on it, you can buy just about anything at just about any time. And remember, although it's a lot of fun to get into debt, it's not nearly as much fun getting out of debt.

Credit cards cause you to think of debt as a natural state.

Once you get on a roll with a credit card, it's tough to stop using it. The idea of debt, which perhaps at one time may have scared you, becomes something you tend to shrug off without a second thought. You figure everyone else has debts when they first start off, so why not you? You tell yourself that having what you want is worth the price of being in debt.

The problem is, you don't know how damaging and stressful debt can be until you're in it. And by that time it's too late. Your preventive measures are gone.

There's the small matter of interest.

Borrowing money, whether on a credit card or from a bank, is expensive. Not only do you have to pay back what you borrowed, you have to pay for the *privilege* of borrowing. It's called interest, and it's not your friend.

Interest is what keeps people in debt, because it never stops growing. The longer you go without paying off your balance, the more your interest builds. Instead of paying off the amount you borrowed each month, you may find yourself paying off just the *interest* on the amount you borrowed. And that can be frustrating.

Credit card companies make a bundle on interest payments. They're in no hurry for you to pay back what you owe. The longer you delay, the more money they make through interest.

That's why credit card companies offer such low minimum monthly payments. You didn't think they were trying to make life easier for you, did you? They're trying to get you to pay as little as possible so that they can keep collecting your interest as long as possible.

Credit Rules

If you decide to apply for a credit card, there are some things you can do to prevent potential problems. Specifically, there are five rules you should live by.

Rule 1: Treat a credit card like a debit card.
A debit card works only as long as you have money in your bank account. Likewise, you shouldn't charge a penny more on your credit card than you know you can pay in full the day your monthly statement comes in.

CRUNCHING NUMBERS

If you borrow money for three years at an interest rate of 18 percent, you will spend the first year and a half paying on the interest alone. By the end of the loan, you will have paid back twice as much as you borrowed.

Rule 2: Stick to your budget.

Know ahead of time what you can and can't afford. Never use a credit card for non-budgeted expenses. That means no "impulse buying." If you have trouble controlling your spending, "ground" your credit cards. Don't let them leave your house.

Rule 3: Pay your credit card bills promptly.

Remember, you will be charged interest on any amount that you don't pay in full by the due date on your statement. That's why it's important to write down your payment due date. If you miss that date even by one day, you will pay a penalty.

Rule 4: Stop using your card as soon as you go over your budget.

If you soar past your allotted spending amount on wings of plastic, you may need to admit to yourself that you're not ready for a card. There's no shame in admitting that. In fact, it's a pretty mature decision to make. If you're not ready to have a credit card, don't give yourself a chance to wreck your budget in the meantime. Get rid of your card.

Rule 5: Pay more than your minimum monthly payment.

This is especially important if you've racked up a debt that will take months to pay off. Remember, your interest will keep growing and growing on any balance you have on your card. The longer it takes you to pay off that balance, the more you end up paying in the long run.

Your Own Set of Wheels

Chapter 4 covers just about everything you need to know about buying cars, so we highly recommend that you check it out. For the purposes of this chapter, though, we've come up with a list of 12 tips designed specifically for someone on a single person's budget.

In no particular order, the tips are as follows.

1. *Think about more than your monthly payments.* A car salesperson can hide all kinds of extras that you may not want in the total price of your car if you're just looking at the monthly payment.

2. *Read the fine print on all sales offers.* For example, if you look at the small type on an ad touting "zero down, no payments for a year," you'll probably find that an extremely high interest rate is being charged during that time, so when you finally do start making the payments, it's even more than you expected.

3. *Ask "What's my monthly income?" not "How much can I afford?"* Your car expenses, including gas and maintenance should account for no more than 15 percent of your Net Spending Income (your take-home pay, minus tithes). That's the figure you should consider when buying a car—and not what price seems "fair."

4. *Get everything in writing.* We're not suggesting that you can't trust a car salesperson. . . . Well, at least not all of them. If a salesperson tells you he or she can give you the car for a certain price, ask for it in writing. If the salesperson hesitates, you can assume that you won't be getting that price.

5. *Don't fall in love with a particular car.* Be prepared to walk away at any time if you don't like the price your salesperson quotes you. You will most likely be able to find a car you like for less money.

6. *Pay cash for the car, if at all possible.* If you can avoid financing—taking out a loan for—a car, you will go a long way toward improving your financial bottom line. The money you would otherwise be spending on car payments could go toward other things, such as college loans or savings.

7. *Don't underestimate the amount of upkeep you'll need to budget for.* Your car expenses don't end with your payments. You'll also need to set aside a significant amount each month to cover preventive maintenance and repairs on your vehicle. If your budget can't handle that extra expense, you might want to rethink your decision to buy the car.

8. *Skip the extras.* You don't always need the extra rust-proofing or the undercoating protection. In fact, if you're not careful, the "add-ons" can increase the price of your car substantially.

9. *Don't forget about car insurance.* Insurance will take another hefty bite out of your monthly budget. Not having liability insurance isn't an option; you're

required by law to carry it. If insurance premiums are too expensive for you, you'll need to reconsider your decision to buy a car.

10. *Do your homework.* Don't buy a car unless you have first investigated it thoroughly. You'll need to know not only its safety and performance records (which can be found in publications like *Consumer Reports*), but what its fair market value is.

11. *Talk to friends and family members.* It's usually a good idea to buy a car from someone you know—or at least from someone who knows someone you know. You're much less likely to be sold a piece of junk or to be cheated out of your money when there's a personal connection involved.

12. *Don't buy a new car.* Your "investment" will lose a significant amount of its value the minute you drive it off the lot. That's why used cars are a much smarter choice.

Insurance

Chapter 8 deals with the topic of insurance in (almost excruciating) detail, so if you're looking for specifics, that's where you should go. For those of you who would prefer to avoid long discourses on double indemnity, we offer the following three-point summary of the insurance needs of a single person living on his or her own.

1. *Singles probably don't need life insurance.* The purpose of life insurance is to provide for people who are dependent on you in the event of your death. If you don't have any dependents, you won't need life insurance (except for burial expenses) until you do. If you do have dependents, your least expensive—and probably best—option at this point in your life is term life insurance. Ask an agent about the specific policy that's right for you.

2. *Get health insurance through your employer.* With the cost of health care today, most people need health insurance. But it's very expensive. That's why, if the company you work for does not offer health insurance, you need to find one that does. Obviously, that's a lot easier said than done. But the amount you'll save in monthly insurance costs and the amount you

gain in benefits will be more than worth the trouble of finding a new employer.

3. *Buy only as much renter's insurance as you need.* Your landlord may require you to carry a certain amount of insurance to cover damages to the unit. The amount you carry above that is up to you. If you don't have a lot of expensive possessions—if you can afford to replace anything you might lose—you don't need a lot of coverage.

One More Thing

Living on your own can be one of the most rewarding experiences of your life. The confidence that comes from knowing you can support and take care of yourself can spill over into other areas of your life, giving you more self-assurance in your career and your interpersonal relationships. Long story short, it can change the way you think of yourself.

So when the time comes for your solo flight, make sure you do it right.

The Buck Stops Here

Think you're an expert on living alone? Here's a quiz to see how much you know.

1. Which of the following is not a good reason to move out of your parents' house?
   a. Your parents tell you to move out of their house.
   b. You have practiced living on a budget successfully for at least three months.
   c. You can get free HBO and Showtime on the cable system across town.
   d. You have a dependable roommate lined up to split expenses with you.

2. What is the best way to practice living on a budget?
   a. Read a how-to book that tells you what to do.
   b. Invest in a state-of-the-art helmet and sensor pads, install the necessary software, and lose yourself in a virtual reality world of budgeting.
   c. Find someone who makes about as much as you do and lives in the type of place you'd like to live and pay his or her bills for a month.
   d. Determine how much money you'll need to live each month, put it into your savings account, and try to get by on what's left.

3. Which of the following would not be considered a necessity for your apartment?
   a. Dishes
   b. Phone
   c. Cleaning supplies
   d. Lava lamp

4. What qualities should you look for in a roommate?
   a. Reliability
   b. Desperation
   c. Unpredictability
   d. Paranoia

5. Which of the following byproducts of living alone is likely to make the biggest difference in your life?
   a. The panic that comes from writing rent checks on an overdrawn bank account
   b. The confidence that comes from knowing you can take care of yourself
   c. The satisfaction that comes from giving all of your deadbeat friends a place to crash
   d. The guilt that comes from convincing yourself you abandoned your parents

Answers: (1) c, (2) d, (3) d, (4) a, (5) b

PARENTING

THE SINGLE PARENT

And Then There Was One

SNAPSHOT

"**Y**ou know what would be a good industry to get in to?" Tammy asked out of the blue as she adjusted the setting on her treadmill. "Divorce counseling."

"Uh oh," Brittany said as she tried to keep pace. "Sounds like someone's having problems collecting child support again."

"No, I'm serious," Tammy replied. "Think about it. Everyone gets marriage counseling before they get married, but no one ever gets divorce counseling when they split up."

"Yeah, I see what you're saying," Brittany said with a laugh. "We could bring experts in to talk about the things nobody ever tells you about life after marriage."

"Exactly!" Tammy squealed. "For instance, I could teach a course on how to convince your ex to pay child support instead of buying a new Mustang to

SNEAK PREVIEW

1. In order to address your financial needs, you must first have a complete understanding of them–which means you must take an inventory of your assets and your liabilities.

2. Because your earning potential is limited by your responsibilities as a single parent, your best strategy for improving your financial health is to reduce your spending in most areas of your budget.

3. There are many resources–both human and financial–available to assist single parents; you just need to know where to look.

impress his 20-year-old girlfriend."

Brittany nodded. "And I could lead a class on how to deal with the fake-sincere people who want to know what went wrong with your marriage."

"How about a seminar on how to convince your daughter that Hamburger Helper is a treat?" Tammy suggested.

"Or a course on how to convince your son that a board game is just as exciting a Christmas gift as a PlayStation 2 system?" Brittany added.

"We ought to draw up a business plan," Tammy suggested with a laugh. "You know what they say about sticking with what you know."

"Yeah, and about making lemonade when life gives you lemons," Brittany added soulfully.

* * * * * * * * * * * * * * *

You're not alone.

That's the first thing you need to know about being a single parent. Whether you've never been married or you're divorced or widowed, you share common struggles with a much larger group of people than you might imagine.

Need numbers to back that up? Try these on for size.

➤ Approximately 10 million homes in this country are headed by single mothers.

➤ Approximately 1.6 million homes in this country are headed by single fathers.

➤ Approximately one out of every three homes in this country is headed by a single parent.

Those stats probably won't do much to ease the loneliness that comes from trying to raise a family on your own. But they should indicate that the financial pressures and problems you face are not unique to you. The fact is, the majority of single parents in this country are struggling with the same kinds of problems and frustrations that you are.

In this chapter you'll find information, encouragement, and practical application suggestions designed to help you tackle the unique financial challenges you face as a single parent.

Take a Peek

The first and perhaps most difficult challenge you'll face is gathering the courage to look closely at your finances. You may tell yourself that what you don't know can't hurt you. In the back of your mind, however, you know that eventually your finances will catch up with you and demand your attention.

CRUNCHING NUMBERS

Approximately 33 percent of all American households are headed by a single mother or a single father.

That's why it's important that you understand exactly where you are financially—what you have, what you pay, and what you owe. (For more information on how to categorize your assets and liabilities, see chapter 2.) Once you've removed your financial blinders and looked at the entire picture of your finances, you'll get a sense of exactly what you need to do.

By the way, the second challenge you'll face is preventing yourself from panicking once you realize the state of your financial affairs. Remember, no situation is hopeless.

With a lot of commitment, sacrifice, and hard work, you can change your financial future, regardless of what your present looks like.

Go-ooo-ooo-aaa-aaa-l!

Your first official act in gaining control over your money is to set some financial goals for yourself. By writing down the details of your current situation and establishing some goals—even small ones—you'll gain a better perspective of your needs and possibly spot some rays of hope when it comes to being able to manage your finances.

Many single parents narrow their financial goals to three:

1. Being able to live within their means

2. Providing for their children's needs

3. Getting out of debt and staying out of debt.

Right now the idea of living within your means—that is, not spending any more than you bring home in your paycheck—may seem like an impossibility. Like countless other single parents, you may be running up your credit card balances or borrowing money just to take care of your family's basic needs each month. And you may feel like you've hit a financial dead end.

But it's not a dead end; it's a crossroads. And if you're willing to continue the journey—as difficult as it may be—you'll eventually find yourself on the road to financial health.

Think of this chapter as a road map.

Budget Considerations

The easiest (and least practical) advice for improving your financial outlook is to make more money. For the purposes of this chapter, though, I'll give you the benefit of the doubt and assume that you're already making as much as possible at this point in your life.

That leaves the more difficult solution of cutting your spending.

In chapters 2 and 3, a monthly budget has been divided into 12 categories. For single parents, each of those budget categories carries its own unique challenges and opportunities. See the appropriate percentages for each budget category on the Percentage Guide, page 382 of the appendix.

Let's take a look at some of those categories to see if there are opportunities for saving money or meeting the specific needs of single parents.

> ## PENNY FOR YOUR THOUGHTS
>
> I'm still not sure what is meant by good fortune and success. I know fame and power are for the birds. But then life suddenly comes into focus for me. And, ah, there stand my kids.
>
> —Lee Iacocca

Taxes

Okay, this isn't an official budget category, according to chapters 2 and 3, but it certainly could be. Taxes play a major role in your finances. And as a single parent, you should be aware of any program that offers tax relief to people in your position.

Earned income credit (EIC) is a tax incentive for low-income working families; it reduces federal taxes to as low as, well, zero percent. In fact, some families receive refunds above what they paid in federal taxes.

To apply for EIC, you'll need to. . .

➤ pick up Schedule EIC forms at your local post office, IRS branch, or on the Web.

➤ ask for a workbook, if one is not included with the forms.

➤ call your local IRS office if you have any questions.

➤ file the form with your federal 1040, 1040 A, or 1040 EZ form.

> ## GLAD YOU ASKED
>
> **I've never had to worry about taxes before, and I wouldn't know a 1040EZ from an R2-D2. Where can I go for help?**
> Check with your local Community Action Agency to see if it offers free tax services to low-income families. If not, talk to your pastor to find out if someone in your church may be able to help you fill out your forms.

Category 1: Housing

Housing is generally the largest budget category, accounting for as much as 40 percent of your Net Spending Income (which is your take-home pay, minus tithes). The following tips are designed to reduce its size in your budget.

Here are seven suggestions for lowering your housing expenses.

1. *Become an apartment manager.* Many apartment complexes offer attractive incentive packages, including free rent and free housing expenses, to their apartment managers. If you think that's a responsibility you could handle, place some calls to local apartment management offices to see if they have any positions available.

2. *Rent one or more bedrooms in your home.* You may know of another single parent, an unmarried person, or a college student looking for a place to live. If you and your kids are comfortable with the idea, determine a fair rental rate and make your home available to a boarder (or two). To avoid

all kinds of problems, make sure that any boarders you take on are the same gender as you. You'll also want to make sure that your boarders don't demonstrate any harmful behavior around your children.

3. *Consider subsidized housing.* At the risk of discouraging you, you probably don't have much of a shot at finding any available subsidized housing. Sometimes there's a waiting list just to *apply* for subsidized housing. Once you've been approved, you will likely have to wait quite a while before a unit becomes available.

4. *Look for a housing co-op.* Though it may seem like the last stand of the hippie communal culture, co-op housing is actually a desirable option for single parents. A housing co-op is a condo or apartment community that is privately owned and regulated by the members who live there. Payments are based on income, so your rent may increase as your income increases. Fortunately, though, each unit has an established maximum payment limit. As is the case with subsidized housing, there are usually long waiting lists for co-op housing. That's why, if you find a co-op you're interested in, it's important to sign up for it as soon as possible.

5. *Contact Habitat for Humanity.* If you're working and have a stable income but still can't afford to buy a home, you might want to consider applying for a Habitat for Humanity house. By putting in "sweat equity"—that is, actually building a home with the help of Habitat volunteers—many single parents who could not purchase homes any other way have become homeowners. For details on requirements and the application process, call the Habitat for Humanity office nearest you.

6. *Investigate low-income, single-parent housing available through nonprofit organizations.* Participating organizations generally offer multiunit facilities that are specifically designed to meet the immediate needs of single mothers and their children for a limited time—usually 24 months. The nonprofit organizations usually require residents to have an educational goal or work training program that can be accomplished within their stay. Budgets are established and rent is charged according to an individual's budget. Some organizations provide child care with their

subsidized housing; others help parents locate subsidized child care. Some programs accept mothers on welfare; others require mothers to work. If you have no other resource for housing you can afford, check around your community to see if there's a single parent housing program available and what the requirements are.

7. *Teach yourself to do simple home repairs.* You can take classes on almost any housing project you can imagine at your local home center store. You can also check your local library for any number of do-it-yourself home repair magazines, such as Family Handyman. It also won't hurt to develop an acquaintance and familiarity with power tools. The more you can avoid using professionals to repair or remodel your house, the more money you'll save.

Category 2: Food

You'll find several tips for cutting your food budget in chapter 3. But if, after doing everything you can to stretch your grocery dollars, you still have difficulty keeping up with your family's food needs, you have some options available to you.

First, you can check with your church to see if they offer a food pantry for people in need. If your church doesn't have a food pantry, they may refer you to an organization that does. Your church may also provide emergency funds or gift certificates for area stores so that you can buy what you need.

Category 3: Auto

The automobile category presents a special challenge for single parents. That's because, without some intervention from outside their own budget, many single parents don't have the resources to replace their worn-out cars.

The cheapest car you'll ever drive is the one you

GLAD YOU ASKED

What can I do to stretch my grocery money as far as it will go?

One of the best money-saving strategies is to buy groceries in bulk. Before you do, though, you'll need to make sure that your freezer is big enough to store large amounts of food. You'll also need to plan your meals so that you can use all of the food before it goes bad. The last thing you want is to have to throw food out. For maximum savings, find someone else to split a bulk purchase with you.

own, but it still needs regular maintenance to keep it running properly. And, unfortunately, auto maintenance doesn't come cheap.

There are some ways, however, to cut your maintenance costs.

➤ Many vocational and technical colleges have auto-repair departments that offer routine maintenance, tune ups, and repairs on cars for little or no cost. (Just make sure that the students are supervised by a qualified instructor.)

➤ Find a family member or friend who is knowledgeable about auto maintenance to help you with routine checks, oil changes, tire and brake checks, and the like. If you're worried about taking advantage of the person's willingness to help, offer to provide a service of your own—including babysitting, chauffeuring, or cleaning—in return.

➤ If your car needs repairs, find a professional mechanic in your circle of friends or relatives who wants to make some money on the side in a home garage—someone who may only charge you for the parts.

➤ Learn all you can about auto maintenance. In time, you may be able to take care of at least some of your car's maintenance yourself. Be sure you know what you're doing, though, before you start monkeying around under the hood. Just to be safe, you might want to have a professional check your work at first.

➤ Find out whether your church offers a car care ministry. A typical car care ministry involves a group of Christians who meet regularly, perhaps once a month on Saturdays at a church parking lot, to perform routine maintenance and minor repairs on the vehicles of single parents or widows.

Keep in mind, too, that not having a car—at least temporarily—is not the end of your world. Public transportation and accommodating friends may get you where you need to go until you can get a car of your own.

Category 4: Insurance

When your funds are limited, life insurance should be a lower priority than health insurance. In fact, depending on your situation, you may not need life insurance at this stage in your life. Remember, life insurance should be used only to provide—never to profit or protect.

If you have children who are grown and on their own, young children who could be cared for by other family members, or investments or retirement funds that could be used to provide for your children if you died, you may not need life insurance.

Before you start ripping up your policy, though, consider this. If your children are still younger than college age, you need life insurance if you have no other resources to provide for them.

If your budget is tight, and you have only a small amount to shell out each month, buy the least expensive insurance coverage you can find. Annual renewable term life insurance provides the greatest death benefit for the least cost. The policy won't accumulate any cash value, but that's okay since you only need it for provision in the event of your death.

As for health insurance, most employers offer a company-sponsored plan and require employees to pay part of the expenses for it. The good news, though, is that they offer several options to help keep the costs low for the employees.

If your children are covered under your health plan or their other parent's health plan, you'll need to find out. . .

➤ what benefits are available

➤ how to process a claim

➤ how much of the uncovered expenses and deductibles you'll have to pay.

If your employer doesn't offer health care benefits, your best bet is to find one who does as soon as you can.

For more information on what kind of insurance you need at this stage of your life, see chapter 8.

Category 5: Debt

If you've recently gone through a divorce, chances are this category took a major hit, thanks to your lawyer bills and other court-related costs. As you've probably

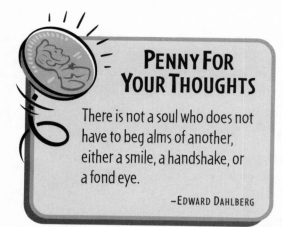

PENNY FOR YOUR THOUGHTS

There is not a soul who does not have to beg alms of another, either a smile, a handshake, or a fond eye.

−EDWARD DAHLBERG

learned, those fees can be hefty.

In chapter 3, it is recommended that you devote no more than 5 percent of your Net Spending Income to paying off your debts. However, that may not be feasible for many single parents.

If you've been subsidizing your income to creditors, you'll find it very difficult to balance your budget. Fortunately, there are some things you can do to change your situation.

1. Contact your creditors with a plan for how much you can pay them each month.

2. Never promise creditors more than you can realistically pay.

3. Pay off your smallest debt first; then add the amount you were paying to the next debt, and do that until all your debts are paid.

4. Recruit the help of a financial advisor through Consumer Credit Counseling to make payment arrangements with your creditors.

5. Back up your words with actions. If you promise to pay something by a certain date, pay it. If you don't follow through on your agreements, you'll be dropped from the Consumer Credit Counseling program. What's worse, you'll be fair game for creditors again.

6. File for bankruptcy under Chapter 13 of the Federal Bankruptcy Act. This provides court protection while your debts are being paid. Keep in mind, though, that bankruptcy does not give you the right to skip out on your financial responsibilities; it only gives you the time to make arrangements to repay them.

7. Reestablish a clean credit record.

Once you get back to square one with a clean record, you can use your newfound wisdom and responsibility to prevent yourself from ever falling into the debt trap again.

Category 6: Entertainment

If you are divorced or widowed, and suddenly faced with the prospect of living on one salary, there's a good chance that you won't be able to provide your children with the recreation they're used to. For example, deluxe family vacations may be a thing of the past.

But that doesn't mean all entertainment must be surgically removed from your life. There are plenty of things you and your kids can—and should—do together strictly for fun.

Here are a few ideas for family fun on a tight budget.

PENNY FOR YOUR THOUGHTS

Independence? That's middle class blasphemy. We are all dependent on one another, every soul of us on earth.

–ANONYMOUS

➤ Take a picnic dinner to a summer play, concert, or symphony in the park.

➤ Check out free events such as puppet shows, art exhibits, or craft fairs at your local library or mall.

➤ Attend local recreation department events such as craft classes, square dances, or sporting contests.

➤ Plan holiday activities, such as baking cookies, making crafts for gifts, or Christmas caroling.

➤ Take advantage of special children's admission prices for museums, festivals, and theaters.

➤ Check out free videos from your local library, pop your own popcorn, and have your own movie night at home.

Organize a babysitting co-op with other parents—not only to give yourself an occasional break but to make sure your kids have regular companions to play with.

Category 7: Clothing

In chapter 3, it is recommended that 5 percent of your Net Spending Income be set aside for clothing expenses. For many single parents, though, that 5 percent figure seems like wishful thinking. When funds are low, the Clothing category is probably one of the first to be sacrificed.

So you're left with the challenge of clothing your family on an extremely tight budget. Fortunately, there are some strategies that can help you stretch your clothing budget.

1. *Organize a clothing exchange.* Pick a theme, such as "children's winter clothes and shoes." Invite several families in your area to participate. Recruit a committee to sort clothes according to size. When you're finished, give leftovers to charity.

2. *Make good use of consignment shops and thrift stores.* Not only can you find good buys if you're an alert shopper, you also can make money on your unwanted items. Call your local consignment shop for an appointment to drop your clothes off.

3. *Buy at yard and garage sales.* For best selection, you'll need to get an early start. You may be surprised at the quality of clothing you can pick up for next to nothing. When the time comes to get rid of your old clothes, organize a sale of your own.

4. *Buy basic colors.* Make sure you get maximum use from the clothes you have. Coordinate your wardrobe around classic, traditional styles you can wear through several seasons.

PENNY FOR YOUR THOUGHTS

In the time of trouble avert not thy face from hope, for the soft marrow abideth in the hard bone.

—HAFIZ

Category 8: Savings

The idea of having leftover funds at the end of the month may seem laughable to you. However, it's vital that you find a way to hang on to at least a few dollars each month to tuck away for emergencies.

Without a savings account, your only other option when unexpected expenses arise are your credit cards. And that's a can of worms that you definitely don't want to open.

One practical way to start saving is to put all of your additional income into your savings account. This would include cash gifts, overtime income, bonuses, garage sale profits, and things like that.

Easier said than done, I know. For a single parent especially, it seems there's always something demanding your financial attention. Even so, you must make savings a priority.

PENNY FOR YOUR THOUGHTS

Children are the anchors that hold a mother to life.

–SOPHOCLES

Category 9: Medical

Unfortunately, one major medical expense can wreak havoc on a single parent's budget. And although there's not a lot you can do to prevent most medical emergencies—aside from preventive maintenance and regular checkups—there are some ways you can deal with overwhelming medical bills.

1. *Share your need.* Let your church and other caring friends know when you can't meet your expenses. Give them a chance to help you.

2. *Explain your situation to your doctor.* Let him or her know your financial predicament before you run up medical bills. Some physicians are willing to provide low-cost service to low-income patients.

3. *Barter for services.* Offer to clean the office, baby-sit, do yard work, and so on, to reduce your medical bills.

4. *Take advantage of local dentist schools.* If you're comfortable with the idea of being part of a dental student's learning process, you can get cleanings, fillings, and other necessary procedures done for about half of what private dentists and orthodontists charge. Just make sure the students are well supervised before you say "Ahhh."

Category 10: Child care

About 40 percent of all single parents are faced with the extra financial burden of paying for some type of child care. The other 60 percent either have families who can help or older children who can baby-sit. Or they work at home, stay at home, or don't have a steady income.

There is no magic formula for making child care expenses fit into your budget, but here are some ideas that might help.

1. *Explore church-based programs.* Some churches offer child care programs with a sliding fee scale for low-income families.

2. *Check out pre-K programs.* In some states, pre-K programs for 4-to 5-year-olds are funded by the state.

3. *Consider the Head Start program.* This government-funded program provides preschool for ages 3 to 5.

4. *Opt for an in-home provider.* Child care providers who work in your home usually charge much less than child care centers.

5. *Start a day care business in your home.* Take matters into your own hands and provide a service for other parents in your area. Benefits include time spent with your kids, companions for them, a safe environment for your children, and tax deductions for a home-based business. Check your local requirements and regulations for operating a child care service.

6. *Start a home-based business.* Stay at home with your kids while you work.

7. *Swap babysitting duties.* This works especially well if you have a friend who works a different schedule than you do.

8. *Contact private schools in your area.* Believe it or not, private schools can be affordable for single parents—if the schools offer scholarship programs. You also may be able to exchange services such as cleaning or preparing food to help pay for tuition.

CRUNCHING NUMBERS

In some parts of the country, full-time childcare can cost as much as $150 a week.

Fare Thee Welfare

One of the toughest decisions you may face as a single parent is whether or not to allow the government to support you financially. For many people, it's a tempting offer. They view government assistance as the most logical way to relieve their financial burdens. They also believe that whatever stigma is associated with going on welfare is a small price to pay for the opportunity to be with their kids, instead of spending most of their day at work.

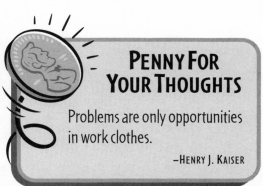

PENNY FOR YOUR THOUGHTS

Problems are only opportunities in work clothes.

−HENRY J. KAISER

But the welfare system isn't the solution. Regardless of what its proponents claim, the system does not encourage independence. In fact, welfare is actually a form of bondage.

For example, under the welfare system, the government decides...

> ➤ whether or not you'll work outside the home.

> ➤ how much you can earn.

> ➤ how many hours you can work.

> ➤ where you can take your child for child care.

> ➤ how much your home can be worth.

> ➤ how much you can save.

> ➤ how much your car can be worth.

> ➤ if you're allowed to receive job training or go to college.

And if you think welfare is a temporary solution to your problems, think again. The system is like a quicksand bog. Once you get in it, it's extremely difficult to get out.

The struggle to break free from welfare has defeated many who try. Some people may claim that once you have a good job, you can give up government assistance with no problem. That simply isn't true. The significant disadvantages for welfare recipients who work keep them stuck in the system.

When you leave the welfare system, you lose several things, including...

> ➤ a monthly check

> ➤ food stamp benefits

➤ Medicaid for you and your children

➤ day care (after the first year)

➤ subsidized housing, if you have it.

On an entry level income, you can't replace those benefits. So the temptation is to give up and go back to the system. However, when you consider the bondage it causes, you'll discover that it's worth it to break free.

Obviously, you need support to get along without welfare. Fortunately, there are some places you can go for help:

➤ your family—including your immediate family and the family of your children's other parent

➤ your church

➤ a trained budget counselor

➤ another single parent who has overcome the obstacles you're facing.

If you haven't yet applied for welfare, don't. Resist the urge to go for the quick-fix solution. Your decision may mean that you and your kids will struggle financially for a while. But in the end, the freedom—and sense of accomplishment—you enjoy will more than make up for those struggles.

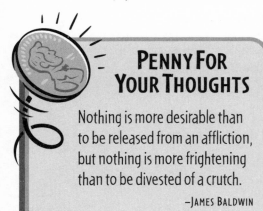

PENNY FOR YOUR THOUGHTS

Nothing is more desirable than to be released from an affliction, but nothing is more frightening than to be divested of a crutch.

–JAMES BALDWIN

If you are on welfare, I urge you to ease your dependence on the government and work toward supporting your kids on your own—with the help of your family and friends, of course. Not only will you eventually be able to experience the satisfaction of providing for your family, you will also set a powerful example for your children.

Random Acts of Kindness

If you're reading this chapter and you're not a single parent yourself, it's likely that you know and care about someone who is. Or it may be that you are the product of a single-parent family. Or perhaps you just have a special place in your heart for people who are often ignored by the rest of society.

Whatever the reason for your interest, know this: You can make a difference in the life of a single parent—and his or her family.

Below you'll find a list of 10 ideas, some of which may spur you into action and others of which may inspire ideas of your own. Either way, it's okay—as long as you do *something*.

PENNY FOR YOUR THOUGHTS

Hope is necessary in every condition. The miseries of poverty, sickness, of captivity, would, without this comfort, be insupportable.

—SAMUEL JOHNSON

1. Write a note of encouragement. Among a stack of bills and notices, a heartfelt letter of admiration and concern will come as a pleasant surprise. And it may just make a single parent's day.

2. Offer to care for a single parent's children for a night. Everyone deserves a break. Even a few hours alone—or with friends enjoying a good time—can go a long way toward restoring a single parent's sanity.

3. Invite a single parent family to your home for meals. Holidays are the most popular time to share your home with others, but don't overlook the single parent's need for fellowship throughout the rest of the year.

4. Offer to coach youth sports. Invite a child from a single parent family to be on the team. Provide transportation to and from practices and games for the child—and parent, if necessary.

5. Offer to take a single parent shopping. Go in together to split the cost of large items or large quantities of an item. Better yet, buy the large quantity yourself and offer half of it to your shopping companion.

6. Purchase inexpensive fun items (such as kites), pack a picnic lunch, and invite a single parent family to the park for a day.

7. When you prepare a meal that can be frozen and reheated, make a double portion. Give the other half to a single parent to use some evening when

he or she doesn't have the energy to cook.

8. Make yourself available as a listener. Sometimes all a single parent needs is a sympathetic ear or a shoulder to cry on. Of course, you'll need to be sure to keep everything you hear confidential.

9. If you can't afford to buy new clothes for a single parent, go through your closet and give him or her some of your own clothes—outfits that you've, ahem, "grown out of" or that you rarely wear anymore.

10. When you rent videos, offer them to a single parent while there is still time left on the rental. What could be better than providing a couple hours worth of entertainment at no extra cost to you? Unless, of course, you wanted to toss in some popcorn and Junior Mints with your gift.

One More Thing

The one thing you can't afford as a single parent is foolish pride. There is a world of resources and assistance available to you and your children. But you must take the initiative in searching them out.

It's not easy to accept the generosity of others—especially if you're not used to being on the receiving end of assistance. Your pride may try to convince you to keep your needs and struggles to yourself. Don't let it. (Think of it this way: Would you help someone in your situation if you knew about it? Right, and so will others if you'll let them know.)

There is no nobility in suffering—especially when the welfare of your children is at stake. Certainly, you should do everything in your power to provide for their financial and emotional needs. But there will come times when you'll need to accept—and perhaps even ask for—help from others.

That doesn't make you a charity case. It makes you someone who can appreciate firsthand the value of kindness and generosity. And it makes you the kind of person who will likely demonstrate those qualities to others as you have the opportunity.

The Buck Stops Here

Think you're an expert on budgeting as a single parent? Here's a quiz to see how much you know.

1. Which of the following is true of one out of every three families in this country?
   a. Believe *Mr. Roger's Neighborhood* inspires violence in children
   b. Complain about their house being "too clean"
   c. Would prefer to see the designated-hitter rule abolished in baseball
   d. Headed by a single parent

2. Which of the following is not a financial goal of most single parents?
   a. Being able to live within their means
   b. Providing for their children's needs
   c. Getting out of debt and staying out of debt
   d. Purchasing a new china set for their formal dinner parties

3. Which of the following suggestions will not help you cut your housing costs?
   a. Teaching yourself to do simple home repairs
   b. Renting a room of your house
   c. Becoming an apartment manager
   d. Opting for the HBO digital cable package instead of the Showtime package

4. Which of the following is not true of welfare?
   a. It's mandatory for all single parents.
   b. Once you're on it, it's difficult to get off it.
   c. It determines the amount of money you can earn.
   d. It allows the government to decide whether you can work outside the home or not.

5. Which of the following would probably not be much help to a single parent?
   a. Preparing a meal that he or she could freeze and reheat at a later time
   b. Providing babysitting service for a night
   c. Complaining about the appearance of his or her child
   d. Writing a note of encouragement

Answers: (1) d, (2) d, (3) d, (4) a, (5) c

CHAPTER 13

Train Children in the Way They Should Go

and When They Are Old, You Can Borrow Money from Them

SNAPSHOT

Kim stared at the envelope she had just opened. She sat motionless, except for her mouth, which dropped open.

"What is it?" Andy asked.

"It's a birthday card for Caleb from my Uncle Maurice," Kim explained. "There's a check for $500 in it."

"Five hundred dollars?" Andy asked. "For a boy who's just turning four? I can't wait to see what he sends when Caleb graduates from college!"

"Can I buy a Happy Meal, Mom?" Caleb asked, looking at his check.

"You can buy a Happy Meal every day for the next year," Andy muttered low enough that his son couldn't hear.

SNEAK PREVIEW

1. The best way to teach your children about finances is to let them observe your financial habits and know your financial goals.

2. Teaching your children the right attitudes toward finances is as important as teaching them how to budget or how to maintain a checking account.

3. Giving your kids responsibility for their own budget is the best way to introduce them to the world of finance.

"Should we let him spend it?" Kim asked. "Maybe take him to a T-O-Y-S-T-O-R-E and let him pick out $500 worth of things he wants?" (Certain words are always spelled out, never spoken aloud, in the Cleese household.)

"Or we could do something boring, like put it into savings," Andy suggested.

"Too bad Caleb doesn't know anything about money," Kim said. "It would be nice to know what he would like to do with it."

* * * * * * * * * * * * * * * *

When he was eight years old, Gary gave his older brother a $20 bill in exchange for a $5 bill. But this was not a case of a youngster being suckered by a mischievous older sibling. The trade was Gary's idea, part of a carefully thought out investment plan. You see, the next day was February 12, Abraham Lincoln's birthday. Gary believed that anything with Lincoln's picture on it, such as a $5 bill, would be worth much more than its normal value on that day. He was so sure of his strategy that he was willing to risk the $20 his grandmother had given him for his birthday.

Cute story, right? (It happens to be true.) On the one hand, you have the magical elements of childhood, when even the most farfetched ideas can seem right and logical. On the other hand, you have the humorous notion of an eight-year-old thinking about an investment opportunity.

But what if we were to change one little part of the story? What if, instead of being eight years old, Gary was *18*? Suddenly the story's not so cute anymore. The idea of an 18-year-old with such a naive financial outlook is a little pathetic and disturbing.

A lot more money sense is demanded from an 18-year-old than from an eight-year-old. But why? What is expected to happen in that 10-year span? Where can kids to go to learn to be financially savvy? Who's going to instruct them? (Hint: Read the title of this chapter again.)

The responsibility of teaching your kids what they need to know about finances falls squarely on your shoulders, like it or not. Protest all you want, but your kids will learn about finances from you, one way or another, and there's not much you can do to change that. The decision you have to make is whether they will learn healthy financial strategies or damaging financial habits.

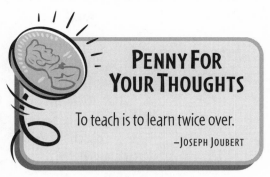

PENNY FOR YOUR THOUGHTS

To teach is to learn twice over.

—JOSEPH JOUBERT

Maybe you spotted the irony of the situation. Your kids are looking to you for financial wisdom, and you're reading a book called *The World's Easiest Guide to Finances*. Don't panic. Remember, nobody's asking you to explain quantum physics to a seven-year-old child. The fact is, if you've ever cashed a check, paid a bill, or set up a budget, you have financial knowledge that your kids can use.

The first step in sharing your knowledge is finding out how much or how little your kids already know about finances.

What Do You Know?

The following list of questions is designed to get your kids talking about financial topics. From these conversations, you should be able to get a fairly accurate picture of what they know and don't know about finances. That information will help you find the best starting place in talking to your kids about their financial future.

For example, if you ask, "Why do we need money?" and your daughter replies, "What's money?" you'll know you need to start with the absolute basics (i.e., "This is a quarter. Don't eat it."). If you ask, "What are taxes?" and your son launches into an impassioned argument for converting your savings into tax-free money market funds, you'll know. . . you're in trouble.

PENNY FOR YOUR THOUGHTS

The excesses of our youths are drafts upon our old age, payable with interest, about thirty years after date.

—CHARLES CALEB COLTON

These questions have been organized according to their level of difficulty, starting with the easiest ones and gradually getting harder. Depending on the age of your kids, you may want to skip the questions at the beginning of the list (to avoid insulting the intelligence of older kids) or at the end of the list (to avoid frustrating younger kids).

1. Why do we need money?
2. How do we get money?
3. What can you do with money?
4. What do banks do?
5. How does a credit card work?
6. How do checks work?
7. What is debt?
8. What is interest?
9. What is a budget?
10. What are taxes?
11. Name the bills our family pays each month.
12. What is a mortgage?
13. How much do we spend on groceries each month?
14. How much money would you need each month to live on your own?

After you've gotten a reading on your kids' financial I.Q., you can start to think about how to fill in the gaps in their knowledge. To do that, though, first you will need to stir their curiosity.

Money See, Money Do

If you believe your kids are going to jump at the chance to learn basic financial principles from you, we would like to take this opportunity to welcome you and the rest of the Cleaver family to the 21st century.

Think of the sports leagues, TV shows, videos, and computer games that are competing for your kids' time and attention. Consider this: If *you* had a choice between ridding the world of computer-generated space zombies or discussing compound interest with your parents, which would you choose?

We're not suggesting that your kids are doomed to financial ignorance for the rest of their lives because they can't pull themselves away from the TV screen. We're suggesting that if you want your financial voice to be heard, you will need to arrange for teachable moments to use it.

The best kind of teachable moments are the ones that allow your kids to be directly involved in what's going on. Instead of giving your kids a three-point lecture on the function of banks in our society, ask them to ride along the next time you go to make a deposit. On the way, start a casual conversation about why putting money in banks makes more sense than keeping it in your house. Show the kids your deposit slip and explain how you filled it out. Let them take turns pushing the button for the funky vacuum tube, if you use the drive-through lanes. When your receipt comes back, ask them to make sure that the amount written on it is the same amount you deposited. (But when they ask why your account balance is so low, change the subject and pretend not to know what they're talking about.)

They may not be ready to pass a banker's exam when they get home, but they probably will have a new appreciation for, and perhaps even an interest in, what goes on in a bank. And that's a great start.

A Backstage Pass to the Adult World

One thing you have going for you as a financial instructor is your kids' natural curiosity about how the adult world functions. Ask your kids if they want to hear about dividend reinvestment strategies, and you'll probably be met with blank stares. Ask them if they'd like to help you pay this month's bills, and you'll probably be met with eager anticipation.

With a little dramatic flair, you can take this concept to the next level by giving your kids the impression that they're getting an exclusive peek behind the scenes of your family's financial empire (or village, as the case may be).

Spread all of your monthly bills on a table and let your kids look through them. Explain what each bill is for. Check out your long distance bill to see how much, say, a call to Grandma costs. Compare your current electric bill with last month's and explain why it went up or down. Ask your kids to read the amount you owe on each bill so that you can write the check for it. While you work, talk about why checks are more convenient than cash for paying bills. Keep the vibe light, loose, and funny.

If your kids aren't careful, they might learn something from the experience. They may come away with a basic understanding of why people use checks and a new awareness that things they take for granted, like electricity and water, actually cost money.

Keep in mind that kids tend to absorb information by osmosis. The more they are exposed to and the closer they are to the action, the more they will absorb.

Once you have your kids' curiosity aroused about financial matters, you can move on to more specific instruction.

Talk the Talk

In order for your kids to take the next step toward financial understanding, they need to learn what certain basic terms mean. Your responsibility is to teach the definitions of these terms in a way that doesn't trigger vocabulary test flashbacks in your kids.

The best way to keep your discussions of these terms interesting is to attach some personal elements to them. For example, when you talk about income, tell your kids about some of the unusual ways you earned money when you were their age. When you talk about savings, tell them about some of the most memorable things you ever did with your money—not just the wise purchases, but the dumb ones as well.

A word of explanation here: In the following paragraphs, you'll find definitions of eight different terms that cover the basic principles of personal finance. But you may notice something different about the wording of these definitions. They might seem a little, well, childish. Don't take it personally; they are just definitions that you can use to explain these terms to your kids.

Income is the money you get. Some of it comes from your allowance, some from birthday or Christmas gifts, some from a job, and some from other places.

Savings is the income you don't spend right away, the money you hold on to for a while. Every time you get a little money, you can add some of it to your savings. After saving for a while, you'll have enough money to buy something you really want.

Some people save for a short time so that they will have enough money to buy a skateboard or Nintendo game. Others save for a long time so that they will have enough to buy a scooter, a Nintendo system, or even a car.

Most adults keep their savings in banks. When you put money for savings in a bank, it's called a *deposit*.

Banks like it when you keep your savings in them. They like it so much that they give you a little extra money each month on top of what you deposit. This extra money is called *interest*.

At first, the interest banks give you may not seem like much. If you have $100 in the bank, you might get 50 cents a month in interest. But the more money you put in a bank and the longer you leave it there, the more interest you will get (this is called compound interest).

Investments are like savings except, instead of putting money in a bank, you buy something, such as land, that you think will be valuable someday. Or you buy part of a company that you think will be successful one day. If the item or property you buy becomes valuable, you can sell it for more money than you paid for it. If the company you invest in makes money, it will share it with you. The more money the company makes, the more it will share with you.

On the other hand, if the item or property doesn't become valuable or if the company doesn't become successful, you won't make any money from them. Even worse, you won't be able to get back the money you paid for them.

Credit lets you buy something now and pay for it later. For example, when you purchase something at a store with a credit card, the store's computer keeps track of what you bought. But instead of making you pay for it right there, the store tells the credit card company how much you spent. At the end of the month, the credit card company sends you a list of all the things you bought and tells you how much money you owe.

Debt occurs when you don't have enough money to pay for the things you buy. Debt is a serious problem for a lot of people. If you buy something on credit and can't afford to pay for it, the people you bought it from won't be very happy.

If they're really mad, they might take you to court and ask a judge to make you sell the things you own to pay what you owe.

A *budget* is a chart that shows all of the money you make each month and all of the money you pay each month (for things like your house, food, and electricity). If you use it right, a budget can tell you where you're spending more money than you should.

Obviously this is not a comprehensive list, but it is a good start. If you can help your kids grasp the basic concept of these eight terms, you'll give them a foundation to build on as they learn more and more about personal finances.

Let's Get Practical

After your kids have learned to talk the talk financially, it's time for them to start walking the walk. The following tips will help you guide your kids as they embark on their own financial adventures.

Make allowances part of the training process.

Unless your kids hit it big in Internet stocks, it's likely that an allowance is their major source of income. As the one who holds the family purse strings, you have the leverage to use your kids' allowance to teach them some valuable lessons about money.

Your first challenge is to give your kids the right amount for their allowance. It should be a large enough sum that they look forward to receiving it, but it shouldn't be so large that it takes care of all their wants and needs. Remember, you want them to learn how to budget and save for the things they want.

It's better to err on the conservative side at first. Otherwise, you may have to explain why you're *reducing* your kids' allowance. As a general rule, taking money away from kids usually doesn't go over well at all.

Just as you get raises at work, your kids should get allowance raises. What kind of boss would you be if you were still paying your employees the same salaries they were making five years ago?

Don't be too extravagant, though. Eventually you'll want to encourage your kids to find part-time jobs outside the home, so you don't want their allowance raises to match their increasing budgets. As your kids get older, their allowance should become a smaller and smaller part of their total income.

You'll also want to use your kids' allowance to teach them the value of work. Don't pay for half-completed jobs. Don't reward laziness. If something isn't done right, dock some pay. Make your kids earn their money. Keep in mind that everything you do with your kids' allowance should reflect the real world as closely as possible, especially its systems of rewards and punishments for employees.

Govern your kids' spending habits.
If your kids are new to the world of consumerism, you will be doing them a favor by setting some ground rules as to how much of their money they may spend at once. Don't make the rules too restrictive, though; you want your kids to experience the freedom of spending their money on what they want to buy. You also want to give them room to make occasional mistakes in their purchases—mistakes they can learn from later.

Encourage your kids to think hard about their spending choices, but don't throw past mistakes at them. You don't want to paralyze their confidence in their own decision-making. When you see them make wise buying decisions, point them out and give them plenty of praise. That's the way they learn.

Your goal is to slowly develop financial discipline and wisdom in your kids. It won't happen overnight; but, if you're consistent, eventually the seeds of responsibility you sow will take root in their lives and yield results in their future financial dealings.

Teach your kids about tithing.
Even young children can understand the concept that everything we have comes from God. Building on that understanding, help your kids see that giving back part of everything we receive is a way of showing that our money is God's. Explain that when we give 10 percent of our income to the church in the offering plate, it's called a *tithe*.

To help give your kids a sense of how much 10 percent of your income is, try using cash for your tithe one week instead of writing a check. Ask your kids to help you stuff the money into the collection envelopes.

When it comes to your kids' tithes, help them recognize the importance of giving their money back to God by requiring them to set aside their tithe before they do anything else with their money. Start this practice early enough with your kids and it may become a habit by the time they hit their teenage years.

Giving your kids money to drop into the collection plate at church or Sunday school is not the way to introduce them to tithing. If it's not their money to begin with, they can't really get a sense of giving it back to God. That's why it's important that your kids start to tithe their own money as early as possible.

To take the concept one step further, ask your church leaders to consider setting up a fund, perhaps through a missions organization, especially for young tithers. Sponsoring a third world child, for example, would be a great introduction to tithing for your kids.

Not a Mouseketeer, a Budgeteer

Once your kids have a basic understanding of what money is and what it can be used for, you can introduce the concept of being a "budgeteer."

We can hear the objections now. *A budget? My son still thinks dirt is an appetizer, and you think he's ready to start allocating his money?*

Relax. We're not trying to raise a generation of preteen accountants and auditors. We're not talking about reviewing complex financial spreadsheets with your 4-year-old. We're talking about teaching your kids that some of their money should be given back to God, some of it should be saved, and some of it can be spent. We're talking about giving your kids a sense of responsibility for the way they use their money.

Your kids' earliest budget should be a model of simplicity. When your kids are between the ages of 3 and 5, set up three piggy banks (or anything that could double as money containers) in their room—one for giving (or tithes), one for savings, and one for spending. Start your kids' budgeting career by having them drop quarters (or dollar bills) in each bank. Explain that whenever they receive money, they should divide it evenly among the three banks.

When your kids reach the age of 6 or 7, try introducing the concept of percentages to their budgets. Explain that 10 percent of all the money they receive should go for tithes, 50 percent should go for savings, and 40 percent should go for spending. Be sure to volunteer your services as "percentage figurer," since your kids will probably have no idea what 40 percent of anything is.

To make budgeting as easy as possible for your kids, give them their allowance money in increments that are easy to divide (break a dollar into change; give four ones and change instead of a $5 bill). To make it a little more interesting and visual, put a picture of whatever your kids are saving for on the savings bank.

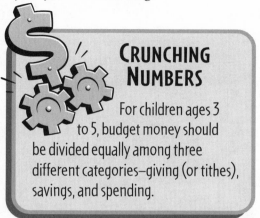

CRUNCHING NUMBERS

For children ages 3 to 5, budget money should be divided equally among three different categories—giving (or tithes), savings, and spending.

When your kids are between the ages of 9 and 12, try setting up a little more complex budget—one that allots 10 percent for tithes, 25 percent for short-term savings, 25 percent for long-term savings, and 40 percent for spending.

For the short-term category, help your kids think of something that will take three to six weeks to save for, based on how much money they generally receive in a week. For the long-term category, help your kids think of something that will take three to six months to save for. Explain that as soon as the waiting period is over, you will take your kids to buy what they have been saving for.

CRUNCHING NUMBERS

For children ages 6 to 8, budget money should be divided among three categories—10 percent for giving (or tithes), 50 percent for savings, and 40 percent for spending.

After your kids have reached their short-term and long-term savings goals a few times, allow them to extend the time periods so that they can target more expensive items. For example, the short-term savings period could be extended to as much as two or three months; the long-term period could be extended to as much as a year.

Be sure to celebrate each successful savings venture. Give your kids a sense of accomplishment when they meet their goals.

This is also a good age to introduce your kids to the concept of recording financial information. Give them notebooks and encourage them to write down their savings' goals (both short-term and long-term) and then keep track of their progress each week.

Your goal is to get your kids in the habit of keeping tabs on their finances. When the time comes for them to make entries in a checkbook register or a savings account book, they will be old pros at the financial recording game.

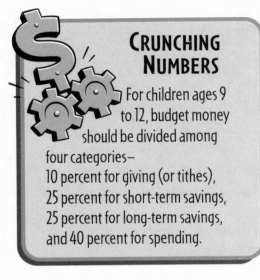

CRUNCHING NUMBERS

For children ages 9 to 12, budget money should be divided among four categories—
10 percent for giving (or tithes),
25 percent for short-term savings,
25 percent for long-term savings,
and 40 percent for spending.

A Budget Fit for a Teen

As your kids enter their teen years, their budgets should reflect their burgeoning maturity. Soon adult expenses will crowd their way into the financial picture. Rather than letting those expenses catch your kids by surprise, help your teens prepare for them by including representative categories in their budget.

For young people ages 13 to 18, income should be divided like this:

10 percent for giving
 5 percent for "community taxes"
25 percent for short-term savings
25 percent for long-term savings
10 percent for expenses
25 percent for spending.

The new "community taxes" category is designed to prepare your kids for the unpleasantness of paying taxes—without actually getting the IRS involved. Here's how to make it work. Set up a "bank" somewhere in your house where your kids' community taxes will be deposited and stored. Join in the fun by committing yourself to matching your teens' contributions each week.

After you've collected a sizable chunk of "tax" money, call a family meeting to decide what to buy with it. Whatever you decide on should benefit your entire family—perhaps a portable stereo for the garage or a DVD of your family's favorite movie.

The new "expenses" category is intended to prepare your kids for utilities and other monthly bills. After you figure out what 10 percent of their income is, find a regular expense that matches that amount. It might be a phone bill (if your kids have a private line), a call-waiting feature that was added specifically for your kids, or a magazine subscription.

When the bills for your chosen expense arrive each month, let your kids take care of them—not only by paying them from their own funds, but by checking the bills to make sure they're accurate and by organizing and filing them in an orderly manner.

> ## CRUNCHING NUMBERS
>
> For young people ages 13 to 18, budget money should be divided among five categories—10 percent for tithes, 5 percent for "community taxes," 25 percent for short-term savings, 25 percent for long-term savings, 10 percent for expenses, and 25 percent for spending.

Checks and Balances

When you picture your kids with a checkbook, does the image fill you with pride or terror? Get used to the idea, because at some point in their teenage years your kids will need to open checking and savings accounts of their own.

When that day comes, you might want to play up the occasion as a "welcome to adulthood" celebration. Take your kids to the bank yourself to help them set up their accounts. Ask a teller or bank official to explain the responsibilities and benefits of the accounts. Encourage your kids to ask any questions they may have.

With checkbooks and savings accounts of their own, your teens are ready for the last step in budget training. Here's how it goes. You spend some time acquainting your kids with your family's budget. You show them where you keep your bills, how you record, and what method you use to pay them. Then you turn over responsibility for your family's budget to them . . . for six months.

GLAD YOU ASKED

Should I help my teenager get a credit card? If so, at what age?

Applying for a credit card is one of the easiest ways for a young person to establish a credit record–something that will prove useful when it's time to buy a house. On the other hand, a credit card in the hands of a teen is a shopping spree waiting to happen. Your best bet is to wait until your teenager consistently demonstrates that he or she can follow monthly budgets before you even bring up the topic of getting a credit card.

The answer to your inevitable next question is, Yes, seriously!

Think about it. When it's time for your kids to learn to drive, what do you do? You risk life, limb, and insurance credit rating, not to mention your car's well-being, to give them experience behind the wheel.

Why not apply that same principle to budgeting and let your kids "climb behind the wheel" of your family's finances? It's a little risky, but the potential rewards are worth the risk. If your kids can learn to manage your family's finances, they will have the confidence and experience they need to manage their own budget later in life.

Beyond Dollars and Cents

In addition to guiding your kids through the practical aspects of personal finance, you need to equip them with a basic sense of what's wise, what's foolish, and what's right, and what's wrong when it comes to money.

Standing in your way are a few problem attitudes that tend to cloud kids'—and adults'—minds. Let's take a look at a couple of these attitudes to see if we can help your kids recognize the danger in them.

Want equals need.

This attitude can be illustrated with a simple sentence: "I need a new bike." If your kids are past the training-wheel stage, chances are you've heard this statement more than once before.

But unless the old bike has been stolen or destroyed, that's probably not an accurate statement. What's usually meant by a sentence like this is, "I want a bike that is newer or more deluxe than the one I have now."

The differences between the two statements are subtle, but significant. Learning to make do with what we have and save for what we want is at the heart of responsible money management.

If we can change "wants" into "needs," we can justify wrecking our budgets to buy them. After all, it was a *need*. . . . That's why it's important to teach your kids to recognize the difference between the two.

To determine whether something is a want or a need, your kids must learn to honestly assess how their lives would be affected if that item were missing from it. For example, a reliable car is a need. If it were missing from your life, you would have problems getting where you need to go. A CD changer in the glove compartment (or trunk) is a want. If it were missing, you would listen to the radio (or cassette player).

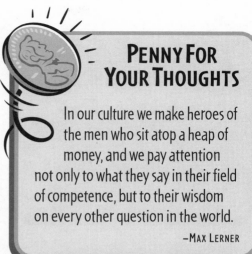

PENNY FOR YOUR THOUGHTS

In our culture we make heroes of the men who sit atop a heap of money, and we pay attention not only to what they say in their field of competence, but to their wisdom on every other question in the world.

—MAX LERNER

Gotta have it now.

This is the true legacy of television advertising: generations of people convinced that having something *now* is worth any price. You can find dozens of rationales for this attitude.

➤ I deserve it.

➤ It will change my life.

➤ If I don't get it, someone else will.

➤ If I don't have it, it will reflect badly on me.

The best way to combat this attitude is to require your kids to wait at least 48 hours before they purchase anything. You want to give them time to get past their initial urge to buy. After the "now" wears off, let your kids rethink whether they've "gotta have it." If they decide they still want it 48 hours later and they have the money, let them buy it.

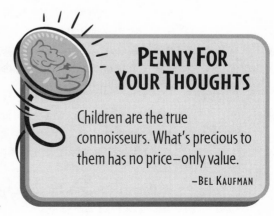

PENNY FOR YOUR THOUGHTS

Children are the true connoisseurs. What's precious to them has no price—only value.

—BEL KAUFMAN

PENNY FOR YOUR THOUGHTS

Children have never been very good at listening to their elders, but they have never failed to imitate them.

—JAMES BALDWIN

Lead by Example

In this chapter, we've focused on things you can say and skills you can teach to help equip your kids for their financial future. But the most valuable contribution you can make to their well-being is as a role model in your financial dealings.

If your kids see you working hard for your money, giving back to God a portion of what He has given you, planning your budget carefully, and maintaining a sense of integrity in all your financial dealings, there's a good chance they will follow in your footsteps.

How's that for pressure?

The Buck Stops Here

Think you've got what it takes to teach your kids about finances? Here's a quiz to see how much you know.

1. Which of the following questions is most likely to get your kids talking about finances?
   a. How conservative should the federal reserve chairman be during an economic upswing?
   b. How can we end the problem of soft money in election campaigns?
   c. Is a flat tax even conceivable in our society?
   d. How do banks work?

2. Why is it not a good idea to give your kids money to drop in the collection plate at church?
   a. They will get in the habit of asking for money anytime they see anyone pass a plate.
   b. There's too much of a temptation for them to pocket it.

c. They don't get a sense of tithing their own money.

d. You're not allowed to claim it as a charitable deduction if someone else actually drops the money into the plate.

3. What is the purpose of the "expenses" category in the budget for teens?

a. To get back some of the money you spend each month trying to keep them fed

b. To prepare them for monthly bills in their adult budget

c. To fill in that extra 10 percent that was left over in the budget as a result of a math error

d. To drive them crazy as they try to figure out what it's for

4. Why should you have your kids write their savings totals in a notebook?

a. To get them used to keeping track of their financial transactions

b. To let you know how much money they have available to borrow

c. To keep them busy for at least 15 minutes

d. To make them feel guilty when that money is gone

5. Which of the following will likely have the longest-lasting effect on your kids' financial decision-making?

a. The example you set for them

b. The career they pursue

c. The type of checking account they choose

d. The how-to books they read

Answers: (1) d, (2) c, (3) b, (4) a, (5) a

Underfunded Undergraduates

SNAPSHOT

"**I** found one!" Kristi's mother called out excitedly. She was grinning as she pointed at the tiny type in the big reference book she was holding. "The Dewey L. Miller Scholarship for freshman women majoring in golf course maintenance."

"Oh, Mom, I hate golf. You know that," Kristi reminded her.

"But you always do a good job when you cut the grass," her mother quipped. "Maybe you have a natural gift for lawn care. Besides, do you really want to let a silly hatred for golf stand in the way of a $2,000 scholarship?"

"Here's another one," Kristi's father interjected in his most serious voice. "The Angus MacLeish Foundation awards a $500 scholarship for the best original bagpipes composition."

"Dad, I play clarinet," Kristi responded with a big sigh.

> ### SNEAK PREVIEW
>
> 1. Most higher education options are pricey, but some are much more expensive than others.
> 2. Scholarships, grants, and student loans can soften the financial blow you take from your college education.
> 3. The more you prepare, financially and academically, before you go to college, the better off you'll be afterward.

"I can't imagine that's much different from playing bagpipes," her dad teased. "For $500, you might want to see what you can come up with."

"How about this one?" Kristi asked sarcastically, pointing to a book on the table. "The Fresh Start organization offers up to $1,500 a semester for high school seniors whose parents are in jail."

"Does it have to be a felony conviction, or can it be a misdemeanor?" her dad asked slyly.

"Look, I really appreciate your help," Kristi peevishly told her parents, "but I think you guys are taking this college financial assistance stuff a little too seriously."

Her mother smiled mischievously as she said, "Honey, we'd really love to talk about this—*after* you finish your bagpipes composition."

* * * * * * * * * * * * * * *

This chapter is no place for the squeamish. In the next several pages, you will be exposed to statistics that may shake you, expenses that may make your skin crawl, and projections that may cause you to pause and think. If you are faint of heart, turn back now. Those who proceed past this point do so at their own risk.

Come with us now, ye who dare. Look upon the horror that is . . . college financing.

Okay, let's not make the idea of affording college any scarier than it has to be. The fact is, you have a variety of choices when it comes to your higher education, some of which you may never have considered before (and some you may never consider again after you finish this chapter).

Let's take a look at some of these different options to see if we can find one that's right for you.

The Road Not Taken

Your first option is not to go to college. (That dull thud you heard in the background was your mother fainting.) That may seem like an unthinkable choice for some people; but for others it makes a lot of sense.

Here's an example. Roger started working with his father in his successful carpentry business when he was 5 years old. Over the years, he became such a skilled craftsman that on his 17th birthday, his father offered him a full-time, salaried position in the company. He gave Roger a year to think about it.

PENNY FOR YOUR THOUGHTS

College [is] a washing machine; you get out of it just what you put in, but you'd never recognize it.

—ANONYMOUS PROFESSOR

Roger knows that he wants to be a carpenter and he loves working for his father. Even though he's always been interested in college, he's not sure he would gain anything from going. His father taught him not only carpentry skills but business skills as well. Roger knows his father's accounting procedures, billing practices, and marketing strategies better than almost anyone else in the company—including those who graduated from college.

Rather than spending money to go to college, Roger could be making money in his chosen career. He would have at least a four-year head start on his peers, financially speaking, and would never have to worry about repaying a financial loan.

Do you think it would make sense for Roger to go to college?

Here's another example. The first generation of kids who grew up with computers are self-reliant do-it-yourselfers. They taught themselves how to write programs, build Web sites . . . and hack into the Pentagon's classified files.

They didn't need books and lectures. They spent hour after hour, day after day, week after week, pounding their keyboards and unlocking the mysteries of the wired world. And in the process, they created potentially lucrative career paths for themselves.

PENNY FOR YOUR THOUGHTS

College education: something that shows a man how little other people know.

—T.C. HALIBURTON

As the Internet changed the way people did business, dot-com companies began popping up like lilies after a spring rain. Suddenly tens of thousands of computer jobs were waiting to be filled—not necessarily by college graduates but by anyone with computer skills.

Many computer-savvy high school graduates were faced with a choice: accept a job with (in some cases) a six-figure salary or start all over as a freshman in school again.

You tell us: which option makes more sense?

Let's be clear here. We're not suggesting that job advancement is the only thing you need to consider when it comes to college. It's not. In fact, most graduates of higher education will tell you that career preparation is only a small part of what college has to offer. There's also the social growth that develops from interacting with a large number of people from many different backgrounds. There's the spiritual growth that comes from applying your faith to new situations and challenges. And there are the friendships you form—the kind that are unlike any other relationships you'll ever have in your life.

Before we get too sentimental and start dragging out old yearbooks and singing our college fight song, let's summarize the issue this way: Unless the career you've chosen requires it, college is not necessarily your best option. If you choose to bypass college, you will miss out on opportunities and experiences that you won't get anywhere else. But if the benefits don't outweigh the drawbacks, college may not be for you—at least not right now.

The Parade of Options

Now that we've gotten that little side trip out of the way, we can move on to the issue at hand. The fact is, you probably wouldn't be reading this chapter if you hadn't already made up your mind that college is right for you.

But which college?

You have, literally, thousands of choices when it comes to your higher education. There are private colleges, state universities, community colleges, Christian colleges, and technical schools. And though the cost of education is different for each school, most colleges and universities can be divided into two general categories: the expensive ones and the really expensive ones.

Let's take a look at the different kinds of schools to see which one fits your needs and your budget.

Private/state universities

If you want a smaller facility, this is the type of school for you. Want to major in upholstery or memorabilia collecting? Try a private or state university. Even if you can't specialize in your chosen field, you probably will be able to take classes that cover the material you're interested in.

Large universities offer educational opportunities that few small colleges can match. Their sizeable endowment funds translate into state-of-the-art facilities and equipment. Their larger campuses provide more varied social interactions. Their sports teams are often competitive on a national level (which might be important to some people).

Of course, bigger isn't always better. Some people complain about the impersonal nature of large universities. Unlike small colleges, where you have a chance to meet and get to know most of your classmates, large colleges leave many people feeling like just another face in the crowd.

GLAD YOU ASKED

What factors, other than price, should I consider when choosing a college?

Your first consideration should be your career plans. Does the school you're considering offer a program that will thoroughly equip you to enter a competitive job market? Beyond that, rely on your instincts. Does the campus seem like a place where you would want to spend the next four years of your life? Do the students seem friendly? Does college life there seem enjoyable?

The average annual cost for tuition, books, and room and board at a state university is approximately $8,500 for in-state students and $11,000 for out-of-state students. The average annual cost at a private university is over $22,000. (But with a little extra effort, you could probably break the $100,000 mark over four years.)

Community colleges

Many people choose to start their undergraduate careers at a community college and then transfer to a state university for their last couple of years. (Most employers don't care where you start your education; most aren't even interested in where you finished it.)

Community colleges give students a chance to test the waters of higher education in a low pressure—and, more importantly, low cost—setting. They allow students

to get acquainted with college-level courses, improve their grades, decide on a major, and save money by living at home.

On the other hand, with their limited budgets, community colleges can only afford to offer a "meat and potatoes" education. If you're looking to specialize in a particular area or if you want experience with more costly high-tech equipment, you'll probably need to transfer to a larger institution to get the training you need.

The average annual cost for tuition and books at a community college is about $2,000. (Take a gander at those rates for state and private universities again, and you'll see why community colleges are a popular choice for financially minded students.)

Christian colleges

Christian colleges provide competitive educational opportunities in a Christian environment. They offer courses like youth ministry, Christian education, and missions; these can't be found in other institutions. But perhaps most significantly, they provide an opportunity for people with a lot of very important things in common to build lasting relationships with each other.

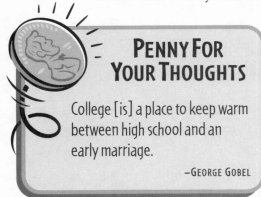

One of the major drawbacks is that most Christian colleges cost a lot, compared to state and community colleges. You have to decide how much a Christian education is worth to you. In addition, even though I don't agree, some people believe that a Christian college environment shelters students from the "real world" and doesn't give them enough exposure to beliefs and ways of thinking that are different from theirs.

The average cost for tuition, books, and room and board at a Christian college is over $13,000.

Vocational/technical schools

Vocational and technical schools offer certification and training in specialized trades, such as plumbing, carpentry, auto mechanics, nursing, welding, and 3-D computer animation. Students get valuable, hands-on experience—often using high-tech equipment—in their chosen career path. Instructors are often working professionals in their fields.

Since many of the students are already working, vocational and technical schools offer flexible hours and shorter courses. Because of the instructors' close links to the business, graduates often have an inside track for apprenticeships and job openings.

Unfortunately, high-tech training doesn't come cheap. Some nine-month courses can run as high as $12,000. Others aren't quite as expensive, but still require a serious outlay of cash.

Will That Be Cash or Charge?

Let's say your parents aren't exactly rushing for their checkbooks to cover your college expenses. Let's say that when the final bill for your education comes due, it has—gulp—your name on it.

Look back at those price tags for the different types of colleges. Multiply those numbers by four if you plan to complete your education in a normal four-year program. (Multiply them by five if you plan to major in frat parties your freshman year.) Add another grand or two to cover inflation costs. Go splash some water on your face; then come back and add everything up.

That's what your college education will cost.

Even if you go to the cheapest school you can find ("Welcome to Fred's Community College"), you'll still be looking at a bill of close to five figures when you graduate.

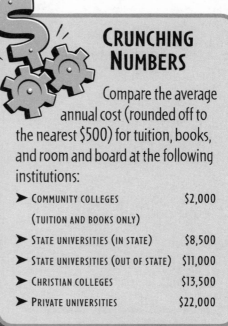

CRUNCHING NUMBERS

Compare the average annual cost (rounded off to the nearest $500) for tuition, books, and room and board at the following institutions:

➤ COMMUNITY COLLEGES $2,000
   (TUITION AND BOOKS ONLY)

➤ STATE UNIVERSITIES (IN STATE) $8,500

➤ STATE UNIVERSITIES (OUT OF STATE) $11,000

➤ CHRISTIAN COLLEGES $13,500

➤ PRIVATE UNIVERSITIES $22,000

If the cost of education seems impossibly high to you, you're not alone. Most students and their families can't afford to pay for college, no matter how long they've been saving for it.

That's why one of the most popular stops on all college tours is the financial aid office. Let's take a look at the three most popular forms of financial assistance for college: scholarships, grants, and student loans.

Scholarships

Probably the best-known type of scholarship is the athletic free ride, an all-expenses-paid trip through college for football players who bench press 350 pounds and for basketball players who can slam dunk from the locker room. These scholarships are paid for by the schools themselves.

GLAD YOU ASKED

What's the best strategy for applying for scholarships?

Avoid the "shotgun" approach, in which you send as many applications as possible out into the void, hoping that one or two of them are on target. Instead, focus your efforts on the scholarships that you have a realistic chance of receiving. You only have time to write so many essays and fill out so many forms. Don't waste that time on long shots.

Generally, the athletes who qualify for these scholarships in major sports don't have to go looking for them. Schools come to them. If, however, you think your athletic prowess in a lower-profile sport such as tennis or golf might impress a college recruiter, ask your high school coach to make some calls on your behalf. It's worth a shot to see if you can get a tryout.

In addition to recruiting the best athletes available, schools also offer scholarships to the brightest students they can find. (The difference is that you don't hear a lot about those scholarship recipients on ESPN.) Obviously the competition for academic scholarships is fierce, but if your GPA is beyond respectable, you may qualify. Check with the college financial aid office for information on deadlines, eligibility, and applications for these scholarships.

Schools aren't the only places to look for financial assistance. Thousands of corporations, organizations, foundations, chambers of commerce, service groups, church denominations, alumni associations, and trade unions offer scholarships based on specific, and sometimes unusual, criteria. Your local library contains dozens of resources that tell you everything you need to know about applying and qualifying for these scholarships.

Grants

Federal and state grants are available to students with financial needs. Forget the jokes about *all* students needing finances. You have to be able to prove that your family can't afford to pay for your education in order to qualify for these grants. And you can't just dress your parents up in rags and have your siblings pretend to be hungry when you apply for the grants, either. You have to show tax records and other official documents.

The good news is that, like scholarships, these grants do not have to be repaid after college. For more information on applying for grants, contact your college financial aid office.

Student loans

Student loans are similar to scholarships and grants, with one minor exception: YOU HAVE TO PAY THEM BACK. For that reason, they should be considered the last resort on the road to college financial assistance.

Many students don't see it that way, however. They consider a student loan to be a necessary evil, a minor bump in the road to a college diploma and eventual financial success.

GLAD YOU ASKED

Should I pay a search firm to find potential scholarships for me?

Nope. Remember, saving money is the issue. Search firms don't have inside information on scholarships and grants that no one else knows about. They are just willing to do the dirty work of slogging through library and Internet resources to find information and opportunities that might apply to you. Keep your money and do the research yourself.

There's a real temptation to underestimate the effect a student loan will have on your post-college finances. You figure that after you graduate you'll get a good job and start bringing home some decent coinage. You figure your student loan will barely cause a ripple in your monthly budget.

And you'll learn the hard way that you figured wrong.

An annual salary of $30,000 or $40,000 may seem like a lot of money to you right now. But are you considering all of the expenses you're going to have when you move out of your parents' house? How much do you suppose you'll be paying for rent, utilities, car payments, and food each month? (Hint: A lot.)

Throw a student loan into the mix and your once-mighty salary is going to start looking awfully weak. At best, you might break even each month. At worst, you might find yourself sinking deeper and deeper into debt as you struggle to pay what you owe.

And please don't make the mistake of underestimating the length of your loan. Don't assume that you'll struggle for a year or so, pay off your debt, and then be home free. That's not how things work. Depending on the amount you borrow, there's a good chance that you will still be making payments on your student loans ten years from now.

Think about that. When you're in your 30s, you may still be paying for classes you took, rooms you stayed in, and meals you ate a decade earlier! That is the reality of student loans.

Money Savers

Even without scholarships and grants, it's possible to graduate from college without a debt that resembles the national debt. The following ideas all involve sacrifice and inconvenience. But when your college career is over, they may turn out to be some of the best decisions you ever make.

Live at home.

For state universities, the average annual cost of tuition is about $3,500. The average annual cost of room and board is about $5,000. Hello, Mom and Dad—goodbye, half your college bill.

What makes this idea especially economical is that while you live at home and attend an inexpensive—well, relatively inexpensive—community college for one or two years, you can work part-time and save money. When you're ready to transfer to a four-year college or university, you will have funds to put toward your bill.

If you're anxious for your freedom and independence, another year or two at home may seem like a life sentence. But that's nothing compared to the eternity of student loan payments.

Try a co-op program.

A co-op program allows you to go to school one semester and work the next. That may sound like a strange arrangement, since it adds another year to a traditional bachelor's degree program. But you can earn over $8,000 annually to apply to your college bills.

CRUNCHING NUMBERS

The average annual cost of tuition at a state university is about $3,500. The average annual cost of room and board is about $5,000.

Most universities have a co-op department that you can contact for details. Usually the department will make every effort to place you in a job related to your chosen field. (Can you say "networking opportunities"?) Unfortunately, there is no guarantee of success. It's also quite possible that you could be placed in a retail sales job or something else quite unexpected. You'll need to investigate the program carefully before you enroll.

Join the military.

Imagine yourself as a lean, mean fighting machine . . . with very little college debt. That's the scenario the U.S. military offers. If you join a reserve unit of any branch of the military or enlist in the Air or Army National Guard, you will receive over $100 a month for attending a weekend drill, plus another $190 for each month you remain in school. Add to that the extra money can you make for summer training, and you're looking at a golden opportunity to pay off your college expenses. In many instances, you can even get your college education paid for in full. Hup, two, three, four . . .

PENNY FOR YOUR THOUGHTS

College: a place where one spends several thousand dollars on an education, then prays for a holiday to come on a school day.

—BOSTON BEANPOT

Check out the Perkins Loan program.

If you have your sights set on a career in government service—law enforcement, the military, or the Peace Corps—or as a teacher in a low-income area, the federal Perkins Loan program can make a big difference in your financial situation. The Perkins Loan works like most other school loans, with one exception. Students who commit to certain government agencies after graduation don't have to repay the loan. Ever.

Find an on-campus job (or two).

Pssst! Want to know a secret about potential employers? They love to see work-study programs listed on an applicant's résumé. Holding down a job while completing your studies demonstrates dedication, discipline, and a strong work ethic, three qualities that make personnel directors drool.

So an on-campus job will benefit you not only in the short-term, by lining your pockets with cash, but also in the long-run by impressing job interviewers.

GLAD YOU ASKED

How many work hours should I schedule for myself each week?

Obviously, the more money you make (and apply to your college bill) now, the less you will have to pay later. But that doesn't mean you should gobble up every available working hour. Not only do you have a lot of studying to do, you have a social life to lead. Work as much as you can, but don't miss out on the college experience in the process.

The key to this money-saving idea is finding a job you like—or at least one that you can hold down without having your studies affected. The great thing about jobs on campus is that they are geared to fit students' schedules and lifestyles. That means bosses are usually understanding around test time.

Depending on your interests and skills, you might find a position in the student information center, dining hall, library, or bookstore. You might land a job as an administrative assistant to a professor. Or you might end up refereeing intramural sports.

Most colleges have job boards where openings are posted. Stake them out. Remember, there are hundreds of other people just like you looking for primo positions. The faster you act, the better chance you have of getting the job that best suits you and your schedule.

Take a year off to work and save money.

There is no age limit for freshmen. People who sit out a year after high school have found that when they do go to college, they have a greater appreciation of the experience. A year in the workforce not only will fatten your bank account, it also will give you some maturity and perspective on life—

things that will come in handy when you finally hit campus.

The most common objection to this idea is that you lose the opportunity to enter school with your friends and peers. But the brutal truth is that there comes a time in everyone's life when they have to go their own way, despite what everyone else is doing.

PENNY FOR YOUR THOUGHTS

College: a mental institution.

—ANONYMOUS

Regardless of which, if any, of these ideas you choose to pursue, remember this: If you genuinely commit yourself to getting a college education as cost-efficiently as possible, you will find ways to do it.

In the Meantime...

If college is still a few years away for you (or your kids), congratulations. You have time to prepare. Make the most of it. Specifically, there are three things you can do now to make your future college application process easier.

Raise that GPA.

You knew this was coming. The better your grades are, the more options you give yourself when college application time rolls around. It's important that you start working now, while your grade point average is still changeable. By the time you're a senior, there won't be a lot you can do to raise your average.

If you set an impressive GPA for yourself, you may be shocked by the number of colleges that send you literature and ask you to consider their campus. Some may even talk of scholarships or financial assistance.

Get involved in extracurricular activities.

Community service and extracurricular activities are almost as important as a GPA to college recruiters. That's why it pays to start building your résumé now. Find some clubs or charities that you would like to get involved with and dive in.

Organize a clothing drive for the homeless. Volunteer at a local retirement home or community center. Try beekeeping. Learn to square dance. Show future college recruiters just how well-rounded you are.

Research, research, research.

No, we're not harping on your study habits again. We're talking about investigating as many different scholarship and grant opportunities as you can find. Earlier we mentioned the various resources available for locating scholarships and grants. You need to spend time with those resources—a lot of time.

Each time you find a scholarship or grant that might possibly apply to you, jot down all of the relevant information. If possible, contact a representative of the organization offering it. See if you can pick up some "inside information" that might help you when you apply.

The earlier you start your search—say, even as early as a couple of years before you're ready to go to college—the more time you'll have to meet the requirements of certain scholarships. Regardless of how obscure a scholarship opportunity may seem (the Sven Errickson Grant for ambidextrous Norwegian flute players), you can bet that there are thousands of students applying for it. The more of a head start you get on the field, the better your chances are of scoring some much needed college funding.

One More Thing

In the midst of all your studying, working, and applying, don't forget to enjoy your college career. These are the best years of your life. Don't let financial worries—or anything else—ruin them.

The Buck Stops Here

Think you're an expert on college finance? Here's a quiz to see how much you know.

1. Which of the following is true of state universities?
   a. By law, they may not charge more than $9,999.99 for tuition, room, and board.
   b. Most of them have strict student dress codes.

   c. They offer a broader range of majors and course options than other types of schools.

   d. Just because a school is named for a state doesn't mean it's actually located in that state.

2. Which of the following is often part of the scholarship application process?
   a. Essay writing
   b. Tap dancing
   c. Chainsaw juggling
   d. Apple polishing

3. What is a grant?
   a. A $50 bill
   b. The award given each year to the nation's top college
   c. A slab of stone, especially popular on college campuses, used for building construction
   d. A form of federal and state financial aid for people with financial needs

4. What is the major problem with using student loans to fund your education?
   a. You get stuck in the worst dorm on campus.
   b. You have to wait until everyone else has registered for classes before you get your turn.
   c. You have to pay the loans back.
   d. You have to wear an embroidered "SL" on your shirt at all school functions.

5. What would you recommend to someone with financial needs who is thinking about going to college?
   a. Pile on the student loans, skip town after graduation, and make the government find you if they want their money back.
   b. Find the best job on campus you can get.
   c. Try to get adopted by a wealthier family.
   d. Buy a lottery ticket.

Answers: (1) c, (2) a, (3) d, (4) c, (5) b

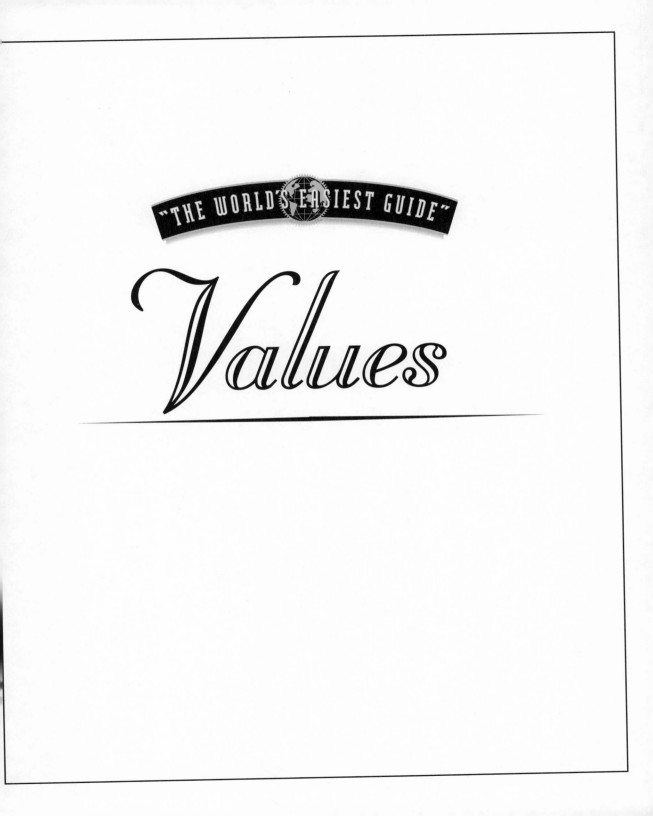

"THE WORLD'S EASIEST GUIDE"

Values

It's All in the Attitude

<u>S N A P S H O T</u>

"**W**hat's with the smile?" Charlotte asked as she sat down at the lunch table with Lindsay.

"You're looking at one debt-free woman," Lindsay explained. "I just paid off both of my credit cards."

"Wow, that's pretty good," Charlotte said. "You had some pretty big bills there for a while, didn't you?"

"Let's just say VISA used to send me hardcover editions of my monthly statements," Lindsay replied.

"You didn't fake your own death and use the insurance to pay them off, did you?" Charlotte quipped.

"Nope, didn't have to," Lindsay retorted. "I just started budgeting my money and using every extra penny to pay off my debts."

"Oh, so you did it the bor-ring way," Charlotte observed.

SNEAK PREVIEW

1. Your attitude toward your finances is every bit as important as budgeting, investing, or any other practical application.

2. It's what you do with your money—and not how much of it you have—that determines how financially successful you are.

3. No matter how bleak your financial situation may seem, you can improve it, even if it's just a little at a time.

"Hey, whatever works," Lindsay said. "Now, not only am I debt free, I also met my monthly budget for the first time ever."

"Are you turning into some kind of upstanding citizen or something?" Charlotte asked.

"I don't know about that," Lindsay said, "but I do know that I like the feeling of being financially stable."

"What are you going to do to celebrate?" Charlotte asked.

Lindsay replied, "Well, one thing I won't do is head to the mall and shop for new clothes. Not anymore!"

* * * * * * * * * * * * * * * *

What You Have Learned

So far in this book you've been told you to . . .

➤ divide your income among 12 different budget categories.

➤ wait until you can afford a down payment of at least 20 percent before you buy a house.

➤ update your will every year or so.

➤ buy used furniture for your first apartment.

➤ stop using credit cards.

So the obvious question is . . . Aren't you getting tired of people telling you what to do?

Your Financial Attitudes

For this chapter, I've ditched the how-to format. Instead, I've come up with a dozen basic tips for maintaining not only a healthy budget but a healthy financial attitude—now and for the rest of your life.

In no particular order, the tips are as follows.

1. Nobody likes an ingrate.

2. Little things mean a lot.

3. With money comes responsibility.

4. Money doesn't buy happiness.

5. Being passive gets you nowhere.

6. It's not what you have; it's how you use it.

7. A lifelong commitment is required.

8. Preparation is everything.

9. Everyone struggles.

10. Bad finances do not make a bad person.

11. Financial lessons are meant to be shared.

12. Things change.

Let's take a look at these nuggets of advice one at a time to see what kind of difference they might make in your life.

1. Nobody likes an ingrate.

In your rush to secure your future, don't lose sight of your present. (Sounds like something from a brokerage commercial, doesn't it?)

One of the problems with financial planning is that it focuses your attention on the things you need and want, at the expense of the things you have. You get so busy figuring out how to afford a bigger house, a new (used) car, and a college education for your kids that you take for granted your current residence, your current vehicle, and your current family situation.

➤ Maybe your house was last renovated during the Nixon administration.

➤ Maybe your car looks like a science fair project on the properties of oxidation.

➤ Maybe your kids' college fund wouldn't cover the gas it would take to drive them to campus.

The fact is, you have a lot to be thankful for.

Financial Blessings

If you have trouble recognizing the blessings in your life, ask your friends and family to point them out to you. Look around at people who are less fortunate than you are. Spend some time thinking about the things you take for granted and how you can start to show your appreciation for them. If you're comfortable with the idea, write some of your thoughts.

For example . . .

➤ The next time you find yourself looking out your front window on a snowy or rainy night, think about the protection your nice warm home offers you every night.

➤ The next time you start to complain about that flivver in your driveway, consider the $10,000 you saved on depreciation this year.

I'm not talking about a mystical communion with inanimate objects; I'm talking about a simple recognition of the fact that you have been blessed with certain material possessions.

True financial success is impossible without a spirit of gratitude. If you can't appreciate what you have now, you won't be able to appreciate anything you get later.

PENNY FOR YOUR THOUGHTS

Do not spoil what you have by desiring what you have not; but remember that what you now have was once among the things only hoped for.

—EPICURUS

2. Little things mean a lot.

If you've ever had a leaky faucet—and seen the resulting water bill—you know that little drips can add up over a period of time. That same principle applies to your financial bottom line.

Small adjustments in your everyday habits eventually will have more of an effect on your finances than, say, a $5,000 tax refund. Saving a dollar here and a dollar there may seem hardly worth the effort when you look at the short-term picture. But, multiply those savings year after year and you'll see that the effort pays off tremendously.

Here's an example. Let's say that by replacing all the light bulbs in your home with lower-watt bulbs you could save 15 percent, or roughly $10, each month on your electric bill.

Ten bucks a month. The cost of a couple value meals at McDonald's. Big deal, right?

Here's another example. Let's say that by turning off the faucet while you brush your teeth or wash dishes you could save 10 percent, or roughly $3, each month on your water bill.

Three dollars a month. The price of a candy bar and a root beer at a convenience store. Yawn.

One more example. Let's say that by using coupons when you shop, you could save $20 a month on your grocery bills.

Twenty dollars a month. Roughly the cost of one CD (with tax). Yippee.

CRUNCHING NUMBERS

If you borrowed $100,000 at 8 percent interest for 30 years to purchase your new home and then paid an extra $100 a month on the principal, you would save over $64,000 in interest and cut almost 10 years off your mortgage.

The point of this little story problem is not that you could save a total of $33 a month ($10 on the electric bill, $3 on the water bill, and $20 on groceries); the point is that you could save $33 a month with little or no effort on your part!

What if you were to add a few money-saving ideas of your own and apply them to other budget categories? How much do you think you could save each month— maybe $100? Still nothing to write home about. Right?

Let's say you took that $100 you saved each month and applied it to the principal of your mortgage. One hundred extra dollars a month, every month—a mere fraction of your actual mortgage payment.

Assuming that you have an average house loan of, say, $100,000 at 8 percent interest for 30 years, that extra $100 a month would eventually save over $64,000 in interest and cut almost 10 years off your mortgage.

Suddenly those "little things" don't seem so minor anymore, do they?

Drip. Drip. Drip.

3. With money comes responsibility.

When you dream about becoming rich—really rich—where does the dream usually end?

➤ On your own tropical island, with you lying in a hammock, watching sunsets for the rest of your life?

➤ In your own Aspen ski lodge, with you huddling around a giant fire after a day on the slopes?

➤ On your own private jet, with you tooling around the world, following no agenda other than enjoying yourself?

For some reason, visions of wealth tend to bring out the isolationist tendencies in people. We imagine ourselves removed from the rest of the world, enjoying life on our own terms, with no cares and no responsibilities.

The difference between the fantasy of wealth and reality can be summed up in one sentence: *To whom much is given much is expected.*

If you have money, you are expected to do good things with it. The more money you have, the higher the expectations are. It's the way our culture is set up. It's the way we are wired. It's the way our tax system is designed. True financial fulfillment can't be found apart from a generous, helping spirit.

If you're struggling to make car payments each month, it may not occur to you to categorize yourself as someone "to whom much as been given"—unless the *much* part refers to debt. But the fact is, we all have a responsibility to use a portion of what we earn to help others, no matter how laughably small that portion may seem at first.

As our earnings increase and our financial outlook brightens, our responsibility grows. And so does the pleasure we receive from giving.

There are traditional and nontraditional ways to help others with your money. For Christians, the tithe—giving 10 percent of everything you earn to the church and its ministries—is a traditional method of using your money in a positive way. Other people have favorite charities that they prefer to donate money and items to regularly.

Nontraditional methods of helping others with your money are limited only by your imagination.

For example, you could . . .

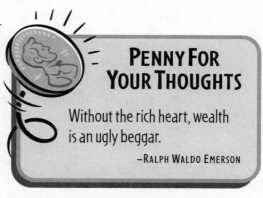

PENNY FOR YOUR THOUGHTS

Without the rich heart, wealth is an ugly beggar.

–RALPH WALDO EMERSON

➤ send money anonymously to a young couple struggling to make ends meet.

➤ buy Christmas presents for some inner-city young people who wouldn't otherwise receive any.

➤ start a college fund for a child in your church who lost a parent.

➤ buy groceries for a single parent family in your community.

Better yet, you could come up with your own ideas.

4. Money doesn't buy happiness.

Blah, blah, blah.

That's what this cliche sounds like to people who don't have a lot of money. Cautionary tales of miserable, messed-up millionaires and lottery winners whose lives are wrecked by their new wealth tend to fall on deaf ears.

They just didn't know how to enjoy their money, is the popular sentiment. *That wouldn't happen to me if I had that kind of dough.*

When it comes to living with wealth, everyone thinks they have it in them to be trailblazers. Everyone thinks they will be the one who finally discovers that elusive connection between money and happiness. Everyone thinks they have calculated the formula that will transform currency into personal fulfillment. Is there is any connection between wealth and happiness?

Since there's no way to determine with any accuracy who's happy and who's not, let's shift our focus and suggest that having money does not solve problems. In fact, it tends to create new ones.

For example, wealthy individuals always face the uncertainty of other people's motives. They learn very quickly that most folks cannot be trusted. They are forced to wonder whether people like them for who they are or for what they own. When you drive an old, high-mileage vehicle and consider dinner *and* a movie a big night out, you tend not to worry about such things.

And no matter how closely you follow the advice in this book, you'll probably never *have* to worry about such things.

The point of this tip is not to warn you against making too much money; it's to warn you not to expect too much of money. Improving your financial bottom line will not necessarily improve your life. It may change your circumstances and your address, but it will not fundamentally change who you are inside or how you feel about yourself.

PENNY FOR YOUR THOUGHTS

It is an unfortunate human failing that a full pocketbook often groans louder than an empty stomach.

—Franklin D. Roosevelt

That's why it's important that you not let your financial growth outpace your spiritual and interpersonal growth. What good is a healthy budget if your soul is sick or if you feel distant from God? What good are discretionary funds (that's what financial types call spending money) if you have no one to help you appreciate them?

Be wise about your finances and find your happiness and fulfillment elsewhere.

5. Being passive gets you nowhere.

If you found out that one of your neighbors was sneaking into your house while you were gone and taking money that you'd left lying around, how long would you let it go on before you finally did something about it?

Though your exact actions might depend on the size of the neighbor, it's a good bet that you wouldn't let such losses continue for very long. After all, you have a responsibility to protect what belongs to you and your family.

What if you found out that your hard-earned money was slowly being drained— not by a kleptomaniac neighbor but by your own faulty budget or unwise buying decisions? Would that affect your commitment to protecting your family's well-being?

Maybe personal finance isn't exactly your cup of tea. Maybe you'd rather attend a paint-drying contest than look for ways to cut your budget. Maybe you'd rather volunteer for exploratory dental surgery than explore methods for scaling back your spending.

If you thought about it long enough, you probably could come up with a hundred different reasons for not taking an active role in changing your finances.

➤ "I have more important things to think about than saving a few pennies."

➤ "I wouldn't know what to do."

➤ "I don't have much will power."

➤ "I don't want to make life miserable for myself or my family."

Certainly no one would argue with these excuses . . . if it weren't for the fact that your financial future is at stake.

You have the power to improve that future for yourself and your family. It doesn't make sense for you to sit idly by while your budget is being destroyed and your debt is digging a hole all around you.

Jump into the fray. Make the tough choices. Learn to sacrifice. Stop the budget hemorrhaging. Fight for what you've been given. Grab the reins of your finances.

It won't be easy, and it won't be enjoyable, but it will be rewarding.

6. It's not what you have, it's how you use it.

How much money does it take to be rich? A million dollars? Ten million? A billion?

The answer probably depends on the person you're asking. A man who's slept in a cardboard box on the street for the past two years might tell you that $1,000 is enough to make you rich. A man who's slept in a penthouse suite for the past two years might tell you that it takes at least $10 million.

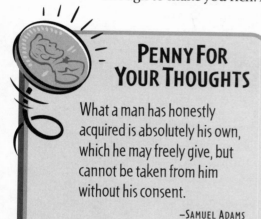

PENNY FOR YOUR THOUGHTS

What a man has honestly acquired is absolutely his own, which he may freely give, but cannot be taken from him without his consent.

–Samuel Adams

Wealth is a matter of perception. That's why you'll never be satisfied if your financial goal is to become rich. No matter how much money you acquire, it will never be enough for you.

A much better financial goal is to use your money to affect the lives of your loved ones, and even people you don't know, in a truly positive way. The obvious advantage of this goal is that it can be accomplished by anyone, regardless of income level.

We're not suggesting that you empty your savings account and take everyone you know out for pizza. That's not necessarily the kind of impact you're looking for. And, to be clear, there's nothing wrong with having money in the bank. In fact, we highly recommend it!

What we're warning against is reveling in your bank statements and treating money like a collectible instead of like a tool. Financial planning is hard work. Why should your banker be the only one who benefits from it?

Remember, saving money is only part of wise financial planning. Knowing what to do with what you save is just as important.

7. A lifelong commitment is required.

You set up a budget. You pay off your debt. You take care of your college bills. You buy just the right amount of insurance. You invest a major portion of your income. You give another major portion away to your church and charities. You write your will.

Then you put your financial ledger away and congratulate yourself on a job well done.

You figure that since you've achieved financial freedom, it's time to enjoy the fruits of your labor—without the constant hassle of watching where every paycheck goes, denying yourself small pleasures, and worrying about whether your monthly spending conforms to the guideline budget.

A month later, you pull out your financial ledger and start figuring ways to pay off the unbelievable debt that accumulated in the past 30 days.

That's the way this financial stuff works. Just when you think you've made it safely to shore, another wave breaks over the top of you and drags you back out to sea.

A question that's probably occurred to you more than once since you started this book is, How long? How long do you have to keep track of your finances? How long do you have to maintain a watchful eye on your monthly budget? How long do you have to restrain yourself from using your credit cards for those oh-so-tempting impulse purchases?

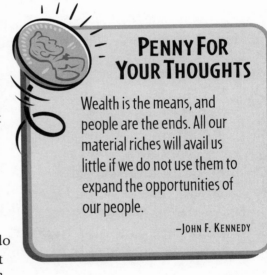

PENNY FOR YOUR THOUGHTS

Wealth is the means, and people are the ends. All our material riches will avail us little if we do not use them to expand the opportunities of our people.

–John F. Kennedy

At what point can you declare victory over debt and other harmful financial tendencies?

Certainly there are a number of variables that figure into the equation—the amount of debt you have to pay off, the interest rate on your mortgage, the percentage of monthly income that you allocate to investments. But if you're looking for a precise estimate, the best way to pinpoint the date would be to say. . . well, never.

That's right, *never*. You will always need to keep an eye on your finances, lest something dreadful happen to them.

Debts and other bad financial habits are like cockroaches; they never really go away. You may get rid of them for a while, but they're always lurking on the fringes of your balance sheet, waiting for you to turn your back or let your guard down for a moment so that they can mount another offensive.

What that means is that there's really no point at which you can say, "Whew! My budget is safe now." As long as you have the ability to make your own financial decisions, there is always a chance that you will make a wrong one—and then suffer the consequences for it.

Buying a retirement condo in Florida when you're 65 can be just as damaging to your budget as buying a fully loaded BMW when you're 25. Debt doesn't offer senior citizen discounts.

We would love to tell you that at age 55 you will receive full budgeting benefits for the rest of your life without ever having to work another day at it. But the brutal truth is that there's no such thing as a retired budgeter.

If you're serious about staying on top of your finances, you're in it for the long haul.

8. Preparation is everything.

How likely is it that the following scenarios (or ones similar to them) could happen to your family?

➤ A night at the local bowling alley ends with a trip to the emergency room and three weeks unpaid vacation when you damage a vertebrae in your back.

➤ You wake up one morning and find a new feature in your living room decor—namely, a half-inch wide crack running from the floor to the ceiling. Your contractor tells you it's the result of your house's crumbling foundation.

GLAD YOU ASKED

No offense, but right now budgeting and watching my finances is nothing but a big pain in the neck. Does it ever get any easier?

As with anything, the more you practice budgeting, the better you'll get at it. More than that, though, the longer you keep a close eye on your finances, the more it will become second nature to you. For example, in time, you won't have to talk yourself out of using credit cards because it won't occur to you to reach for them when you want something.

➤ The neighbor who fell and broke his wrist while helping you shovel your driveway last winter informs you that he's suing you for damages and for pain and suffering.

These are the types of unexpected occurrences that prey on unsuspecting budgets, pouncing on them at their most vulnerable point and ripping them to shreds.

How safe is your budget from such an attack?

When finances are tight, people have a tendency to budget for expected expenses and hope for the best. Unfortunately, when the odds catch up with them and an unexpected expense hits, the effect is often devastating.

That's why it's important that you set aside a healthy portion of your income in a savings account so that you can use it to sustain you and your family during times of unexpected hardship.

CRUNCHING NUMBERS

Ideally, you should set aside 10 percent of your monthly Net Spending Income for savings.

It's not just money that will help you survive these circumstances, though. You also need a plan of action—a step-by-step guide on what you should and shouldn't do, depending on the situation.

The only way to create such a plan is to anticipate different circumstances and scenarios that might affect you and your family.

For example, what would you do if . . .

➤ your spouse lost his or her job?

➤ your house burned down?

➤ your car was totaled?

The more specific ideas you come up with, the easier it will be for you to apply them, if it ever becomes necessary.

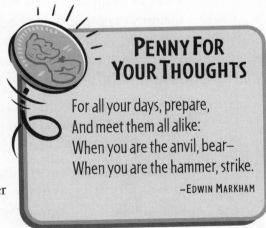

PENNY FOR YOUR THOUGHTS

For all your days, prepare,
And meet them all alike:
When you are the anvil, bear—
When you are the hammer, strike.

—EDWIN MARKHAM

In the case of the burned-down house, you might make sure that you have a copy of your insurance agent's name and number somewhere other than your home, in case that information is lost in the fire. You might also make arrangements with a friend or family member to make sure that you have a place to go, if such a situation were ever to occur.

Remember, the ability to weather an occasional crisis often means the difference between financial success and failure.

If you need a second opinion, ask a Boy Scout. He'll tell you that being prepared just makes good sense.

9. Everybody struggles.

Imagine how different this world would be if everyone's financial status were public record. Picture an Internet site where you could enter the name of, say, the chairman of your church board to find out how much of a tithe he's really giving each month. Or you could enter the name of your next door neighbors to find out how they afforded the fancy new deck and swimming pool.

Chances are, you'd be shocked at what you would find—not necessarily about your board chairman or your neighbor but about most people.

What you'd find is that your struggle with finances places you in an overwhelming majority of people. In fact, many of your friends, family members, coworkers, and fellow church members are probably dealing with financial crises that make yours pale in comparison. You'd discover that even your (seemingly) wealthiest acquaintances are not immune to serious money problems.

We're not suggesting that you take pleasure—or even comfort—in other people's misfortune. We're merely pointing out that you are not alone in your struggles, despite the fact that it may feel that way sometimes.

No one wants to admit that they struggle with finances. People who have no qualms about revealing every embarrassing thing they did in high school or every major physical ailment they've suffered draw the line at financial disclosure. They consider it "too personal."

Unfortunately, if more people were willing to talk about their financial problems, many of them would find the help they need—perhaps from people who lived through and overcame the same problems.

So we're letting the cat out of the bag. Everyone struggles with finances. Do with that information what you will.

10. Bad finances do not make a bad person.

The reason people don't want to talk about their money problems is that there's a stigma attached to financial insecurity. People who can't afford to pay their bills are often categorized as lazy, greedy, or unintelligent.

The irony of such thinking can be found in the title of the previous tip: Everybody struggles. You'd have to be a hardcore pessimist to believe that *everybody* is lazy, greedy, or unintelligent.

The real reason most people struggle financially is that they've never been taught how to handle their money. It's not laziness, greed, or stupidity; it's a lack of education.

You may be embarrassed about your financial circumstances. That's okay. Most mistakes *are* embarrassing. However, you should not be ashamed of your circumstances.

The fact that you haven't quite got a grip on your finances does not make you any less of a person. Remember, character is built in the midst of struggle. And though you may not be able to use character to pay your phone bill, you'll find that it has longer-lasting value than, say, a year-end bonus. When your money problems are gone, your character—who you are inside—will still be around.

GLAD YOU ASKED

How do I start a conversation about financial struggles without embarrassing myself?
Your best bet is to start with something general and safe—perhaps the high cost of houses or cars or golf clubs or child care. From there, you might mention some of your personal struggles to afford things you want. Then invite your conversation partner to do the same. As you get more and more comfortable with the topic—and with each other—you will find yourself sharing more vulnerable aspects of your financial situation.

Believe it or not, you may look back on your struggling years fondly some day. And when you do, chances are you'll like the person you recall being.

11. Financial lessons are meant to be shared.

Let's say that with a lot of hard work, planning, and sacrifice you manage to turn your financial situation around—or at least experience some success in paying down your debt or building up your savings.

PENNY FOR YOUR THOUGHTS

There is no man in this world without some manner of tribulation or anguish, though he be king or pope.

–THOMAS A KEMPIS

What's your next step?

How about being a *role model*?

Hey, now wait a minute—don't slam the book shut until you see what's coming next.

Remember all those people mentioned earlier—the overwhelming majority who are struggling with money issues? Isn't it possible that they could benefit from your financial experiences and mistakes?

You don't have to become a budget evangelist and travel from city to city, spreading the good news of debt reduction and guideline percentages. You don't have to drive around with a bumper sticker on your car that reads, "I paid off all my debts. Ask me how."

Just be sensitive to the needs of others. Learn to share your financial experiences in a nonthreatening, non-offensive, and nonjudgmental way. Make a difference in someone's life with as little fanfare as possible.

12. Things change.

Don't mistake your present financial situation for your future financial situation. No matter how bad things look right now, there is no reason to believe that you are beaten.

With determination, courage, sacrifice, and a little guidance from this book, you can and will improve your financial outlook.

You may not become a millionaire. You may not even get rid of your debts for years to come. But you will see just enough light at the end of the tunnel to give you hope.

And hope is what's important, because once you lose sight of it, once you determine that where you are now is where you will be for the rest of your life, you resign yourself to financial failure.

And you'll never find out how close you were to success.

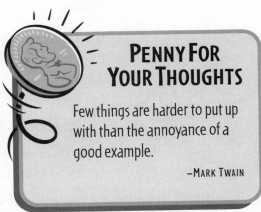

PENNY FOR YOUR THOUGHTS

Few things are harder to put up with than the annoyance of a good example.

—MARK TWAIN

That's the thing about despair: you know how bad things are, but you have no idea how close things are to being good.

For example, can you say for sure that you won't . . .

➤ get a promotion that increases your salary by 20 percent?

➤ be offered a job that pays double what you're making now?

➤ benefit from a federal tax cut to the tune of $2,000 a year?

➤ open your own successful small business?

➤ make a small investment that produces a major return?

➤ discover oil while hunting one day, strike it rich, and move to Beverly Hills?

PENNY FOR YOUR THOUGHTS

When water covers the head, a hundred fathoms are as one.

—PERSIAN PROVERB

Okay, forget that last one.

The point is, you can't say with any assurance that one or all of these things won't happen to you. None of them are unprecedented. In fact, most are fairly common occurrences. And even if they don't happen to you, there's a good chance that something equally exciting, and equally life changing, will.

That means you have cause for hope. It may be tough to spot sometimes when the bills are piled high, but it's there.

The Buck Stops Here

Think you're an expert on finances? Here's a quiz to see how much you know.

1. What are the "little things" that can mean a lot to your budget?
   a. $500 bills
   b. Lottery tickets
   c. Finance fairies
   d. Money-saving changes to your everyday routine

2. What responsibility comes with having wealth?
   a. Wearing an ascot
   b. Joining a country club
   c. Talking like Thurston Howell III on Gilligan's Island
   d. Using your money to help others

3. What does true financial freedom require?
   a. A 10 percent down payment
   b. A lifelong commitment
   c. A minimum monthly balance of $500
   d. A Mercedes

4. What does everybody struggle with?
   a. Finances
   b. Trigonometry
   c. The sticky strip across the top of CD jewel boxes
   d. Saying "I'm sorry"

5. What is the best way to share the financial lessons you've learned with someone else?
   a. Making them read all your favorite advice on finances
   b. Show righteous anger about the mess the person has made of his or her life
   c. In a nonthreatening, non-offensive, and nonjudgmental way
   d. With a sly grin on your face that lets the person know you are a financial expert

Answers: (1) d, (2) d, (3) b, (4) a, (5) c

Give and Take

SNAPSHOT

"What's that junk all over your table?" Ann asked, pointing to a large pile of brochures and leaflets.

Amy rolled her eyes. "That's the result of my bright idea to contact a couple of charitable organizations to ask if they had any suggestions about what I could do with some money that I wanted to donate."

"You didn't!" Ann said.

"I did," Amy laughed, shaking her head. "They must have passed my letter around to every charity in the Northern Hemisphere."

"And this is the stuff you're getting?" Ann asked, running her hands over the pile.

"Yeah, that's about one month's worth right there," Amy estimated.

"The Ragweed Anti-Defamation League?" Ann questioned, picking up one of the brochures.

> ## SNEAK PREVIEW
>
> **1.** Giving is as vital to a healthy financial outlook as saving or investing.
> **2.** The attitude that motivates you to give is as important as the gift itself.
> **3.** Many Christians believe they have a responsibility to give 10 percent or more of their income to the church for God's work.

"They believe ragweed has been unfairly cast in a negative light because of allergies," Amy explained. "They want to see it referred to as a sneeze enhancer."

"Uh huh," Ann said, picking up another brochure. "People for the Ethical Treatment of Bald Men?"

"They represent the rights of the follicly challenged."

"I see," Ann replied, holding up a leaflet. "And what about Paper First?"

"They're a radical organization dedicated to outlawing staplers and paper clips. They believe sheets of paper are meant to be loose and free. They oppose anything that restricts that freedom."

"So have these brochures helped you make up your mind about what to do with your money?" Ann asked.

"Yes, they have," Amy replied with a smile. "I decided that my money is going to the A.N.S.F."

"What's that?" Ann asked.

"Amy's New Stereo Fund."

* * * * * * * * * * * * * * * *

"Don't be so selfish."

"Give some to your sister!"

"Let your brother play with that!"

"I hope you brought enough for everyone."

"You need to learn to share."

Sound familiar? If we'd all listened to our parents and teachers as children, we wouldn't need a chapter on giving, would we? (Not only that, we'd be eating vegetables with every meal, sleeping in tidy rooms, and wearing clean underwear 24-7.)

No matter where you come from or what your background is, chances are you have memories of being told to share something of yours with someone else. What you may not have realized is that those nagging authority figures from your youth weren't just trying to keep you from becoming a spoiled brat. They were also laying the groundwork for an important future financial concept: giving.

What's Mine Is…Yours?

Let's get the obvious question out of the way first—the one you may or may not have had the guts to ask as a kid.

Why?

Why should you be expected to share what's rightfully yours with other people—especially the things you've *earned*?

Because I said so, that's why!

Oops, sorry. Just having a childhood flashback. But there are several convincing reasons why you should give some of what you have to people who are less fortunate than you. Here are just a few of them.

Reason #1: You can.

It's that simple. You give because you are able to give.

Regardless of how poor you may consider yourself, the fact is that if you have a steady income you have something to share. You may not have *a lot* to share, but you do have something.

Even $5, given at the right time, could make a difference in someone's life. Set aside $5 a week for a month and you've got $20 to give away. And while parting with a couple of sawbucks every 30 days may not land you on the cover of *Philanthropy Weekly*, it is a significant gesture. In some areas of the world, $20 will feed a family of four for a month.

What minor changes would you have to make to your daily routine to set aside $5 a week? Drink water instead of soda a couple days a week? Bring a lunch from home instead of eating out? Forego a bag of chips or a candy bar from the vending machine?

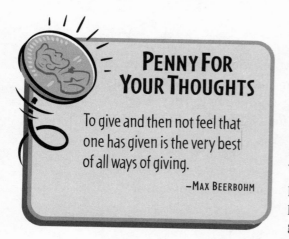

When you think about what that money could mean to someone else, it's hard to argue with making a few small sacrifices here and there.

You've probably heard the expression, "To whom much is given, much is expected." What you may not have realized was that *whom* included you. When you see photos or video footage of true poverty, it's tough to deny that you've been given plenty. So the question becomes, What are you going to do with what you've been given?

Reason #2: You've benefited from the generosity of others.

"I've never accepted a penny of charity in my life!" you may be protesting. And that may be true. But keep in mind that not all gifts have monetary value.

Regardless of how self-sufficient you may consider yourself, chances are you've been on the receiving end of someone's generosity. Few people make it through this world untouched by others.

For example...

➤ Has someone ever taken the time to explain a new concept to you?

➤ Has anyone ever taught you a new skill?

➤ Have you ever received a meaningful compliment?

➤ Has someone ever encouraged you when you weren't so sure of yourself?

If you answered yes to any of these questions, you've benefited from the generosity of others; so, you know firsthand what a difference a simple gesture or a small sacrifice can make in someone's life.

Reason #3: It's good for the soul.

Have you ever seen the look on the face of a little girl who's been raised in extreme poverty when she receives a beautiful new dress for Christmas? Have you ever seen the expression of a little boy who's never been given anything in his life when he finds out that he has tickets to see his favorite pro sports team play?

If you've ever seen those expressions, you'll never forget them. If you haven't, I highly recommend the experience. The words *simple pleasures* will take on a whole new meaning for you.

One of the great things about being created human is that you have the ability to take pleasure in other people's joy. If you've ever cried while watching a Hallmark commercial, you know what I mean. So, in a sense, when you give with the right frame of mind you also receive.

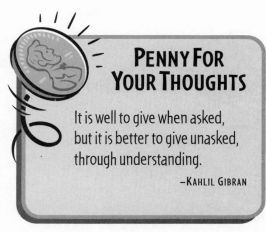

PENNY FOR YOUR THOUGHTS

It is well to give when asked, but it is better to give unasked, through understanding.

–Kahlil Gibran

Reason #4: What comes around goes around.

"Give, and it will be given to you" is the biblical way of putting it. That's not to say that you can expect a dollar-for-dollar return on your charitable donations. It's just that generous people often get a taste of their own medicine—usually when they expect it least but need it most.

Put it this way. Someday you might be in need. Who's to say that it won't be someone you've helped in the past who will come to your assistance?

Reason #5: It sets a good example.

If you have children, show—don't just tell—them how to share. You can establish a powerful precedent for them by generously giving your family's resources to people in need. If they can see the effect your generosity has on other people's lives, they may be inclined to follow your example when they have income of their own to share.

Even if you don't have children, your generous spirit may inspire others to follow your example—whether you realize it or not. What better legacy could you ask for yourself?

Reason #6: It's tax deductible.

If all of these feel-good reasons are making you slightly nauseated, let's get mercenary for a moment and look at the bottom line. Giving money away makes financial sense. Your friends at the IRS smile on what they call *charitable deductions*. In fact, they like it so much that they allow you to reduce the amount

PENNY FOR YOUR THOUGHTS

Charity: bestowing on a poor man something he could otherwise fish from your rubbish can.

—ANONYMOUS

of taxes you owe, based on the amount you give away.

That's an offer you can't refuse. In case you haven't noticed, the United States government throws tax breaks around like manhole covers. The fact that it rewards giving money away would suggest that charity is an important part of our national identity. (Call it Reason #6.5—Giving money to people who are less fortunate than you is patriotic!)

As reasons for giving go, to get a tax break doesn't exactly rate high on the nobility chart; but, in the interest of full disclosure, you should at least be aware of it.

Reason #7: What else are you going to do with it?

How would you finish this sentence? *Instead of giving a portion of my income to help people in need, I would much rather use it to*_____.

It's a tough blank to fill in, isn't it? The fact is, giving a portion of your income to help people in need is the ideal way to use your money.

Watch Your Attitude

Some nerve, huh? First I overwhelm you with a list of reasons why you should just give away a portion of your hard-earned money. Now I'm trying to tell you what kind of *attitude* you should have when you do it. Next thing you know, I'll be telling you how to sign your name on the checks you write.

But the fact is, your attitude in giving is just as important as the gift itself. When giving is done with the wrong spirit or motivation, the gift becomes meaningless—maybe not to the recipient, but certainly to the giver. And that's a shame, especially since there's so much pleasure and satisfaction to be found in helping others. The following are some tips for developing the right giving spirit.

Don't expect any favors in return.

Remember, if there's a string attached, it's not a gift—it's either a bribe, a transaction, or a loan. And there's nothing particularly generous about any of those things. When you give, it should be with no expectations of rewards or repayment. Consider it money well spent and forget about it.

Don't expect a lot of gratitude or recognition.

What can you legitimately expect if you donate money to an established organization? A form letter thanking you for your gift, a receipt for tax purposes, and a preprinted envelope to use for your next donation.

If you give your money to an individual, you very likely can expect about the same thing—except for the form letter, receipt, and envelope.

The point is, some people know how to show their gratitude and some people don't. If you're looking for a ticker tape parade or a commemorative plaque with your face framed by the words "Friend of the Downtrodden," you'll have to find a way to add a handful of zeros to the end of your next donation. A $3 million gift makes you a noted philanthropist. A $30 check makes you donor number 34078.

Don't underestimate how uncomfortable it is for people to accept gifts.

Most giving is done long distance, in a semi-anonymous manner, using envelopes and checks. Occasionally, though, you may have an opportunity to give directly to a person in need; and if you're not prepared for the experience, you may come away from it disappointed and maybe even a little angry.

An odd dynamic occurs when you give money directly to another person. On one level, the person may be grateful for your help. On another level, though, the person may be ashamed of his or her financial situation or even resent the fact that you have money to give.

Most folks can't accept money from another person without swallowing a fair amount of pride. So don't be surprised if you don't get the show of gratitude you may have expected.

Don't make people prove themselves worthy of your gifts.

If you're going to give money to someone, give it. Don't make people jump through hoops to "earn" your gift. Don't attach unreasonable demands to your financial support. Don't say, "I'll give you money if. . ." or "I'll help you out as long as you don't. . ."

PENNY FOR YOUR THOUGHTS

Let him that desires to see others happy, make haste to give while his gift can be enjoyed, and remember that every moment of delay takes away something from the value of his benefaction.

—Samuel Johnson

If you have a moral concern about where your money might go—for example, if you suspect that it might be used to buy drugs—it's probably a good idea not to give it. If you're looking for some personal expectations to be met, though, you're not giving with the proper attitude.

Who Needs Some Cash?

One thing's for sure: you won't have to look far to find people willing to take your money off your hands. In fact, you may need to invest in a lion tamer's whip and chair to keep yourself from being mauled by overeager would-be recipients. Everyone from the Committee for Safer Nacho Chips to the Euro Disney Preservation Society to the Ballroom Dancers Retirement Fund would all love to get their hands on any extra rubles you may care to send their way.

With so many options available, how can you possibly make an informed decision about where your money should go?

The first thing you need to do is think about the needs, struggles, causes, and issues that are closest to your heart. Christians, for example, give highest priority to God's work—specifically, His work in and through the church. As part of their commitment to God's work, they give a portion of their income to their churches each week. (More will be said about this specific kind of giving, called *tithing*, later in the chapter.)

What Is Close to Your Heart?

Beyond the church, though, there may be other needs or causes that you feel especially strong about because of your own experiences or circumstances.

For example...

> ➤ If your niece is battling leukemia, you may want to support cancer research or recovery programs.

➤ If your best friend was seriously injured in an accident in which alcohol played a role, you may have strong feelings about preventing and punishing drunk driving.

➤ If you needed the help of grants and scholarships to attend college, you may have a desire to assist other financially strapped students by contributing to the scholarship fund of your alma mater.

➤ If an after-school program kept you off the streets and out of trouble when you were growing up, you may feel a sense of obligation to help keep the program going for other at-risk kids.

By supporting causes that are meaningful to you, you get to share in the enjoyment of the good that is accomplished—or may be accomplished someday— with your gift. That's a lot better than sending money to some faceless organization because you feel like you're expected to.

The number of nonprofit organizations is growing every day. If you don't already know of one dedicated to a specific need or cause, a quick search on the Internet should give you the information you need to start your search.

GLAD YOU ASKED

There are so many causes I'd like to support, if only I had the money. How can I decide which one is best for me?
Try thinking in terms of who needs it most. For example, you may want to support your alma mater's scholarship fund. But if your school already has a war chest of tens of millions of dollars, your money probably would be more valuable to a smaller organization or one that is not quite as well funded.

Do Your Homework

See if you can spot the problem in the following sequence.

1. Drought conditions in East Africa result in massive starvation.

2. The Food for Everyone Organization (FFEO) sponsors a 30-minute infomercial describing the plight of the children in East Africa.

3. Late one night Alec watches the infomercial and is moved by what he sees.

4. Alec sends a check for $100 to the Food for Everyone Organization to help the children of East Africa.

5. The FFEO deposits Alec's check and uses $25 of it to buy food and supplies and send them to the children of East Africa.

6. The $25 worth of food and supplies, along with other donations, are distributed among the starving children of East Africa.

Did you recognize the problem? Did you notice that something disappeared between steps #4 and #5? Look at it again and you'll see that $75 of Alec's generous donation vanishes like a snowflake in an open flame.

Welcome to the wonderful world of operating costs.

A (Big) Piece of the Action

In basic terms, *operating costs* are the funds an organization uses to run its day-to-day business. Some organizations have small operating expenses; others have super-size costs.

In terms of excitement, discussing the internal financial structures of various nonprofit organizations ranks right up there with attending latex-paint-drying competitions. However, in this case, operating costs is a subject you should care about. Here's why.

If you give money to help a particular group of people—the starving children of East Africa, for example—you want as much of that money to get to those people as possible. You don't want your hard-earned income paying for a corporate jet or a new logo design for Food for Everyone.

But that's what happens when you send your money to an organization with excessive operating costs. You're paying for things like office furniture, new carpeting, and printing costs for junk mail appeals for more money.

Although the 75 percent that Food for Everyone took out of Alec's donation may be a bit high, it's not unusual to find organizations that spend more than 50 percent of the money they receive on operating costs.

That's why it's important to investigate as many organizations as possible before you offer any of them your financial assistance. You want to know that the organizations you choose to support will direct your money where you intend it to go.

You should be able to find several resources at your local library that rate nonprofit organizations according to their giving percentage and operating costs. These resources will come in handy when it's time to narrow your search for causes to support. If your library doesn't have any such resources, typing in a few key words for an Internet search should yield the results you're looking for.

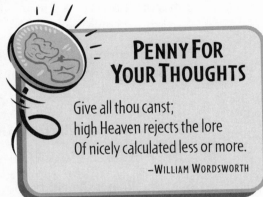

PENNY FOR YOUR THOUGHTS

Give all thou canst;
high Heaven rejects the lore
Of nicely calculated less or more.

–WILLIAM WORDSWORTH

The Hunt for Red Flags

Though a generous spirit should guide everything you do, there are times when giving can be counterproductive. Put simply, some organizations and individuals should not receive your money.

Many people learn to recognize these dicey organizations and individuals only after they've been burned by them—often more than once. To help prevent you from making the same mistake, the following are "red flags" to look for—clues that should tip you off to the fact that you're dealing with people you probably shouldn't be dealing with.

Red flag organizations

It was mentioned earlier that you should investigate organizations before you give them access to your funds. The more thorough your investigation is, the more secure you can feel about your gift being in good hands.

Obviously the first red flag is *an organization with a big operating cost*. A charity that spends too much on itself probably doesn't exist to help others. And even if its heart is in the right place, it may be too bloated—or worse, too inept—to be of any real help to needy people.

The second red flag is *an organization that is cagey with its details*. The fact is, there are some things you should know before you give your money away. If an organization is unwilling to give you the information you need, it's probably not worthy of your donation.

Here are some questions to ask the next time you talk to a representative of a charity or a service organization.

> ➤ What is the history of your organization?

> ➤ What were the circumstances of its founding?

> ➤ What effect has it had on the world since it was started?

> ➤ What is the philosophy of your organization?

> ➤ Who specifically do you help and how?

> ➤ What percentage of the donations you receive goes to the people in need? What percentage goes to your operating costs?

If you find that an organization's representatives can't answer your questions, or if they respond in ways that raise some doubts in your mind, keep your checkbook safely tucked away.

The third red flag is *an organization that solicits donations door to door or over the phone*. That's not to say that everyone who rings your doorbell or interrupts your dinner is a scam artist out to drain your bank account. Some legitimate organizations do use these methods to solicit funds.

However, it's your responsibility to make sure that the people you give money to are who they say they are and work for whom they say they work for. You can do this by asking a few questions like the ones we listed above. The more legitimate details you ask about, the more likely you are to catch a person in a lie.

For example, if someone claims to be collecting for the Red Cross but can't remember what the organization's logo looks like, he or she is probably being less than truthful with you.

Red flag individuals

When you're dealing directly with needy people, the first red flag to look for is *suspicious behavior.* Obviously one of the things you want to guard against is supporting drug addicts with your money.

But since few addicts wear name tags identifying themselves as addicts, and since many of them will say or do anything to get money for a fix, it can be hard to get the truth from them. When someone begins to tell you his or her woes before hitting you up for cash, your best strategy is to ask for details.

For example, let's say a young woman on the street tells you that she needs money to help her sick child. Before you reach for your cash, ask her a few simple questions to help you determine whether she's telling the truth.

> ➤ What's your child's name?

> ➤ What's wrong with your child?

> ➤ What did the doctor recommend?

> ➤ What kind of medicine does your child need?

You don't have to assume the role of grand inquisitor—or even prosecuting attorney. You'll notice that there's nothing particularly threatening about any of the questions. All of them are quite conversational.

But if the mother seems confused or irritated by the questions or has difficulty remembering her story, you would be wise to keep your suspicions—and your money—to yourself.

The second red flag to look for with individuals is *freeloading.* Even the most compassionate book ever written says, *"If anyone is not willing to work, then he is not to eat, either"* (2 Thessalonians 3:10 NASB).

There is nothing noble or fulfilling about being a meal ticket for someone who is too lazy to make it on his or her own. With so many truly needy people in the world, there is no reason to support someone whose chief affliction is an allergy to work.

How Will You Be Paying for That?

If you're serious about becoming a giver, one of the obvious decisions you'll need to make is what form your gifts will take. Here are a few of the options you might consider.

Cash

The advantage of giving cash is that it can be put to use immediately, and it allows you to remain anonymous, if that's how you prefer to give. The drawback is that when you give money, there's no record of the gift. That's why it's not a good idea to send cash through the mail. You won't know for sure whether it reached your intended destination or whether it was pocketed by someone else along the way.

Check

A check or money order gives you a record of your gift, which is an especially helpful thing to have when tax time comes. Most IRS auditors won't accept your memory of giving a $100 bill to a guy in a homeless shelter as proof of your charitable donation.

Stock

Maybe you would prefer to open your portfolio to your favorite charitable organizations. Shares of stocks, bonds, and mutual funds are all legitimate gifts and may even be preferable to cash.

Real estate

Although the thought may never have crossed your mind, it is possible to donate property—including your house—to your favorite charitable organization. If you ever become a land baron, that might be a helpful thing to know.

Fire Up the Creative Juices

Only traditional forms of giving have been mentioned, but there is no law that says you have to be traditional in your generosity. Your possibilities for giving are limited only by your imagination.

To help you understand, the following is a list of ten creative giving ideas that may help expand your concept of what a charitable contribution is.

1. Buy school clothes for a needy family in your area. (You'll need to find out the sizes.)

2. Buy Christmas presents for a family who's struggling to make ends meet and deliver them anonymously on Christmas morning.

3. Buy a semester's worth of school books for a college student.

4. Buy a little extra food each time you go to the supermarket and deliver each month's surplus to a local food pantry.

5. Pick up as many used coats and blankets as you can find at garage sales and thrift shops and deliver them to the local homeless people before the first cold snap of the year.

6. Buy, cook, and deliver Thanksgiving meals to several needy families in your area.

7. Offer to match the amount of college funds a young person earns over the summer.

8. Buy a group of tickets to a sporting event and invite kids from a local orphanage to join you. (Many sports organizations will give you a discount rate if you explain what you're doing.)

9. Team up with a sharing-minded friend and offer to match each other's pledge to a certain charity.

10. Organize a neighborhood garage sale/car wash and donate the proceeds to a specific fund drive.

> ### GLAD YOU ASKED
> **Is it possible to donate money after I die?**
>
> Is it ever! Many people include their favorite charities in their wills. Trusts, such as the charitable remainder trust, can provide a steady flow of income for Christian ministries and charitable organizations for years after your death. (For more information on how to get a will or set up a trust, see chapter 9.)

If none of these specific ideas appeals to you, that's okay. Our goal is simply to get you thinking "outside the box" when it comes to giving.

The Big Money Problem

Let's say an unexpected chunk of change falls into your lap and you decide you want to share your good fortune. And let's say the gift you're thinking of has a few more zeros than your checkbook is used to. (Okay, it's not a likely scenario, but it is possible.)

If making a large donation falls into uncharted territory for you, there are a couple of things you'll need to keep in mind.

You're going to become very popular.

This is especially true if the circumstances of your windfall are high profile, such as winning a contest or a court settlement. When word gets out, you can expect to hear from everyone you've ever said "Hi" to since the fifth grade. You'll have third cousins twice removed calling you to relive the "good old days"; and while they're on the phone they may just happen to mention their need for a couple thousand dollars to get back on their feet again. Even your old friends may start treating you like you're someone new.

If you're not careful, such sudden attention can cloud your judgment. And before you know it, you'll have money flying in all directions, trying to help old friends who didn't even know you existed when your bank account was small.

Beware of sharks.

Greedy long-lost relatives are minor concerns, compared to some of the predators that will surface when word of your financial gain gets out. Some of these predators may take the form of investment advisors; others may pawn themselves off as charity representatives. But their goal is the same: to relieve you of as much of your money as possible.

Earlier it was mentioned that you need to investigate organizations before you commit money to them. This is especially true when the amount you're considering giving away includes a comma.

Stick with what you know.

If you're faced with the dilemma of making a large donation (which, on the dilemma scale ranks right up there with choosing a place to display your Oscar or deciding what to wear for your date with a supermodel), your best bet is to focus on what you're already familiar with.

Talk to your church, your alma mater, and charities you've supported in the past to see if there are special projects that you can help fund.

More Than Money

Money is not the only thing you have to give. In fact, it's not even the most valuable asset you have to offer. You can benefit others by giving a portion of your time, energy, and talents as well.

We all know that time is a precious commodity in our nonstop world. With your family, career, church, and other responsibilities all vying for your waking hours, you probably have very little. . . blah, blah, blah.

You're busy. I'm busy. Everybody's busy. So what? That doesn't mean you can't carve out a few spare minutes of your day to help people in need.

If you were willing to give just one percent—*one*, mind you, the closest to zero you can get—of your time to help people less fortunate than you, that would work out to about 15 minutes a day. The obvious question, then, is what could you do in 15 minutes to help someone else?

The answer is, probably not a lot. But what if you saved up 15 minutes each day for a week? By the weekend, you'd have over one and one-half hour of your time to donate. And there are plenty of organizations that would love to fill those 90-plus minutes for you.

Giving Rather Than Getting

What would that mean for your schedule?

➤ Canceling a golf game?

➤ Giving up a couple hours of overtime?

➤ Foregoing a movie or video?

CRUNCHING NUMBERS

If you donated one percent of your time to helping people in need, it would work out to just over one hour and 40 minutes a week.

The one area that wouldn't have to be affected is the time you spend with your spouse or family—if you find an activity that can involve everyone. Talk about spending quality time together!

There's certainly no shortage of ways to spend your available time. Depending on your preferred level of activity, you could. . .

➤ help build a house with an organization like Habitat for Humanity.

➤ help renovate and paint a youth center.

➤ help clean up an abandoned lot so that a new park can be built.

➤ solicit donations at intersections or in front of supermarkets.

➤ make necessary telephone calls or help with other office work.

➤ help a young couple develop a budget.

The best way to spend your donated time is to find a role that lets you use your talents, skills, and gifts. For example. . .

PENNY FOR YOUR THOUGHTS

The silver ore of pure charity is an expensive article in the catalogue of a man's good qualities.

—RICHARD BRINSLEY SHERIDAN

➤ If you know how to write, you might volunteer to put out a newsletter or handle correspondence.

➤ If you have computer expertise, you might volunteer to hook up a system or write some software.

➤ If you're good with people, you might volunteer to serve as a mentor to an at-risk teen.

A Specific Kind of Giving

An area of giving that is misunderstood by a lot of people is tithing. If you didn't grow up in the church, you may wonder what's the deal when people drop money in those little collection plates. Is it. . .

➤ a gratuity for the ushers?

➤ a bribe for forgiveness?

➤ a way of showing off your wealth?

➤ a betting pool run by the deacons and elders?

➤ spending money for the pastor's wife?

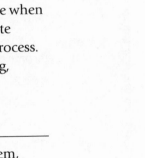

CRUNCHING NUMBERS

The average American Christian currently gives 2.5 percent of his or her income to God's work.

Actually, the answer is much more profound than you might imagine. Christians believe that everything they have comes from God. They view the tithe as a way of giving back a portion of what God has given them to carry out His work in and through the church.

When people go to church, they put their cash or check in the offering plate when it is passed. Some people prefer to give anonymously with cash; others write checks. Some churches include preprinted envelope slips to simplify the process. Many churches send out monthly, quarterly, or annual statements of giving, which can be used for tax purposes.

The Tithes That Bind

In addition to their desire to give back a portion of what God has given them, Christians cite several other reasons for tithing, or giving 10 percent, of their income. For example, they suggest that. . .

➤ tithing is a way of passing God's love on to others. They believe that since God is generous, He transforms His followers into generous givers as well.

➤ tithing is a way of dedicating all of their money to God and including Him in every area of their finances.

➤ the Bible makes a strong case for tithing. They believe that passages such as Malachi 3:1-12 in the Old Testament and Hebrews 7:1-10 in the New Testament suggest that tithing with the proper motives invokes God's blessings.

➤ tithing funds the internal workings of the church. Everything from staff salaries to the utility bills are paid from the tithes and gifts of church members. Churches are tax-exempt, which means they don't have to pay taxes on what they receive. But that doesn't mean they get other things free. Everything from the water for drinking fountains to the elements for communion costs money.

➤ tithing funds other ministries as well. Most churches sponsor a variety of service and outreach organizations. Many churches have their own teams of missionaries that they support both financially and spiritually. Ultimately, these important functions of the church are paid for by the support of its members.

GLAD YOU ASKED

Should my tithe be 10 percent of my gross income (before taxes) or 10 percent of my net income (after taxes)?

The easiest way to answer that is to ask whether you want God to bless your gross income or your net income. The point is, if you're trying to cut corners in your budget, your gift to God is not the place to do it. The Bible does not lay down any specific guidelines for tithes. But ask yourself this question: Why wouldn't you give 10 percent of your gross income to God? Is it more than He deserves? Are you afraid of giving Him too much?

Let's Talk Numbers

The word *tithe* means "tenth." Many Christians take that definition literally and give one-tenth of everything they earn back to God in the form of their weekly church offerings. That includes not only salary but any unexpected bonuses, dividends, or gifts they may receive.

Many Christians take the concept of tithing one step further. They believe that giving 10 percent of their incomes back to God is just the starting point. As a result, they practice what is called sacrificial giving.

Sacrificial giving involves purposefully foregoing some wants and desires to support the work of God.

Some people may use the money they would have spent bowling or golfing or eating out to make a special donation to a specific church need. Others may give up a new car, boat, swimming pool, or even a house. It all depends on the person and the circumstances.

Call it a radical priority readjustment.

One More Thing

If you've never made giving a habit, you may find it strange to think that handing over your hard-earned money can be more satisfying than keeping it yourself. But don't knock it until you've tried it.

Once you see what your money can do for other people, you'll experience a sense of satisfaction and fulfillment that's impossible to describe. Go ahead, give it a shot.

# The Buck Stops Here

Think you're an expert on giving? Here's a quiz to see how much you know.

1. Which of the following is not a good reason to share what you have with people less fortunate than you?
   a. You have enough to share.
   b. You've benefited from the generosity of others.
   c. You set a good example for others.
   d. You can make your enemies extremely jealous.

2. Which of the following financial tasks requires the right attitude?
   a. Writing a check for your electric bill
   b. Giving money to a person in need
   c. Balancing your checkbook
   d. Getting change for a $20

3. If an organization is cagey about the details of its operations, what should that tell you?
   a. It's probably part of a covert CIA operation.
   b. Its record keeping leaves a lot to be desired.
   c. It's probably not the place you should give your money to.
   d. It has an admirable stance on privacy issues.

4. Which of the following is true of donating your time to a charity organization?
   a. Your family will resent you for it because it takes away from the time you spend with them.
   b. Once you get involved with charity people, they will demand more and more time from you until they possess your every waking second.
   c. You are guaranteed to be bored out of your skull.
   d. You don't need to make an unreasonable time commitment to make a difference.

5. Which of the following is true of tithing?
   a. Many Christians believe that they should give 10 percent of their income back to God.
   b. When the collection plate comes around, you have the option of giving or taking from it.
   c. It's a form of gambling.
   d. Most churches frown on it.

Answers: (1) d, (2) b, (3) c, (4) d, (5) a

The Wisdom of the Ages

SNAPSHOT

"**B**oy, I just don't know about this investment," Scott fretted. "It seems a little risky."

"Strike while the iron's hot," Jeff said. "That's what Jack Singleton advises."

"Who's Jack Singleton?" Scott asked.

"You don't know who Jack Singleton is?" Jeff gasped. "He's only the biggest name on Wall Street these days. He's been on all the morning talk shows lately promoting his new book."

"'Strike while the iron's hot' is enough to get you on morning talk shows now?" Scott asked.

"Hey, a lot of people made money off his advice, including yours truly," Jeff countered. "Even Frank Sharp endorsed his strategy."

"Oh, well, if it's good enough for Frank Sharp, it's good enough for me," Scott said with a confident

SNEAK PREVIEW

1. Finance is not an amoral concept; there are elements of right and wrong in almost every financial decision you make.
2. Determining what's right and wrong in any given financial decision often requires careful examination of both your means and your motives.
3. The only way to truly appreciate and enjoy your financial assets is to acquire and use them ethically.

nod. "Just one question. Who's Frank Sharp?"

"Have you ever *heard* of the stock market before?" Jeff questioned. "Frank Sharp practically ran Wall Street in the mid-90s. His slogan was 'Buy now, pay later'."

"I'll bet that landed him on a few talk shows, didn't it?"

"Make fun all you like," Jeff said. "But he made millions from it."

"What big shot endorsed his strategy?" Scott asked.

"I think it was Michael Nelson," Jeff replied.

"And what was *his* slogan?"

"Go for it!" Jeff said.

"And he made millions too?" Scott asked.

"Oh, yeah."

Scott threw up his hands. "Don't you ever wish you had a little more *substantial* advice to help guide your finances? Something a little more profound than 'Go for it'?"

"What do you mean?" Jeff asked.

"I'm saying maybe we should get back to more timeless truths," Scott suggested. "The kind of wisdom that's been around for centuries."

"What did you just say?" Jeff asked.

Scott shrugged. "I said we should get back to timeless truths."

"Oh, that's *good*," Jeff marveled. "Have you ever thought about writing a book?"

* * * * * * * * * * * * * * *

You can learn a lot of useful information from financial gurus and investment advisors. Things like what to do in certain markets. How to evaluate your portfolio. When to sell an under-performing stock. How to use the word *amortize* correctly in a sentence.

But if it's guiding principles for your entire financial life you're searching for, you'll need to look beyond the current crop of Wall Street golden children.

For the kind of advice that addresses your actions *and* your motives, you'll need to go back to a time before there was such a thing as minute-by-minute updates from the New York Stock Exchange on your home computer.

You'll need to go back to a time before there was such a thing as non-professional interest in the New York Stock Exchange.

You'll need to go back to a time before there was such a thing as the New York Stock Exchange.

You'll need to go back to a time before there was such a thing as New York.

There are certain bits of wisdom and advice that simply transcend time, place, and context. They are as applicable today as they were thousands of years ago. And they will still be applicable when our dollar goes the way of the denarius.

I'm going to close this book by spotlighting 10 such pieces of timeless financial advice.

1. More Valuable Than Gold

Unfortunately, not everyone recognizes the value of wisdom. You can see for yourself the next time you're in a restaurant. When the check comes, turn it over and write "The truth is always the strongest argument" (or some other nugget of wisdom) on the back. Then give it to your waiter or waitress in lieu of cash and see what happens. Chances are, the manager will be at your table faster than you can say, "Just kidding."

Wisdom may be a long way from acceptance as a monetary unit, but that doesn't decrease its value in your life.

Actually, comparing wisdom to finances is a little misleading. They're more like companions than competitors. The only difference is their stand-alone potential. Wisdom without money retains 100 percent of its value. Money without wisdom loses a good 99 percent of its value.

Without wisdom, making the right decisions about your money becomes difficult, if not impossible. Wisdom is what helps you determine. . .

➤ the difference between needs, wants, and desires.

➤ which investment opportunities will best meet your financial needs at a given time.

➤ which charities and nonprofit organizations are most deserving of your financial assistance.

➤ how to budget your money each month.

➤ how much time to devote to financial matters.

That's why your quest for wisdom should always outpace your quest for money. You can find useful bits of financial knowledge and wisdom everywhere from the Old Testament (where the proverbs spotlighted in this chapter come from) to the advice of your parents and other people whose opinions you trust.

Contrary to what you might assume, the need for wisdom does not decrease as your bank accounts and portfolio grow. In fact, it's safe to say that the more money you have the more wisdom you need.

PENNY FOR YOUR THOUGHTS

Blessed is the man who finds wisdom, the man who gains understanding, for she is more profitable than silver and yields better returns than gold. She is more precious than rubies; nothing you desire can compare with her.

–PROVERBS 3:13-15

2. Safety in Numbers

When it comes to planning your family's financial future, hardcore do-it-yourselfers need not apply. Regardless of how confident you are in your budgeting and investing abilities, if you don't seek input from experts and others who know more than you do, you will fail eventually.

And if you're not careful, your crash will be spectacular.

As you seek quality financial counseling, there are three tips you should keep in mind.

a. Choose a wise counselor.

Sure, it sounds like a headline from *Duh!* magazine. And it raises a couple of rather obvious questions.

➤ *How do you measure the amount of wisdom someone possesses?* After all, it's not the kind of question you usually pose in an interview ("On a scale of 1 to 10, how wise are you?").

➤ *How much wisdom is enough?* How do you know whether you should settle for a certain level of wisdom or keep searching for someone wiser to counsel you? You'll need some criteria to help you reach a decision.

Where a financial counselor is concerned, your best strategy is to compare his or her advice with conventional wisdom—even if you have to do some investigating to find out what the conventional wisdom is.

If you find some discrepancies between what your counselor recommends and what other experts advise, ask your counselor to account for them. If he or she is at a loss to offer an explanation, or if he or she seems unfamiliar with other financial strategies, you may want to consider finding a new counselor.

b. Go with a team approach.

No one can specialize in the many different areas of finances. Taxes, securities, stocks, bonds, real estate, and other financial categories all have their own intricacies and nuances. And it's those details that make it difficult for a general advisor to give you the specific information you need.

That's why, as your financial horizons expand, you should consider using multiple advisors, specialists in each field. Believe it or not, the best place to find such a stable of advisors is through recommendations from your current financial counselor. If your counselor is threatened by your desire to see other advisors, it may be a tip off that he or she doesn't really have your best interests at heart.

PENNY FOR YOUR THOUGHTS

Plans fail for lack of counsel, but with many advisers they succeed.

–PROVERBS 15:22

c. Use your own judgment.

Among the gaggle of advisors vying for your financial trust, don't let your own voice be drowned out. Whenever you receive any financial advice, you should weigh it against your own opinions, preferences, and reservations.

In some cases, the advice will coincide with your own opinions, allowing you to pursue it without a second thought. In other cases, the advice you receive may not seem right to you—for reasons you may not even be able to put your finger on. It's important that you not ignore or discount your uneasy feelings.

If something your financial advisor recommends doesn't seem right to you, don't pursue it. Get a second opinion, then a third, and so on, until you have a sense of peace about your decision.

Remember, it's not your counselor's financial future at stake; it's yours—and your family's.

3. Ant Lessons

If we were to publish an Ant Edition of this book, we could probably reduce our printing costs by leaving out chapter 7, on preparing for the different seasons of life. Ants are world-class preparers. They wouldn't need to be told to set aside provisions for a later day. That's what they're all about.

It's this preparation, this willingness to sacrifice a portion of today's comfort for tomorrow's needs, that you would do well to emulate.

This is not to suggest that you should. . .

➤ work weekends and cancel your vacation plans to gather resources for the future.

➤ work your fingers to the bone collecting and storing away assets.

➤ send your stress level off the chart by constantly worrying about tomorrow.

➤ lose sight of what's important today.

What it does suggest is that today's surplus is tomorrow's provision. If you don't invest it while you have the chance, you may not get a second one.

4. Servants and Masters

What is freedom?

What does independence mean to you?

No, this isn't a Fourth of July essay contest. It's an attempt to get you thinking about the "invisible" bonds that can restrict you just as surely as handcuffs and leg irons can.

We're talking about financial loans, which have the unique ability to make you feel free while they tighten the screws on your future. While you're busy focusing on the advantages and freedoms offered by a new house or car, you may overlook the financial burdens you're creating for yourself—not to mention the dependence you create for yourself on your creditor.

There's no getting around the fact that borrowing money puts you at the mercy of other people (or institutions). Here's how it works. In exchange for a loan, you are obligated to...

➤ write a check for the amount your creditor requires.

➤ make sure that check arrives before the date your creditor schedules.

GLAD YOU ASKED

How can I achieve the proper balance in preparing for the future—not being too lackadaisical or too obsessive?

Your best friend in this case is a good budget. If you do your calculatin' and figurin' right, you can determine just how much you'll need to set aside each month for investments in order to accommodate the retirement lifestyle you prefer. Once you have that figure (or figures, since they will change at different stages of your life), you'll have a target range for your efforts. Then you won't have to wonder about whether you're doing too much or too little preparation.

➤ pay the penalty your creditor demands if you fail to meet your initial obligations.

Although that may not seem like unreasonable servitude, it certainly doesn't seem much like freedom, either.

It's not just a matter of making payments, though. When you borrow money, you place yourself under the shadow of financial ruin. If, in the future, your creditor decides to call in its loan, you have little choice but to pay what you owe. If you can't, well, that's where the financial ruin part comes in.

PENNY FOR YOUR THOUGHTS

The rich rule over the poor, and the borrower is servant to the lender.

–PROVERBS 22:7

You may rightly point out that we're not living in the Depression Era and that the likelihood of a creditor calling in a loan is remote. But you can't deny the fact that it is a shadow on your financial horizon.

The bottom line is that if another person (or institution) has the power to seriously affect your financial bottom line, you can't claim independence. That's why relieving yourself of debt—achieving true financial freedom—should be at the top of your to-do list.

5. The Big Score

If you were making a list of the top-10 cliched movie plots, you'd have to include the one in which a retired thief/cat burglar/bank robber comes out of retirement to pull one last job. If you've sat through your share of these adventures, you know that it's always the promise of "one big score" that lures the criminal out of retirement.

It's that same "one big score" mentality that guides many people's financial planning decisions. How else do you explain lottery jackpots of more than $100 million?

There are two problems with gearing your financial future toward achieving one big payoff.

First, the more desperate you become to make your one big financial score, the more likely you will be to violate your own ethical code—or even the law—to get it. It's not all that difficult to convince yourself that the end justifies the means if the end is a financial windfall. The sad fact is that if you're willing to do anything to have a lot of money, chances are you'll succeed.

Second, if you do manage to make a big score—if you come into a great deal of money at one time—there's a good chance that you won't be able to hang on to it.

At the heart of the issue is the concept of appreciation. If you've worked hard for your money and watched it grow over a period of years—even decades—you'll have an appreciation for that money and an awareness of its true value.

In the case of a sudden windfall, many people find that the money seems somehow unreal and, as a result, easier to spend. That's why it's not uncommon to hear of big lottery winners who are forced to declare bankruptcy only a few years after their moment of glory.

"Slow but sure wins the race" is not just the moral of the old tortoise and hare fable; it's also an important financial guideline. The strategy of setting aside a little cash each month certainly doesn't have the same kind of drama or excitement as the strategy of plotting for one big score. (It's safe to say that responsible budgeting isn't likely to become a movie cliche in the near future.)

But it makes a lot more sense in the long run.

6. The Untouchables?

You're walking with your spouse on a deserted city street. It's late, and you're trying to find your car. Suddenly a gunman steps out of the shadows, points a gun at your chest, and demands your money. When you reach into the inside front pocket of your coat, the gunman panics, thinking you're going for a gun. He shoots you at point-blank range, sending you sprawling backward, and runs off into the night.

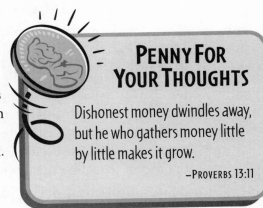

PENNY FOR YOUR THOUGHTS

Dishonest money dwindles away, but he who gathers money little by little makes it grow.

–PROVERBS 13:11

While your spouse fumbles with a cell phone, trying to remember the number for 911, you put your hand to your chest and are surprised to find no blood there. You reach into your front pocket again and pull out your wallet, which is stuffed beyond capacity with $100 bills. Embedded in the wad of bills you find the bullet that was meant for your heart.

There you have it—the only example we could think of in which your money could protect you from tragedy.

The truth is, no matter how wealthy you become, you're still vulnerable to the same problems, setbacks, and devastation that befall most people. Your money may give you access to better resources—including medical care—but it can't shield you from physical, emotional, or (ironically) financial ruin.

All it takes is one. . .

➤ stock market fluctuation

➤ natural disaster

➤ devastating personal loss

➤ string of minor incidents

. . . to destroy what you may have once considered "fortified" or "unscalable" (to quote the proverb).

We mention this not to send you scrambling for Prozac, but to warn you not to put too much faith in your money.

7. The Surety Thing

Here's a little story for you. Todd wanted to buy a car, but his credit rating was—well, let's just say creditors weren't standing in line to loan him money. But he really wanted this car. He had to have it. He was the front runner for a sales position with a cutting-edge software firm, and he needed reliable transportation in order to cover his sales territory.

With no money and no credit, he had only one place to turn: his college roommate, David. David was a successful businessman who had managed to make a comfortable life for himself and his family since graduation.

When Todd called to explain his situation, David looked out at his two cars in the driveway and felt sorry for his old roommate. "Sure," he said, "I'll cosign a car loan for you."

PENNY FOR YOUR THOUGHTS

The wealth of the rich is their fortified city; they imagine it an unscalable wall.

—PROVERBS 18:11

[Cue dramatic music.]

Three months later, David started getting past-due notices from the dealership where Todd had purchased the car. When he called Todd to ask about it, the person who answered the phone explained that Todd had skipped town when he wasn't offered the sales position he was expecting. Todd hadn't left a forwarding address, and the person didn't know when or if he was ever coming back.

David tried to call the dealership to explain the situation, but the representative he talked to informed him that he, David, was responsible for the debt since he had cosigned for the loan. David felt a knot tighten in his stomach as he tried to think of a way to explain to his wife how they could afford to add another car payment to their monthly budget.

We can take the conclusion of this story as far as necessary to drive the point home. We could tell you that the extra payment proved too much for David's family's budget and that their house, cars, and furniture were repossessed, leaving them with no place to go and no way to get there. We could tell you that David's business went bankrupt. We could tell you that he and his family now operate— and live out of—a hot dog vending cart at the local Little League baseball field.

But that would be a little too dramatic.

The point is, David and his family felt the effects of his ill-considered cosigning decision for years. David learned a little too late that tying your financial future to anyone else's (other than your spouse's, of course) is not a good idea.

Cosigning is not the only financial no-no associated with what's known as surety, though. In fact, it's not even the most common.

A good working definition of surety is "taking on an obligation to pay for something at a later time without having a *certain* way to pay it." In other words, when you sign surety for a debt, you pledge your future.

And that would be fine and dandy—if you had a guarantee as to what your future holds. But since few (read: none) of us are blessed with omniscience, that's a tough guarantee to get.

Being *reasonably confident* that you'll be able to make future payments isn't good enough. Look at the first four letters of the word again: S-U-R-E. Unless you have the funds—or the collateral—to cover the entire amount of a loan, you can't borrow money without violating the surety principle.

Go ahead, ask the obvious question: According that definition, wouldn't most home mortgages qualify as surety?

PENNY FOR YOUR THOUGHTS

Do not be a man who strikes hands in pledge or puts up security for debts; if you lack the means to pay, your very bed will be snatched from under you.

—PROVERBS 22:26-27

In answering that question, we need to consider the complexities of—

Aw, let's just be blunt. Yes, most home mortgages *do* qualify as surety.

If you or your spouse were to lose your job— through no fault of your own, we might add—you would probably have a hard time making your mortgage payments. And with no collateral to use in lieu of cash, you would be staring at a house full of surety.

If you've already committed yourself to some form of surety, whether it's a mortgage or a cosign, there's probably not much you can do about it now, aside from paying off your debts as soon as possible. It's important, however, that you not make the same mistake again. If you don't commit yourself to eliminating surety from your financial dealings now, you may never do it.

8. First Things First

Which is more important, your financial health or your physical health?

What if the choice was your financial health or your emotional health?

How about your financial health or your spiritual health?

In terms of priority, where do your finances rank in your life? (Hint: If it places any higher than fourth among the choices we just mentioned, it's time to rethink your priorities.)

Throughout this book we've emphasized the importance of sacrifice, particularly in the area of budgeting. However, that sacrifice should not extend to your physical, emotional, or spiritual health. Quite frankly, the money—whatever the amount—is just not worth it.

GLAD YOU ASKED

Does that mean I should never borrow anything?

Not necessarily. It is possible to borrow money without running into surety problems. The key is to make sure you have collateral to cover the loan, in case you're unable to repay it. If the lender is willing to accept your collateral in lieu of payment—should that become necessary—you can borrow the money with a clear financial conscience.

There are three questions you need to consider as you strive for financial health and success:

    a. What good is wealth if you're not physically able to enjoy it?

    b. What good does it do to satisfy your financial needs if the process itself leaves you miserable?

    c. Biblically speaking, what good will it be for you if you gain the whole world, yet forfeit your soul?

There are some things in life that money can't buy. (Relax, this isn't a VISA commercial.) But because those things are free, you may tend to underestimate their value or overlook them altogether.

Don't make that mistake. Keep tabs on your physical, emotional, and spiritual

PENNY FOR YOUR THOUGHTS

Do not wear yourself out to get rich; have the wisdom to show restraint. Cast but a glance at riches, and they are gone, for they will surely sprout wings and fly off to the sky like an eagle.

–PROVERBS 23:4-5

well-being as closely as you watch your finances. If not for your own sake, for the sake of your family.

9. While You Were Sleeping

Hardly seems fair, does it? You work your entire life to become financially secure. After you achieve your goal, you take a little break. And before you know it, everything you've worked for is gone.

This proverb doesn't just apply to physical rest, though. It's also applies to mental lapses. There may come a time in your financial "career"—perhaps after you receive a couple of healthy dividends—when you start to become impressed with your financial prowess.

As a result, you may start cutting corners in your financial practices. For example, instead of doing research on investment possibilities, you may start relying on your gut instincts. You may let your guard down and start considering opportunities that ordinarily you would have dismissed as too risky. You may get lazy in your financial habits.

And that's when you're primed for disaster.

PENNY FOR YOUR THOUGHTS

A little sleep, a little slumber, a little folding of the hands to rest–and poverty will come on you like a bandit and scarcity like an armed man.

–PROVERBS 24:33-34

Another recipe for disaster is placing too high of a priority on comfort and relaxation. Enjoying "down time" is not a fatal character flaw by any stretch of the imagination. But there is a need for moderation.

This is an especially important concept for retirees to grasp. There is nothing wrong with relaxing and enjoying your post-career years—as long as relaxation and enjoyment are not your primary goals. If you get too caught up in taking it easy, you'll leave yourself vulnerable to the "poverty" and "scarcity" the proverb warns against.

And don't forget: Financial ruin at age 65 is much more devastating than it is at age 35.

10. Slippery Slopes

In the financial trenches, there will be plenty of opportunities for you to cut some ethical corners or to mire yourself in the so-called "gray areas" between what's obviously right and what's obviously wrong.

For example, you might. . .

➤ conveniently "forget" to report certain non-traceable forms of income on your tax form.

➤ persuade an unsuspecting buyer to pay more for your car than you know it's worth.

➤ choose to invest in a hot company whose product or services you consider to be morally objectionable (for example, a pharmaceutical company that markets an abortion pill).

They say a word to the wise is sufficient, so our word to you is this: Don't take that first step.

Commit yourself to rigid ethical standards where your finances are concerned. Once you cross that line the first time, no matter how "minor" the offense may seem, you make it easier to cross it again and again.

And you may be surprised and shocked to discover how far and how fast your morals fall in pursuit of the almighty dollar.

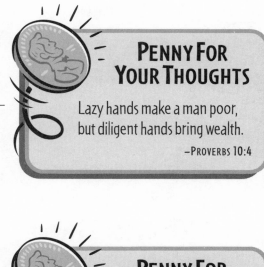

PENNY FOR YOUR THOUGHTS

Lazy hands make a man poor, but diligent hands bring wealth.

–PROVERBS 10:4

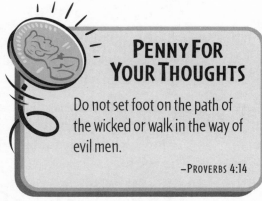

PENNY FOR YOUR THOUGHTS

Do not set foot on the path of the wicked or walk in the way of evil men.

–PROVERBS 4:14

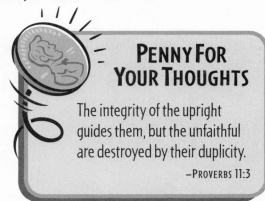

PENNY FOR YOUR THOUGHTS

The integrity of the upright guides them, but the unfaithful are destroyed by their duplicity.

–PROVERBS 11:3

Your best strategy for avoiding this fate is to establish an accountability with both your spouse and your advisor regarding your financial decisions. Establish a relationship of openness and honesty regarding your financial actions and motives.

When your financial accountability partners question a decision, listen to them. Make sure that your heart is in the right place before you do anything.

One More Thing

Many people would like to sneak finances in as the third element in the old aphorism that all's fair in love and war. But the fact is, it's no more true about finances than it is about love or war.

Quite simply, there is a right way and a wrong way to earn and manage your money. And if you don't maintain a sense of ethics and priority in your financial dealings, you will never be truly satisfied with, or fulfilled by, what you have.

The Buck Stops Here

Think you're an expert on time-tested financial advice? Here's a quiz to see how much you know.

1. According to the Book of Proverbs, what is more valuable than silver, gold, and rubies?
   a. Wisdom
   b. Platinum
   c. VISA
   d. Playoff tickets

2. Which of the following is not a lesson we can learn from an ant?
    a. Preparation is a continuous process.
    b. Sidewalk cracks make perfect home construction sites.
    c. Future needs take precedence over present enjoyment.
    d. There are different seasons of life that must be accounted for.

3. In which of the following areas is wealth least effective?
    a. Ensuring that you have a place to live when you retire
    b. Assisting in your kids' education
    c. Shielding you and your family from tragedy
    d. Getting you tickets to a playoff game

4. What's wrong with surety?
    a. Scientists have discovered that it's extremely vulnerable to heat and moisture, making it a poor building material.
    b. Many people are unsure of the correct pronunciation of the word and end up calling it "ceretti."
    c. Many people confuse it with cockiness and conceit and may tend to resent you for it.
    d. It requires you to pledge to repay funds without having a way to actually repay them.

5. Why is it so dangerous to relax and take it easy once you've achieved financial success?
    a. Science has proven that stress is vital to good physical health; without it, we can't survive.
    b. Other people may assume you're rubbing their noses in your good fortune and take offense.
    c. You may unwittingly make yourself vulnerable to a sudden reversal of fortune.
    d. That's when careless accidents usually happen—the kinds of things that can land you in a hospital for a couple of months.

Answers: (1) a, (2) b, (3) c, (4) d, (5) c

Appendix

TABLE OF CONTENTS

From Financial Bondage to Financial Freedom!

Place a ✓ by Your Degree of Financial Difficulty	My Financial Symptoms (Underline the symptoms you are experiencing)	Which Action Steps Leading to Financial Freedom Do You Need to Take? (Underline steps that apply)
On the Verge of Bankruptcy?	Personal assets liquidated; possible jail time; credit record impacted for 10 years; sleepless nights; depression; withdrawal from family and friends.	Pray and praise God in your circumstances; forgive everyone; take responsibility for your actions; develop a plan to repay everyone; be honest with all creditors.
Severe Financial Distress?	Threatening phone calls and letters from creditors; lots of arguments over money; credit cards "maxed" out; begin working two or three jobs.	Pray; immediately seek counsel from CCCS at 1-888-771-HOPE; contact creditors, explain situation, propose a budget along with your plan for repayment; stop using credit cards right now.
Living Above Your Means?	Expenses exceed income; only able to make minimum payments; handle emergencies with credit cards; no savings; peer pressure.	Pray; contact your church (or Crown at 1-800-722-1976) to locate a volunteer budget counselor; learn what parts of your budget are being overspent and reduce spending; start saving.
Living At Your Means?	Income = expenses; "surprises" consistently prevent any attempts to save; lots of worry, anxiety, and fear about the future.	Pray; get on budget; stop using credit cards that aren't paid in full each month; avoid impulsive purchases and set a goal of saving 3-6 months income; reduce spending.
Living Below Your Means?	Income greater than expenses; bills consistently paid on time; regular savings; 3-6 month emergency fund has been established.	Pray; fine-tune your budget to maximize surplus; seek discernment in meeting needs of others; become informed about investment opportunities; testify to God's work in your life.
Ah, Yes! Financial Freedom	No worries about debt, investments, or material things; consistently using surplus funds for meeting needs of God's people; inner joy in abundance.	Pray; commit to teaching your children and others the wise principles of money management from God's Word; testify to God's good work in your life.

Common Money Problems

❏ Can't sleep at night

❏ Feel guilty

❏ Financially broke (or close to it)

❏ Panic attacks

❏ In trouble with IRS

❏ Feel abandoned

❏ Can't pray

❏ Depressed

❏ Lonely

❏ Ashamed

❏ Don't know what to do

❏ No future or hope

❏ Frightened

❏ Angry at self

❏ Too much pressure

❏ Looking for a way out

❏ Embarrassed

❏ Stressed out with spouse

❏ Threatening calls from creditors

❏ Stressed out with kids

❏ Dread of opening the mail because of bills

❏ Thoughts of running away

❏ Can't take anymore

❏ Blame others

❏ Angry with others

❏ Bitter outlook on life

❏ Feeling punished by God

❏ Dread of tomorrow

❏ Rejection from family

❏ Rejection from church members

❏ Numb emotionally

❏ Discouraged

❏ Try hard, but just can't get ahead

❏ Feel like a failure

Creating My Budget for Vacation

Transportation there and back $_____
(gas, airfare, car rental, and so on)

Lodging $_____

Meals $_____

Recreation $_____
(fishing tackle, green fees, shopping, and so on)

Souvenirs $_____

Miscellaneous $_____

Total estimated vacation expenditures $_____

Total divided by 12 months
equals amount to save each month $_____

Creating My Budget for Christmas

Name   Approximate Amount for Gifts

_____

_____

_____

_____

_____

_____

_____

_____

_____

_____

_____

_____

_____

_____

_____

_____

_____

_____

Estimated total for all gifts $ _____

Total divided by 12 months
equals amount to save each month $_____

Variable Expense Planning Worksheet

Plan for those expenses that are not paid on a regular monthly basis by estimating the yearly cost and determining the monthly amount needed to be set aside for that expense. A helpful formula is to allow the previous year's expense and add 5 percent.

	Estimated Cost		Per Month
1. Vacation	$_____	÷ 12 =	$_____
2. Dentist	$_____	÷ 12 =	$_____
3. Doctor	$_____	÷ 12 =	$_____
4. Auto	$_____	÷ 12 =	$_____
5. Annual Insurance	$_____	÷ 12 =	$_____
(Life)	($_____	÷ 12 =	$_____)
(Health)	($_____	÷ 12 =	$_____)
(Auto)	($_____	÷ 12 =	$_____)
(Home)	($_____	÷ 12 =	$_____)
6. Clothing	$_____	÷ 12 =	$_____
7. Investments	$_____	÷ 12 =	$_____
8. Other	$_____	÷ 12 =	$_____
	$_____	÷ 12 =	$_____

Percentage Guide for Family Income

(Singles and Families)

	SINGLE ADULT[1] Living Alone		SINGLE PARENT		FAMILY OF FOUR[2]	
GROSS INCOME	23,000	32,000	15,000	25,000	35,000	55,000
1. Tithe	10%	10%	10%	10%	10%	10%
2. Taxes[3]	21%	24%	6%	6%	14.9%	19.9%
Net Spendable percentages numbers 3 through 13 below add to 100%						
NET SPENDABLE INCOME	15,870	21,120	12,600	21,000	26,285	38,555
3. Housing	40%	38%	40%	38%	36%	30%
4. Food[4]	6%	6%	15%	14%	12%	12%
5. Auto	15%	15%	15%	14%	12%	14%
6. Insurance	4%	4%	3%	5%	5%	5%
7. Debts	5%	5%	4%	5%	5%	5%
8. Entertainment/Recreation	8%	7%	4%	4%	6%	7%
9. Clothing	5%	5%	5%	5%	5%	6%
10. Savings	5%	5%	5%	5%	5%	5%
11. Medical/Dental	5%	3%	5%	5%	4%	4%
12. Miscellaneous	5%	7%	4%	5%	5%	7%
13. Investments[5]	2%	5%	—	—	5%	5%
If you have the Education expense below, the percentage shown must be deducted from a budget category above.						
14. Education/Child Care[6]	3%	7%	—	—	6%	5%
15. Unallocated Surplus Income[7]	—	—	—	—	—	—

This guide is designed to help you begin to establish a budget. The Gross Income figures shown serve as common ranges for Single Adults, Single Parents, and a Family of Four. However, education, experience, and geographic location often cause incomes to vary greatly.

Nevertheless, individual needs and incomes should not prompt you to depart too far from the suggested guideline percentages. Be conservative as you make any adjustments upward or downward.

[1] *If a single adult has a roommate, allocations for items such as Housing might be reduced considerably.*

[2] *Family of Four percentages can also be used for Head of Household family of three.*

[3] *Tax category percentages include Social Security, federal, and a small estimated amount for state, based on 1999 rates. (Single Parent rates are for year 2000.)*

[4] *This percentage does not include the reduction that would result from food stamp or food bank use.*

[5] *This category is used for long-term planning such as retirement or college education for children.*

[6] *This category is added as a guide only. Some parents have alternate ways to meet the need through family or scholarship programs. However, if you do have this expense, the percentage used must be deducted from other budget categories.*

[7] *This category is used for surplus income received from irregular child support, yard sales, gifts, or bonuses. This would be kept in the checking account to be used within a few weeks; otherwise it should be transferred to an allocated category.*

How Much Monthly House Allowance Can You <u>Really</u> Afford?

Your Gross Income Per Year	Your Net Spendable Income Per Year –NSI–	Your Net Spendable Income Per Month –NSI–	Housing Allowance Per Month (% of NSI)
$25,000	$21,225	$1,769	$672 (38%)
$45,000	$32,445	$2,704	$865 (32%)
$65,000	$44,330	$3,694	$1,108 (30%)
$85,000	$54,570	$4,548	$1,364 (30%)
$115,000	$71,185	$5,932	$1,720 (29%)

How to Buy a House

The Fasters' Strategy	The Goal: Own a $100,000 home	The Wisers' Strategy

$ 101,037.55
- $ 10,000.00
= $ 91,037.55 @ 8.5%
   for 30 years = $700.00
	House
	Down Payment
	Balance
	Terms
	Monthly Payment
		$66,458.12
		- $10,000.00
		= $56,458.12 @ 8.5%
		   for 10 years = $700.00

		In 10 years, the Wisers own the $66,458 home and have paid $27,541 in interest. Total payback on the loan = $83,999.

	Next, the Wisers purchase their $101,037.55 home, using their $66,458 as a down payment, with the same terms.	$ 101,037.55 home
		$ 66,458.12 down
		$ 34,579.43 mortgage @ 8.5%
		   for 5 years and 1 month =
		   $700 payment

	Total payments of the Wiser's House #2=	$42,706.79 ($34,579.43 principal + $8,127.36 interest)
	After 15 years and one month, the Wisers own their $101,000 home and begin to invest their former house payment. Amazingly, the Fasters still have 14 years, 11 months before they will own their home!	The Wisers invest $700 in mutual funds at an average return of 8% for the next 14 years, 11 months = $125,300.00 in payments $ 114,627.24 interest $ 239,927.24 total
30 years later $252,000.00 $160,962.45 -0- -0- $101,037.55 $101,037.55	Amount paid for the house Total interest paid Difference in total paid Investments after payoff Home equity Total gain	30 years later $136,705.91 $ 35,668.36 $115,294.09 $239,927.24 $ 101,037.55 $340,964.79

Explanation of the "How to Buy a House" Example

1. Both families, the Fasters and the Wisers, desire to own a $100,000 home. For simplicity, the actual sales price of the homes computes as $101,037.55.

2. Both families will spend exactly the same monthly amount on the house payment: $700 (principal and interest only).

3. Both families put $10,000 down on the purchase price of their homes.

4. The Faster family immediately purchased their dream home at the terms shown.

5. The Wiser family purchased a home of lesser value ($66,458.12) at the same interest rate (8.5 percent) as the Fasters but with an identical monthly payment of ($700).

6. In 10 years, the Wisers paid off their home, sold it, and purchased their dream home at exactly the same price as the Fasters: $101,037.55. Their mortgage, however, was only $34,579.43.

7. By continuing to make $700 house payments each month, the Wisers paid off their dream home in only 5 years and 1 month. In contrast, the Fasters (really?) still had another 14 years and 11 months before their dream home would be paid off.

8. Living up to their name, the Wisers immediately began to invest their old house payment ($700) in a mutual fund that averaged 8 percent return each year.

9. At the end of the 30th year, both families owned their dream homes.

10. The Wisers, however, were substantially better off than the Fasters. Through their investments, they saved $125,300 ($700 per month for 179 months) and earned $114,627.24 of interest on those deposits.

11. The Wisers ended up with $239,927.24 in the mutual fund, with interest accruing at the rate of $1,584.47 a month when the Fasters made their last house payment. Not bad.

How Much Monthly Car Payment Can You Really Afford?

Your Gross Income Per Year	Your Net Spendable Income Per Year –NSI–	Your Net Spendable Income Per Month –NSI–	Housing Allowance Per Month (% of NSI)
$25,000	$21,225	$1,769	$124 (7%)
$45,000	$32,445	$2,704	$176 (6.5%)
$65,000	$42,250	$3,520	$246 (7%)
$85,000	$54,570	$4,548	$296 (6.5%)
$115,000	$71,185	$5,932	$386 (6.5%)

Assumptions Behind the Chart

1. It is assumed that you are paying a 10 percent tithe and your appropriate percentage of income taxes.

2. The chart assumes you will only spend 50 percent of your overall Automobile allowance on the car payment, with the other 50 percent spent on gasoline, insurance, repair, maintenance, license, and replacement costs.

3. Keep in mind that the budget guidelines are only guidelines; they are not laws. You may choose to exceed the recommended percentage for spending in this category; just be aware that you must deduct the degree of your overspending from another budget category.

How Much Monthly Credit Card Payment Can You Really Afford?

Your Gross Income Per Year	Your Net Spendable Income Per Year -NSI-	Your Net Spendable Income Per Month -NSI-	Debt Payment Per Month (5% of NSI)
$25,000	$21,225	$1,769	$88
$45,000	$32,445	$2,704	$135
$65,000	$42,250	$3,520	$176
$85,000	$54,570	$4,548	$227
$115,000	$71,185	$5,932	$296

Assumptions Behind the Chart

The chart above only provides a reference point for payments on credit card debt. Remember that this budget category, as explained on your Monthly Income and Expenses Worksheet, includes not only credit cards but student loans, personal loans, and other forms of debt repayment.

My Credit Card Payments at a Glance

Credit Card Account Name	Monthly Payment	Interest Rate	Balance Due
Card 1			
Card 2			
Card 3			
Card 4			
Card 5			
Card 6			
Card 7			
Card 8			
Card 9			
Card 10			
Card 11			
Card 12			
Total monthly payments =	_____	**Total of all balances =**	_____

Using the chart on the previous page, what is the suggested amount for credit card payments? $ _____

-minus-

Your monthly payments $ _____

_____

Equals amount over or under budget $ _____

My Credit Card Payments at a Glance

Credit Card Account Name	Monthly Payment	Interest Rate	Balance Due
Card 1			
Card 2			
Card 3			
Card 4			
Card 5			
Card 6			
Card 7			
Card 8			
Card 9			
Card 10			
Card 11			
Card 12			
Total monthly payments =		**Total of all balances =**	

Using the chart on the previous page, what is the suggested amount for credit card payments?

$ _____

-minus-

Your monthly payments

$ _____

Equals amount over or under budget

$ _____

A Proven Strategy for Conquering Credit Card Debt (How the Millers Did It)

Credit Card	Balance	Interest Rate	Minimum Monthly Payment
VISA	$5,500	10.5	$110
MasterCard	$3,000	13.5	$80
Sears	$1,100	18.0	$65
Shell Gas	$750	9.5	$35
Nordstrom	$500	21.0	$25
J.C. Penney	$295	21.0	$15

How the Millers' Strategy Worked

Step 1: The Millers made the necessary adjustments in their lifestyle in order to stop using credit cards.

Step 2: By selling excess items at yard and garage sales, they generated extra cash. They sold newer automobiles in favor of older cars, thus lowering their monthly car payments. The extra cash was diverted to the Debt Reduction category of their budget.

Step 3: The Millers arranged their credit card debts in order: greatest balance and highest interest rates to least, as pictured above.

Step 4: While making minimum payments on all the accounts, the Millers concentrated on paying off accounts with the small balances and highest interest rates first.

Step 5: When one account got paid off, they closed it and rolled that payment into the next smallest account. The following notes illustrate the example above.

➤ By limiting spending in other budget categories, the Millers discovered they could pay $150 toward their J.C. Penney bill. In two months, the bill was paid off and the account closed.

➤ The Millers then rolled the $150 they had been paying to J.C. Penney over to their Nordstrom bill, increasing their monthly payment from $25 to $175 ($25 minimum payment + the $150 they had been paying on the J.C. Penney account). At this rate, the Nordstrom bill was paid off in three months.

➤ Next in line was the Shell gas bill. They took $175 they had been paying to Nordstrom, combined with their normal $35 payment, and began paying $210 a month on Shell. In no time that account was paid off and closed.

➤ Next was Sears. The Millers took the $210 a month they had been paying on Shell, combined it with their monthly payment of $65, and began paying $275 a month on Sears.

➤ Thus the Millers attacked one account at a time.

What Is Required for This Strategy to Work

1. You must be committed to living debt free. No fudging.

2. As a result, you must be willing to make the lifestyle changes necessary to free more cash flow for debt reduction. You may have to prayerfully consider selling cars, recreational vehicles, and perhaps even your house. Everything with regard to lifestyle must "go on the table." This is major financial surgery, not a Band-Aid approach. Seek God's wisdom and leading in these matters (see John 16:13).

3. Stop using credit cards. If you can't resist the temptation to use them, cut them up. No strategy to conquer credit card debt will work in the long run if you continue to use credit cards.

4. Rejoice in the steps you are taking toward financial freedom!

5. Begin by paying off debts that have the combination of highest interest rates and lowest balances.

6. When an account is paid off, close it, and roll that payment amount into the next account in line for elimination.

7. Consider shopping for credit cards that allow you to transfer balances with low introductory interest rates.

8. If you're in major credit card trouble, seek assistance from the Consumer Credit Counseling Service at 1-888-771-HOPE. They may be able to intercede with your creditors on your behalf to negotiate lower monthly payments.

My Credit Card Debt Elimination Strategy

Credit Card Account Name	Monthly Payment	Interest Rate	Balance Due
Card 1			
Card 2			
Card 3			
Card 4			
Card 5			
Card 6			
Card 7			
Card 8			
Card 9			
Card 10			
Card 11			
Card 12			

Directions: Organize this debt list (as well as you can) with the largest balances toward the top (Card 1) and smallest balances toward the bottom (Card 12). Also, do your best to list the accounts with the highest interest rates toward the bottom of the list (Card 12).

CONCENTRATE on paying off the account at the bottom of the list first, and systematically work your way to the top!

How to Use the Growing-in-Giving Chart

The chart below is provided to help you track actual progress in giving. To use the chart, follow these simple steps.

1. Locate the Annual Income figure closest to your earnings.

2. The chart reflects giving percentages of 2.5, 5, 7, 10, 12, and 15, calculated on gross income.

3. Both an annual amount and monthly amount of giving are reflected on the chart.

4. One box has been blackened as an illustration. A family earning $35,000 a year is shown giving 7 percent of their income to God's work. This amounts to $2,450.00 a year, or $204.16 per month.

5. The average American Christian currently gives 2.5 percent to God's work.

Growing-in-Giving Chart

Annual Income	Giving Period of Time	Average American Christian 2.5%[1]	5%	7%	10% **The Tithe	12%	15%
$15,000	Month	$31.25	$62.50	$87.50	$125.00	$150.00	$187.50
	Year	$375.00	$750.00	$1,050.00	$1,500.00	$1,800.00	$2,250.00
$25,000	Month	$52.08	$104.16	$145.83	$208.32	$250.00	$312.48
	Year	$625.00	$1,250.00	$1,750.00	$2500.00	$3000.00	$3,750.00
$35,000	Month	$72.91	$145.82	$204.16	$291.64	$350.00	$437.46
	Year	$875.00	$1,750.00	$2,450.00	$3,500.00	$4,200.00	$5,250.00
$45,000	Month	$93.75	$187.50	$262.50	$375.00	$450.00	$562.50
	Year	$1,125.00	$2,250.00	$3,150.00	$4,500.00	$5,400.00	$6,750.00
$55,000	Month	$114.58	$229.16	$320.83	$458.32	$550.00	$687.48
	Year	$1,375.00	$2,750.00	$3,850.00	$5,500.00	$6,600.00	$8,250.00
$65,000	Month	$135.41	$270.82	$379.16	$541.64	$650.00	$812.46
	Year	$1625.00	$3,250.00	$4,550.00	$6,500.00	$7,800.00	$9,750.00
$75,000	Month	$156.25	$312.50	$437.50	$625.00	$750.00	$937.50
	Year	$1875.00	$3,750.00	$5,250.00	$7,500.00	$9,000.00	$11,250.00
$85,000	Month	$177.08	$354.16	$495.83	$708.32	$850.00	$1,062.48
	Year	$2,125.00	$4,250.00	$5,950.00	$8,500.00	$10,200.00	$12,750.00

[1] Ronsvalle, John and Sylvia. *Behind the Stained Glass Windows: Money Dynamics in the Church*, p. 36, Baker Books, Grand Rapids, MI.

Life Insurance Needs Worksheets

Step 1 – How Much Money Do You Make Now?

Primary Wage Earner Annual Income $__80,000__

     +

Other Wage Earner Annual Income $__20,000__

     =   Total Annual Income $__100,000__

                                                                (Line 1)

Step 2 – How Will Your Expenses Decrease?

Annual Amounts No Longer Required

Estimated Living Cost (for the deceased) $__15,000__   (includes food, cars, clothing, and so on)

Savings reduction $__2,400__

Investments reduction $__10,000__

Taxes reduction $__16,000__

Other_____ $_____

                     Total = $__43,400__

                                                       (Line 2)

Income Required to Maintain
the Family's Standard of Living   (Line 1 – Line 2) = $__56,600__

                                                               (Line 3)

Step 3 – How Much Income Will You Have?

Annual Income Available

Social Security survivor's benefits $__18,000__

Your (surviving spouse's) income $__20,000__

Retirement plans $__5,000__

Investments $_____

Other_____ $_____

                     Total = $__43,000__

                                                       (Line 4)

Step 4 – How Much More Money Will You Need (if any)?

Additional Annual Income Required to Support Family

                     (Line 3 – Line 4) = $__13,600__

                                                                     (Line 5)

Step 5 - One Way to Make Up the Difference

Invest a Lump Sum of Money to Provide Needed Income (Invested at 10 percent interest) (Line 5 x10) =	$____136,000____ (Line 6)

Step 6 - List One-Time Expenses You'll Face

Lump Sum Requirements

Debt Payments	$____50,000____
Funeral costs	$____10,000____
Estate tax and settlement costs	$____3,000____
Education costs	$____60,000____
Other_____	$_____
Total =	$____123,400____ (Line 7)

Step 7 - Assets You Can Liquidate

Assets Available to Liquidate

Real estate	$____18,500____
Stocks and bonds	$_____
Savings	$_____
Other_____	$_____
Total =	$____18,500____ (Line 8)

Step 8 - Deduct Liquid Assets from One-Time Expenses

Subject Line 8 from Line 7 = (This is the amount you will need for one-time expenses)	$____104,500____ (Line 9)

Step 9 - Here's How Much Life Insurance You Need

Add Line 6 (the lump sum you need to invest) to Line 9 to calculate the amount of life insurance you require to meet your financial plans in the event of an untimely death.

Line 6 =	$____136,000____
+ Line 9 =	$____104,500____
Total =	$____240,500____
	(This much life insurance needed)

Life Insurance Needs Worksheets

Step 1 – How Much Money Do You Make Now?

Primary Wage Earner Annual Income $_____

\+

Other Wage Earner Annual Income $_____

=   Total Annual Income $_____

(Line 1)

Step 2 – How Will Your Expenses Decrease?

Annual Amounts No Longer Required

Estimated Living Cost (for the deceased) $_____ (includes food, cars, clothing, and so on)

Savings reduction $_____

Investments reduction $_____

Taxes reduction $_____

Other_____ $_____

Total = $_____

(Line 2)

Income Required to Maintain
the Family's Standard of Living   (Line 1 – Line 2) = $_____

(Line 3)

Step 3 – How Much Income Will You Have?

Annual Income Available

Social Security survivor's benefits $_____

Your (surviving spouse's) income $_____

Retirement plans $_____

Investments $_____

Other_____ $_____

Total = $_____

(Line 4)

Step 4 – How Much More Money Will You Need (if any)?

Additional Annual Income Required to Support Family

(Line 3 – Line 4) = $_____

(Line 5)

Step 5 – One Way to Make Up the Difference

Invest a Lump Sum of Money to Provide Needed Income
(Invested at 10 percent interest) (Line 5 x10) = $_____
                                                     (Line 6)

Step 6 – List One-Time Expenses You'll Face

Lump Sum Requirements
   Debt Payments $_____
   Funeral costs $_____
   Estate tax and settlement costs $_____
   Education costs $_____
   Other_____ $_____
                              Total = $_____
                                          (Line 7)

Step 7 – Assets You Can Liquidate

Assets Available to Liquidate
   Real estate $_____
   Stocks and bonds $_____
   Savings $_____
   Other_____ $_____
                              Total = $_____
                                          (Line 8)

Step 8 – Deduct Liquid Assets from One-Time Expenses

Subject Line 8 from Line 7 = $_____
(This is the amount you will need for one-time expenses)   (Line 9)

Step 9 – Here's How Much Life Insurance You Need

Add Line 6 (the lump sum you need to invest) to Line 9 to calculate the amount of life
insurance you require to meet your financial plans in the event of an untimely death.

                    Line 6 = $_____
                  + Line 9 = $_____
                       Total = $_____
                       (This much life insurance needed)

CHECKLIST OF IMPORTANT DOCUMENTS

REAL ESTATE RECORDS

Records for Property Located at	Type of Record	Dated	Location of Document

AUTOMOBILE RECORDS

Title & Registration for Vehicle	Title Number	Dated	Location of Document

LIFE INSURANCE POLICIES

Policy on Life of	Policy Number	Company	Location of Document

BANK, SAVINGS & LOAN OR CREDIT UNION RECORDS

Name of Institution	Type of Account	Account Number	Location of Document

SAFE DEPOSIT BOXES

Box Registered in Name of	Name of Institution	Box Number	Location of Keys

CHURCH RECORDS

Type of Record	Record for (Name)	Date of Event	Location of Document

MILITARY RECORDS

Type of Record	Record for (Name)	Date of Event	Location of Document

OTHER IMPORTANT PAPERS

Type of Record	For	Dated	Location of Document

CHECKLIST OF IMPORTANT DOCUMENTS

WILLS

Will for	Dated	Attorney	Location of Will

POWER OF ATTORNEY

Power of Attorney for	Power Given to	Dated	Location of Document

BIRTH CERTIFICATES

Certificate for	Date of Birth	Certificate Number	Location of Certificate

DEATH CERTIFICATES

Certificate for	Date of Death	Certificate Number	Location of Certificate

MARRIAGE LICENSES

License for	Date of Marriage	Certificate Number	Location of Document

DIVORCE DECREES

Divorce Decree for	Date of Divorce	Decree Number	Location of Document

SOCIAL SECURITY RECORDS

Social Security Records/Cards for	Social Security Number	Date Received	Location of Document

An Example: Budget Percentage Guidelines Worksheet

Salary for guideline = $ __35,000__ /year[1]

GROSS INCOME PER MONTH			$ __2,917__		
1. Tithe	(_10_ % of Gross)	($ _2,917_)	=	$	292
2. Tax	(_14.9_ % of Gross)	($ _2,917_)	=	$	435
NET SPENDABLE INCOME			$ __2,190__		
3. Housing	(_36_ % of Net)	($ _2,190_)	=	$	788
4. Food	(_12_ % of Net)	($ _2,190_)	=	$	263
5. Auto	(_12_ % of Net)	($ _2,190_)	=	$	263
6. Insurance	(_5_ % of Net)	($ _2,190_)	=	$	110
7. Debts	(_5_ % of Net)	($ _2,190_)	=	$	110
8. Entertainment/ Recreation	(_6_ % of Net)	($ _2,190_)	=	$	131
9. Clothing	(_5_ % of Net)	($ _2,190_)	=	$	110
10. Savings	(_5_ % of Net)	($ _2,190_)	=	$	110
11. Medical/Dental	(_5_ % of Net)	($ _2,190_)	=	$	110
12. Miscellaneous	(_4_ % of Net)	($ _2,190_)	=	$	87
13. Investments	(_5_ % of Net)[2]	($ _2,190_)	=	$	110
14. School/ Child Care	(_6_ % of Net)[3]	($_____)	=	$	
TOTAL *(Cannot exceed Net Spendable Income)*				$	2,192[4]
15. Unallocated Surplus Income[5]	($ __N/A__)	=	$		

[1] *Refer to the Budget Percentage Guide for Family Income for percentage guidelines.*
[2] *Consider the given obligations at this income level, there is no surplus for investing long term.*
[3] *For this example, this percentage has not been factored into the total percentages shown for net income.*
[4] *Because of rounding to the nearest dollar, this figure may not match the Net Spendable Income exactly. You may add or deduct the difference from any category total to make an exact match.*
[5] *This category is not part of the budget system but can be used to record and show disbursements.*

Index